Language and Creativity

The art of common talk

Do we just use language? Or do we create it?
Who says only a genius can be creative?
What do our everyday conversations tell us about ourselves?

Creativity in language has conventionally been regarded as the preserve of institutionalised discourses such as literature and advertising, and individual gifted
minds. *Language and Creativity* explores the idea that creativity, far from being
simply a property of exceptional people, is an exceptional property of all people.

Drawing on a range of real examples of everyday conversations and speech,
from flatmates in a student house and families on holiday to psychotherapy sessions and chat-lines, the book argues that creativity is an all-pervasive feature
of everyday language. Using close analysis of naturally occurring language,
taken from the unique, 5-million-word corpus held at the University of Nottingham, *Language and Creativity* reveals that speakers commonly make meanings
in a variety of creative ways, in a wide range of social contexts and for a diverse
set of reasons.

In this ground-breaking book, Ronald Carter builds on previous theories of
creativity, and offers a radical contribution to linguistic, literary and cultural
theory. A must for anyone interested in the creativity of our everyday speech.

Ronald Carter is Professor of Modern English Language in the School of
English Studies, University of Nottingham. He has published extensively in the
fields of applied linguistics, literary studies and language in education.

'Professor Carter has always recognized that casual spontaneous conversation is extraordinarily rich and creative in the way its speakers use the resources of their language. Thanks to the CANCODE corpus he has been able to document this creativity with dialogue taken from real life. In this new book, Ronald Carter examines the notion of creativity as it appears in different cultural and historical contexts, but with the main focus still in spoken language. The book affords major insight not only into "common talk" but through and beyond this into the nature of language in general.'

Michael Halliday, University of Sydney, Australia

'Ronald Carter's book is a fresh and thoughtful probing of one of the most neglected topics in contemporary language studies, using the insights provided by the CANCODE corpus, and firmly locating its subject within an inter-disciplinary aesthetic perspective. It is a major step forward in conversation analysis, and gives a deserved recognition to the remarkable linguistic creativity that exists in all of us.'

David Crystal, University of Wales, Bangor, UK

'Ronald Carter's new book *Language and Creativity: The Art of Common Talk* is a delight to read. The book clearly demonstrates through the analysis of real spoken speech that people are deeply creative in what they say and how they say it. Carter outlines concrete ways for identifying creative aspects of talk and what this type of language reveals about human thought more generally. Few books offer this range of insights into language, thought, and creativity. Carter's book represents the best in interdisciplinary studies on the art and science of ordinary talk.'

Raymond W. Gibbs, Jr., University of California, Santa Cruz, USA

'This book is a sustained and rigorous examination of creativity in the diversity of language. Conscious of how the concept of creativity itself is culturally and historically defined, the author eschews a limited argument about relativism in favour of one about relevance. Ronald Carter digs deep to demonstrate how creativity inhabits the demotic and the everyday in a wide variety of linguistic acts. He situates creativity on a continuum with the literary, and thus not as something intrinsically separate or defined in antithesis to the ordinary uses of language. Indeed what is so remarkable about this book is the way it continually reveals to us just how creative and artful we are in our everyday language use, and in this regard it is a deeply enriching work, and one that surprises and delights in its revelation of the sheer ingenuity of human interactions. *Language and Creativity: The Art of Common Talk* breaks new ground, and yet it always keeps the reader in mind: as it travels across the new terrain, it maps its movements with absolute clarity and coherence.'

Philip Martin, De Montfort University, Leicester, UK

Language and Creativity

The art of common talk

Ronald Carter

Routledge
Taylor & Francis Group

LONDON AND NEW YORK

First published 2004
by Routledge
2 Park Square, Milton Park, Abingdon, Oxon OX14 4RN

Simultaneously published in the USA and Canada
by Routledge
270 Madison Avenue, New York, NY 10016

Routledge is an imprint of the Taylor & Francis Group, an informa business

© 2004 Ronald Carter

Reprinted 2006, 2007, 2008

Typeset in Perpetua by The Running Head Limited, Cambridge
Printed and bound in Great Britain by
Antony Rowe Ltd., Chippenham, Wiltshire

British Library Cataloguing in Publication Data
A catalogue record for this book is available from the British Library

Library of Congress Cataloging in Publication Data
Carter, Ronald, 1947–
Language and creativity: the art of common talk / Ronald Carter.
  p. cm.
Includes bibliographical references and index.
1. Creativity (Linguistics) 2. Sociolinguistics. I. Title.
P37.5.C74C37 2004
401'41–dc22   2003015366

ISBN 0–415–23448–4 (hbk)
ISBN 978–0–415–23448–1 (hbk)
ISBN 0–415–23449–2 (pbk)
ISBN 978–0–415–23449–8 (pbk)

Contents

List of illustrations   vii
Acknowledgements   xi

Introduction   1

PART I
Backgrounds and theories   15

1   Approaches to creativity   17

2   Lines and clines: linguistic approaches   53

PART II
Forms and functions   87

3   Creativity and patterns of talk   89

4   Figures of speech   115

PART III
Contexts and variations   145

5   Creativity, language and social context   147

6   Creativity, discourse and social practice   170

Appendix 1 A note on transcription and corpus analysis   219

Appendix 2 New words for old   222

Appendix 3 CANCODE publications 1994–2003   227

References   231
Index   249

Illustrations

Figures

1.1 A systems view of creativity   39
2.1 Talking voices and creative patterns   80
A2.1 Distribution of new words   224

Tables

3.1 Creativity and dimensions of discourse   111
5.1 CANCODE text types and typical situations in which they
     might be found   150
5.2 Mapping creativity and social interactional context   165
6.1 Mapping creativity and social interactional context: Matrix 1   206
6.2 Mapping creativity and social interactional context: Matrix 2   207
A1.1 Transcription codes   220
A2.1 Distribution of new words   225
A2.2 Creative morphemes and categories   225

In general the arts establishment connives to keep alive the myth of the special, creative individual artist holding out against passive mass consumerism . . . Against this we insist that there is a vibrant symbolic life and symbolic creativity current in everyday life, everyday activity and expression – even if it is sometimes invisible, looked down on or spurned. We don't want to invent it or propose it. We want to recognise it – literally re-cognise it . . .

We are thinking of the extraordinary creativity of the multitude of ways in which young people use, humanize, decorate and invest with meanings their common and immediate life space and social practices – personal styles and choice of clothes, selective and active use of music, TV, magazines, decoration of bedrooms; the rituals of romance and subcultural styles; the style, banter and drama of friendship groups, music-making and dance . . . There is work, even desperate work in their play.

(Willis *et al.*, 1990: 1–2)

Literature lives within language and language within everyday life. The study of literature must live within the study of language, and the study of language within the study of the everyday mind . . .

These assumptions are deadly. Common language expressing common thought is anything but simple, and its workings are not obvious. Special language expressing special thought is an exploitation of the common and to be analyzed only in relation to it.

(Turner, 1991: 4, 14)

Acknowledgements

Many, and perhaps most, creative accomplishments in this world are neither the products of single individuals working in isolation nor the products of historical geniuses but are instead the products of several people working in intended or unintended collaboration.

(Harrington, 1999: 144)

It is now standard practice to make something close to an Oscar acceptance speech in book acknowledgements. And this book is no exception. It cannot be otherwise, since the more I reread the book the more I realise I haven't really done that much by myself.

Above all, I owe much, and much more than he will himself acknowledge, to Michael McCarthy, friend, collaborator, fellow-traveller and co-director of the CANCODE project. Mike has over the past twenty years provided all manner of points of inspiration for my own work, and in work we have done together; the many conversations, exchanges of ideas and joint seminars we have had mean, as a quick look at the bibliography for this book will demonstrate, that, not just in a metaphoric sense, this book is as much his as mine. Several of the chapters here contain voicings, tracings and in some cases liftings from papers we have co-authored, and I am grateful to Mike for allowing me to use them co-creatively in this book. I also owe much to Chris Candlin, who has provided inspiration to and encouragement of many, many academics in the field of applied linguistics and is simply the best editor and critical commentator on the work of others that I have had the pleasure to work with. Much of the work in the following chapters derives from Chris's own work on creativity over the years, and I have benefited greatly from innumerable conversations with him and for his encouragement to me in this work – which dates back to an American Applied Linguistics Association conference in Baltimore in 1994. I also owe more than they may imagine to Guy Cook, John McRae and Rob Pope, whose work on literary language, creativity and language play has been a constant source of encouragement and inspiration during the writing of this book. Rob Pope was generous enough to allow me to see an advance copy of a manuscript for a forthcoming book (Pope, forthcoming) from which I not only learned much but also filched some excellent quotations. And particular thanks go to Svenja Adolphs for helping me with innumerable corpus searches and for allowing me to draw on articles and conference papers which we have co-written.

Other friends from whom I have learned much and whose sharing of ideas and of their own work and general help to me in the field of language and creativity is greatly appreciated include Lynne Cameron, Sandra Cornbleet, Zoltán Dörnyei, Angie Goddard, Jo Guy, Michael Halliday, Craig Hamilton, Jean Hudson, Rebecca Hughes, Claire Kramsch, Michael Lewis, Janet Maybin, Louise Mullany, Bill Nash, Luke Prodromov, John Richmond, Norbert Schmitt, Paul Simpson, John Sinclair, Peter Stockwell, Brian Street, Michael Toolan and Janet White. Michael Lewis has continued to send me examples from his own corpus of everyday creative language use and allowed me to use some examples here.

I also thank Svenja Adolphs, Chris Candlin, Guy Cook, Ray Gibbs, Angie Goddard, Michael Lewis, Mike McCarthy, John McRae, Ben Rampton, Peter Stockwell and Joan Swann for providing detailed comments on the draft manuscript of this book, or parts of it, and for continuing to show interest and send me examples, references and other relevant material. Any errors which remain are entirely their fault and I accept no responsibility whatsoever.

In writing the book I am indebted to Cambridge University Press, most particularly to Colin Hayes and Jeanne McCarten, for their support and for granting me permission to use examples from the CANCODE corpus, collected between 1993 and 2003. Without the Cambridge University Press's financial support and belief in the whole CANCODE project, this book would probably not have been possible. My thanks also go to Annie Jackson and David Williams at The Running Head for their professionalism and expertise during the production process of the book and to Fran Brown for creatively helping me out of all kinds of holes by her exemplary copy-editing work.

Particular thanks go to Louisa Semlyen, Christy Kirkpatrick and Kate Parker at Routledge for their continuing patience and encouragement and for simply being a delight to work with. Last but by no means least, my thanks to Jane Carter and our children Matthew, Jennifer and Claire for combining an appropriately healthy scepticism about books like this with constant and continuous loving support.

Parts of this book have been previously published, and thanks go to the following sources for allowing me to reprint previously published material, suitably revised and modified for publication in this book. To Oxford University Press for: 'Discourse and creativity: bridging the gap between language and literature', in G. Cook and B. Seidlhofer (eds) *Principle and Practice in Applied Linguistics*, Oxford (1995): 303–23 (with Michael McCarthy) and 'Talking, creating: interactional language, creativity and context', in *Applied Linguistics*, 25, 1 (2004): 62–88 (with Michael McCarthy); to Sage Publications for 'Common language: corpus, creativity and cognition', in *Language and Literature* 8, 3 (1999): 195–216; to Trentham Books for 'Creativity and a corpus of spoken English' in S. Goodman, *et al.* (eds) *Language, Literacy and Education: A Reader*: Stoke-on-Trent (2003): 247–62 (with Svenja Adolphs). Thanks also go to Birmingham University for inviting me to give the second Sinclair Open Lecture in May 2002 on the topic of Language and Creativity, a version of which was published in 2003 by the Department of English Language and Literature.

CANCODE and Cambridge University Press

This book has made use of the Cambridge and Nottingham Corpus of Discourse in English (CANCODE). CANCODE is a 5-million-word computerised corpus of spoken English, made up of recordings from a variety of settings in the countries of the United Kingdom and Ireland. The corpus is designed with a substantial organised database giving information on participants, settings and conversational goals. CANCODE was built by Cambridge University Press and the University of Nottingham and it forms part of the Cambridge International Corpus (CIC). It provides insights into language use, and offers a resource to supplement what is already known about English from other, non-corpus-based research, thereby providing valuable and accurate information for researchers and those preparing teaching materials. Sole copyright of the corpus resides with Cambridge University Press, from whom all permission to reproduce material must be obtained.

Ronald Carter
Nottingham, July 2003

Introduction

The genesis of the book

In the Beginning was the Word.

Starting points for books can often be accidental. It was several years ago now when the starting point for this book was found, somewhat unpropitiously, one dark and slightly misty autumnal morning as I was making my trolley-pushing way towards the check-in of a local regional airport. My eye was caught by a single line of red and blue letters spread out across a large glass-fronted placard. They were arrayed in a straight line against a plain white background. The letters were the letters of the alphabet. Momentarily intrigued by the sight of the alphabet occurring in this form and in this context, I looked more closely, not at first noticing that one of the letters was missing and that its absence was accentuated by a gap between the letter *p* and the letter *r*, more or less as follows:

abcdefghijklmnop rstuvwxyz

Closer inspection revealed, of course, that the placard was an advertisement for an airline which counted among the proclaimed benefits of travelling business class the fact that there were no 'queues' at its check-in desk and that check-in for passengers with hand luggage only could be undertaken automatically by a machine.

Several minutes later when I was sitting in the departures lounge my thoughts were disturbed by the person next to me, a young Irishman who was holding a child (a little girl about 18 months of age) in his arms and moving her rhythmically back and forth while gazing intently into her eyes and occasionally rubbing his nose against hers. He was softly singing nursery rhymes which I had long forgotten having sung to my own children but which were soon recalled almost verbatim with a surprising immediacy.

Hickory, dickory dock
The mouse ran up the clock
The clock struck one

The mouse ran down
Hickory, dickory dock

Diddle, diddle dumpling my son John
Went to bed with his trousers on
One shoe off and one shoe on
Diddle, diddle dumpling my son John.

Later that same day I found myself in a seminar discussing with a group of teachers some differences between spoken and written English, and during the course of the discussion I put the following short conversational exchange (extracted from a computer-based corpus which I had been compiling) onto a projector in order for us to examine some of the ways in which spoken discourses utilise lexical vagueness ('a bob or two', 'things', 'and stuff', 'and things'). Almost involuntarily I became distracted by the repetition of the word 'bob/Bob', a feature of this text to which I had not previously paid any particular attention:

[Three students in Bristol are talking about the landlord of a mutual friend]

   A: Yes, he must have a bob or two.
   B: Whatever he does he makes money out of it, just like that.
   C: Bob's your uncle.
   B: He's quite a lot of money erm tied up in property and things. He's got a finger in all kinds of pies and houses and stuff. A couple in Bristol, one in Clevedon I think.

I began to consider why the word 'bob' was repeated, why there appeared to be no straightforward semantic connection between the two 'bobs', what kinds of attitudes and feelings may have been aroused for the speakers by the particular choice of echo and just how conscious or otherwise such a choice might be.

These three seemingly unconnected instances are provoking and I have since then begun increasingly to puzzle over them and to explore the parallels and points of connection between them. The first example, the *no queue* advertisement, is relatively easily recognisable as an instance of the widespread uses of striking wordplay and imaginative textual semiosis designed to capture a reader/viewer's attention. Very often too, as here, the message is inexplicit and some interpretative work is required to work out its meaning. In this example there is a deliberate focus on the message in that the text draws our attention by breaking with expectation. Thus, the letters of the alphabet have an established order which is broken here by a missing letter, the interpretative work centring on creative deviation from a norm. The alphabetic sequence breaks and re-forms, but only after the reader/viewer, who has of course to be predisposed to do such things, has come to read a new and original slant on the meaning of the text. The text of *no queue* is a widespread and culturally pervasive example of creativity in everyday communication. Its basic textual strategies are familiar and have been the subject of a number of recent seminal linguistic studies (see Cook, 2000).

The second example is different in so far as the content is less transparent; indeed, it would take undue amounts of imaginative energy to work out a meaning for many of the words and phrases in these nursery rhymes. For example, what are the meanings in this context of *diddle* and *dumpling*? They have established dictionary definitions but their normal referential meaning seems to be suspended in this instance, particularly since the remainder of the text asks us to forgo any formal logical understanding of why John might go to bed dressed in trousers while alternately dispensing with a single shoe. And about the mouse which runs up and down a clock seemingly in order to coincide with the striking of the hour, the less said the better, particularly when it does so to the beat of the barely intelligible *hickory dickory dock*.

The communicative purpose of the nursery rhymes is of course not so straightforward or conventional as the *no queue* advertisement. The context of the young Irish father singing when in close physical proximity to his daughter is crucial. The content of the message matters less than its communicability. It is performed rather than 'read'. The sounds and movement of the rhyme, especially its repetitions, powerfully override the referential meaning. Both nursery rhymes are representational before they are referential, their primary purpose being to represent and, by representing, to help to create a relationship, here a close physical relationship. The patterns of sound, lexis and grammatical structure are familiar and they are repeated, reinforcing rather than re-forming a way of seeing and doing. In its way each nursery rhyme is as creative as the *no queue* text, although, because repetition is conventionally seen not to be inventive, in many societies the advertisement would be more highly valued for its creative use of language.

The third example is more intriguing still, and in ways which go a long way beyond my initial preoccupation with the communicative functions of vague language and with the differences and distinctions between the lexico-grammar of spoken and written discourse. This spoken exchange deviates from familiar existing patterns in particular ways. Take, for example, the ways in which idioms are used. Idioms are regularly fixed in their form (for example, you can take a short sleep by *having forty winks* – though not 'fifty' or 'thirty-nine' winks), but in this exchange the idiomatic patterns are re-formed and extended so that the established idiom *to have a finger in every pie* is creatively transmuted into *He's got a finger in all kinds of pies and houses and stuff.* On the other hand, other idioms such as *Bob's your uncle* serve, as I have already suggested, a more echoing function, repeating a previous form, at least in terms of the word *bob*. The speaker appears to choose to repeat or at least to echo the pattern in order to concur with the previous speaker. There is a clear ideational content to the exchange here, for the speakers are talking about the relative wealth of a local landlord, but, as in the example of nursery rhymes, some of the language choices create a convergent relationship, in particular by negotiating and reinforcing a certain way of seeing things.

Notice, too, the rhetorical figure of understatement. When speaker A states that the landlord *must have a bob or two* he is implying that he is wealthy. The phrase is close to idiom of course, and is in a way one of a memory store of fixed expressions from which speakers select, but the choice is none the less marked as one which invites the other speakers not to take what is said only at its most literal but also to evaluate what is said. Indeed, across this whole conversational extract, short though it is, there is not only a pervasively creative wordplay, but the wordplay is doing more than merely displaying or achieving a focus on content. It is introducing a more affective element into the discourse by creating attitudes and by creating and reinforcing relationships. And as I have deliberated on this extract, a further intriguing feature is the precise nature of the echo of the word *bob/Bob* which originally and almost involuntarily attracted my attention. There is no clear semantic parallel between a coin (*bob*) and a name (*Bob* even in idiomatic form) and so the parallel is established either accidentally or by means of an altogether more subliminal configuration – a possibility which requires psychological as well as social or cultural explanation.

In exploring these questions further I have become more engaged by examples 2 and 3 than by example 1. Example 1 is a written text, and discussions of creativity and wordplay in relation to written examples are relatively widely available, and especially in recent years from a more linguistic point of view. As already mentioned, there are books which analyse the linguistic formation of advertisements and such books continue a line of stylistic analysis of creative language use going back almost a century to the first linguistic analyses of the language of literary texts. Such sources are valuable in that continuities and commonalities between written and spoken texts cannot be denied, and frameworks drawn from the analyses of text 1 can be of considerable value in the analyses of texts such as text 2, which exists (in written form as a record or as a prompt to memory) to be spoken or sung, and text 3, which is exclusively a spoken exchange, though that too, for the particular purposes of this book, is written out as text.

In undertaking these explorations I have been fortunate to have access to a corpus of spoken English, the CANCODE corpus (the Cambridge and Nottingham Corpus of Discourse in English), which is one of the largest of its type in the world. The details of this corpus are described in more detail in chapter 4. The main purpose of its compilation has been to provide a research resource from which better understandings of the differences between spoken and written English could be obtained in order to develop better-grounded materials for the teaching of English grammar and vocabulary. Yet, as this work has progressed, one salient and striking feature of the corpus samples appearing daily on my computer screen has been the frequency with which examples similar to that of text 3 are observed.

The following week

The following week, back at the office and having decided that these issues must wait until more data can be assembled, I was working on specific aspects of spoken grammar as part of a chapter of a new grammar of English for

Cambridge University Press (Carter and McCarthy, forthcoming). I was using the CANCODE corpus of spoken English and was scrolling through several screens of corpus data looking for examples. My attention became drawn to a particular sequence in a conversational exchange between flatmates. The contextual background to this corpus data is as follows.

[Four friends are meeting at <S 02>'s house. Following on from a prolonged stretch of casual conversation, <S 02> diverts the attention to some DIY task. Two of the friends are attempting to drill a hole in a wall in order to put up shelves: <S 01> secretary: female (31); <S 02> scientist: female (31); <S 03> unemployed: female (28); <S 04> production chemist: male (29); <S 03> and <S 04> are partners.]

    <S 03>: Have you finished screwing it in then?
    <S 02>: [laughs] Well no. [unintelligible]
    <S 03>: [unintelligible] again.
    <S 02>: We've all had a go.
    <S 04>: Yeah. Go on you have a go.
    <S 03>: It's quite hard.
    <S 02>: It's it's getting there. You can do alternate turns but then your wrist starts to hurt.
    <S 03>: Mm.
    [laughter]
    [unintelligible]
    <S 01>: It's cos you can't get a foot in. If you could get a decent er lean on it.
    <S 03>: It doesn't happen fast enough for me.
    [unintelligible]
    <S 03>: Ah. I can't move that at all. Am I exceptionally weak and crap?
    <S 01>: Yeah. It was just an exceptionally large screw for a small hole I think.
    <S 02>: Oh dear. I wouldn't wanna do that.
    [laughter]
    <S 02>: I'll heave it.
    <S 01>: It's not moving at all Margaret.
    [unintelligible]
    <S 03>: We'll put this [unintelligible] away now and never touch it again.
    [laughter]

As my attention gradually shifted from the grammatical properties to the creative properties of language, I began to consider questions about the ways in which language was being used and how far the examples did or did not correspond with the examples provided on that misty day the previous week. I began to consider the extent to which the exchange might be regarded as 'literary', not least because of the way figures of speech and wordplay normally considered to be the preserve of written, literary discourse were appearing with a particular density. I began to consider the functions and purposes to which such language was being put. I asked to what extent it was a reflex of the context (a group of friends), or of the subject matter (DIY or *do-it-yourself* home maintenance), a discourse containing many words with tendencies towards sexual puns and scatological humour, of which the word 'screw' is the most common example. I questioned to what extent the creativity serves to establish solidarity in the group, and whether the creativity in a mixed group such as this is in any way marked by the gender of the speakers. I also began to consider whether there are material differences in the way in which creativity operates in this extract of spoken English when compared with the more standard instances of written creative language which I was more accustomed to studying.

The exchange also inverts common assumptions that language use is wholly for ideational reference and for 'purposeful' transactional communication. The participants here are creating an alternative reality in which, albeit momentarily, representation takes over from reference. The event does not lead to increased knowledge on the part of the participants and the point of the exchange is not necessarily to prompt action or to transfer information. The laughter and obvious pleasure derived by the group as a result of the wordplay is sufficient justification for the exchange. And, in contrast, the extract also reminded me how often this kind of sexual wordplay and banter can also be used for competitive purposes, for purposes of insult or to put someone down. Although I do not believe that to be the case here, creativity with language does not always function for collaborative purposes.

I began to ask more questions and, in particular, to search for further instances in the corpus. As the corpus grew to 5 million words in total, I began to see ever more instances in a wider range of discourse contexts. I began to conclude that creativity is a pervasive feature of spoken language exchanges as well as a key component in interpersonal communication, and that it is a property actively possessed by all speakers and listeners; it is not simply the domain of a few creatively gifted individuals.

But is it creativity? More questions

Further searches in more data led to further questions. The searches revealed the complex nature of the topic of creativity, pointing to a need to question pretty fundamentally what exactly it means when a stretch of language is described as creative.

The following example from a conversational extract from the CANCODE corpus further prompts some of these questions about the precise nature of creative features of spoken language use. Chief among these features are examples of the repetition already noted above, but there are also other features to note.

[Extract from a conversation involving three art college students. The students are all female, are the same age (between 20 and 21) and share a house in Wales. Two of the

students (<S 01> and <S 03>) are from the south-west of England and one (<S 02>)
is from South Wales. They are having tea at home on a Sunday.]

<S 03>: I like Sunday nights for some reason. [laughs] I don't know
          why.
<S 02>: [laughs] Cos you come home.
<S 03>: I come home+
<S 02>: You come home to us.
<S 03>: +and pig out.
<S 02>: Yeah yeah.
<S 03>: Sunday is a really nice day I think.
<S 02>: It certainly is.
<S 03>: It's a really nice relaxing day.
<S 02>: It's me earring.
<S 03>: Oh lovely oh lovely.
<S 02>: It's fallen apart a bit. But
<S 03>: It looks quite nice like that actually. I like that. I bet, is that
          supposed to be straight?
<S 02>: Yeah.
<S 03>: I reckon it looks better like that.
<S 02>: And it was another bit as well, was another dangly bit.
<S 03>: What . . . attached to+
<S 02>: The top bit.
<S 03>: +that one.
<S 02>: Yeah. So it was even.
<S 01>: Mobile earrings.
<S 03>: I like it like that. It looks better like that.
<S 02>: Oh what did I see. What did I see. Stained glass. There w=, I
          went to a craft fair.
<S 01>: Mm.
<S 02>: C=, erm in Bristol. And erm, I know. [laughs] I went to a craft
          fair in Bristol and they had erm this stained glass stall and it was
          all mobiles made out of stained glass.
<S 03>: Oh wow.
<S 02>: And they were superb, they were. And the mirrors with all
          different colours, like going round in the colour colour wheel.
          But all different size bits of coloured glass on it.
<S 03>: Oh wow.
<S 02>: It was superb. Massive.

(See Appendix 1 for an explanation of the symbols used in this book for the
transcription of speech extracts.)

According to Deborah Tannen in her book on everyday talk *Talking Voices*,
repetition is a key component in what she terms the 'poetry' of talk. 'Repetition
is a resource by which conversationalists together create a discourse, a relationship, and a world. It is the central linguistic meaning-making strategy, a limitless

resource for individual creativity and interpersonal involvement' (Tannen, 1989: ch. 3). For example, key exchanges in the extract (numbered 1–3 below) involve linguistic repetition across speaking turns. But, as will be seen, the repetition is not simply an echo of the previous speaker. The forms include both verbatim phrasal and clausal repetition, and repetition with variation (for example, the addition of the word 'relaxing' in extract 2). This patterning with variation includes both lexical and grammatical repetition (the repetition of the word *bit* or *like* – in its different grammatical realisations as verb and preposition – as well as repetition of the determiner *that* in extract 3). It includes pronominal repetition with variation '*I* come home/*you* come home' (extract 1) and phonological repetition with variation (for example, *bit/better* in extract 3). Repetition is evident here in varied linguistic ways and it may not be stretching things too far to say that in the forms which are created here there is indeed a poetry of talk.

Extract 1

        <S 02>: [laughs] cos you <u>come home</u>.
        <S 03>: I come home.
        <S 02>: You <u>come home</u> to us.

Extract 2

        <S 03>: Sunday is <u>a really nice day</u> I think.
        <S 02>: It certainly is.
        <S 03>: It's a <u>really nice</u> relaxing day.

Extract 3

        <S 03>: I reckon it looks better <u>like that</u>.
        <S 02>: And it was another <u>bit</u> as well, was another dangly <u>bit</u>.
        <S 03>: What . . . attached to+
        <S 02>: The top <u>bit</u>.
        <S 03>: +<u>that one</u>.
        <S 02>: Yeah. So it was even.
        <S 01>: Mobile earrings.
        <S 03>: I like it <u>like that</u>. It looks <u>better like that</u>.
        <S 02>: <u>Oh what did I see</u>. <u>What did I see</u>. Stained glass. There w=, I
                      went to a craft fair.
        <S 01>: Mm.

But on their own the forms only take us so far. The main creative functions seem to be in the dialogic building of a relationship of accord between the speakers, the extensive repetition here creating what might be termed an affective convergence or commonality of viewpoint. These relationship-reinforcing worlds are created in other ways too: for example, by means of backchannelling, e.g. *Oh lovely, oh lovely*; *yeah, yeah*; by means of interpersonal grammatical forms such as tails . . . *They were superb, they were*; and by means of affective exclamatives *Oh wow*. The exchanges are also impregnated with vague and hedged language forms (for example, *fallen apart a bit, the top bit, I reckon*), and a range of evaluative and attitudinal expressions (often juxtaposed with much laughter) which further support and creatively adapt to the informality, intimacy and solidarity established between the three speakers.

I noted above, however, an expectation that when the the word 'creative' is employed it entails uses which are marked out as striking and innovative. Conventionally, this involves a marked breaking or bending of rules and norms of language, including a deliberate play with its forms and its potential for meaning. Such a use occurs in the above exchange towards the end of the extract, as the topic switches to discussions of the earrings worn by one of the girls. The earrings are 'dangly' rather than fixed and clearly move all over the place as she talks. They are also large and bright. The word *mobile* is metaphorically linked with the word 'earrings'. There is a pun on the meaning of 'mobile' (with its meaning of movement) and the fixture of a *mobile* – meaning either a brightly coloured dangling object which is often placed over a child's bed or cot to provide distraction or entertainment, or else a piece of moving art.

This usage is a more conventional instance of linguistic creativity involving changes in, to and with the language. It also seems on the surface to be of a different order to the repetitions and echoes noted above. To what extent is this kind of creativity different from the echoes and repetitions created by the girlfriends? If it is different, how and why is it different and is it differently valued? And, to adapt the subtitle of this book, is it or is any of it art?

Yet more questions

The extent of the evidence for the existence of creativity in daily spoken communicative exchanges and interactions has become compelling, and over the past few years I have returned many times to that happenstantial day at that airport and to the examples I encountered there of common language uses in everyday communication. And I have continued to explore and excavate, asking, among other questions: why creativity is conventionally seen largely as a written phenomenon; how spoken and written creativity differ; what their respective purposes are; whether speakers are conscious or unconscious of what they do; whether there are degrees of creativity, with some instances to be more highly valued than others; how and why creativity in common speech often seems to be connected with the construction of a relationship and of interpersonal convergence; whether spoken creativity is confined to particular sociocultural contexts and to particular kinds of relationship; what the implications are for our understanding of creativity when something is planned and worked over several times (the *no queue* advertisement), when folk memory and multiple rehearsals affect the spoken performance (the nursery rhyme) and when the discourse is largely spontaneous, unplanned and improvised chat (the Bristol landlord discussion and the art students casually talking on a Sunday afternoon).

As examples from the CANCODE data have multiplied, so have yet more questions about the nature of the data and the extent to which the many types and forms of these data can be termed creative. Throughout these early investigations what continued to strike me, and still does strike me most forcibly, is the fact that patterns and forms of language which as a student of literature I had readily classified as poetic or literary can be seen to be regularly occurring in everyday conversational exchanges.

The mere existence of such features does not, however, make the exchanges 'literary' or creative. Nor can we automatically infer that the speakers themselves are being creative or that they think of themselves as creative, though in the examples given so far the participants are clearly doing more than simply transacting information or simply socially interacting. Do we not expect there to be much more evidence of new coinages and linguistic inventions, and at the least language use which is strikingly different from the ordinary which prompts us to see things in new ways, layering in the memory and providing pleasure at the moment of use and upon recall? Can creativity be at the same time both an exceptional and an ubiquitous phenomenon? Is it art or artful or both? Can it be both? And, if creativity is pervasive in everyday language and life, is everybody creative to the same degree? Are some people more creative than others? And, in terms of methodology, how much does the analyst notice which the participants do not and vice versa? If some creative patterns such as repetition and echoing are claimed to be more below the level of conscious awareness, then what is the nature of the evidence which the analyst offers?

So, what exactly does constitute creativity in this type of language use? The Sunday afternoon example involving the art college students shows in varying degrees the creation of mutuality and a creative use of words and patterns in speech. Are such features to be seen in terms of social purposes and functions? Can they be explained wholly by means of linguistic analysis? Given the extent of work on the psychology of creativity and on creativity as a psychological phenomenon, is it best to define such uses of language with reference to psycholinguistic paradigms, as an aspect of a poetics of mind? And then, from a perspective of a cultural history of word meaning, how stable is the word 'creative'? Does it vary over time and culture or are there continuities in the meaning of the word which will help in the discussion of the kinds of forms and uses seen so widely in the samples collected?

Most importantly, for me, what part does social context play in these processes? For example, how significant is the context of friendship, membership of a cultural group, a father–daughter contact, the identity of an individual in relation to other individuals? On the above evidence creativity is clearly contextually framed and conditioned. What does this mean for our discussion?

Why this book and what is its main point?

As I researched further I discovered innumerable books on creativity, in particular in the context of written, especially literary, text but found that very little
had been written on *spoken creativity*. What explorations of the language of
spoken creativity there are have been limited by the particular preoccupations
and research paradigms of linguistics in the twentieth century. Although a rich
body of work exists in the fields of ethnolinguistics and poetics and in work on
language and anthropology, many descriptive frameworks are modelled on the
basis of written rather than spoken examples.

In some traditions, too, the preoccupation with invented sentences and the
testing of such sentences for grammaticality has not helped investigation of data
which are naturally occurring, which go beyond the level of the individual sentence, and which contain many of the features of spoken performance such as
slips of the tongue, false starts, hesitations, pauses, interruptions and the like.
Such features are inevitably not to be found when tidied up and anaesthetised
examples are the basis for analysis, and when referential and ideational uses of
language are privileged over affective, interpersonal and emotive uses. Although
there are cultural conventions in contemporary Western societies which do not
assign positive value to emotions, it is perhaps still surprising that the interpersonal and emotive features which are most marked in spoken data have not
been subjected to extensive analysis.

Of course, such preoccupations and research paradigms have to a considerable degree been occasioned by the limitations of available audio-recording
technology and, as we have seen, this situation is changing rapidly. Similarly, the
development of computer-assisted corpus linguistics, which embraces analysis
of extensive quantities of language, facilitates the analysis both of stretches of
text and of predominant patterns within such texts, including examples of
'common talk'. At the same time, however, the development of new frameworks for the analysis of spoken language and of the widespread creativity
within such examples is needed. I have thus come to the topic inspired by what
I began to see in the corpus, but with broad research questions rather than
narrow hypotheses to investigate.

The main point of the book is to explore creativity in everyday spoken
English. In doing this I look closely at the kinds of examples given in this introduction, believing that it is time to describe such data more closely and in the
conviction that creativity is not the exclusive preserve of the individual genius,
that, fundamentally, creativity is also a matter of dialogue with others and that
the social and cultural contexts for creative language use need to be more fully
emphasised. In this book I try to take some steps in this direction, although it
is new and complex territory and there will be and have been times when I
wish I had not encountered that provocative cluster of examples on that (symbolically) misty autumnal day.

The organisation of the book

The prologue at the start of chapter 1 focuses on the notion of common talk and the values which surround it, providing in the process a focus for the core questions raised in this introduction. Chapters 1 and 2 review a range of research paradigms for the study of creativity, beginning with a review of work in the discipline of psychology. The aim is to explore what different disciplines make and have made of the subject, and to see what work from other disciplines may have to offer to linguistic approaches to the topic. Existing studies of creativity as a linguistic phenomenon focus mainly on written artefacts, produced by individuals whose creative processes mark them out as uniquely inspired. With some exceptions, existing research paradigms, while often insightful and revealing, do not offer many frameworks for the analysis of creative spoken language in general, of interpersonal creativity, or of creativity as a phenomenon of daily demotic social exchanges. Studies which do offer help with theorisation of everyday creativity include: research into the cultural variability of creativity, especially in non-Western, non-individualist cultures; research into language play; research into literariness as a cline or gradient of creative language use. All these studies are reviewed and evaluated in the light of some of the main questions raised in this introduction. But, overall, it is to the studies with a more social or discoursal orientation that I turn, as the main theoretical ground is laid.

Chapters 3 and 4 set out the main issues and questions which are raised by the data in the CANCODE corpus. These chapters combine practical analysis and theoretical debate. They offer further descriptions and analysis of the main patterns found in the data, with a particular focus on parts of speech and on patterns of repetition and echoing brought about in the process of affective, interpersonal exchanges. A whole set of figures of speech such as metaphor, metonymy, idiom, and hyperbole are discussed in the context of the everyday discourses in which they most commonly occur. The existence of such patterns forces upon us key questions which impact both on linguistic and literary-aesthetic theory.

Chapter 5 describes the main corpus of spoken data on which many of the examples for the book are based. The organisation of the corpus, the procedures for data collection, the ways in which the data are organised generically, are discussed and evaluated. Analysis across the contextually shaped organisation of the CANCODE corpus also reveals further that creativity is to be located in a wide range of everyday communications, that it is closely linked to humour and wordplay, that it involves affective and interpersonal language choices, and that it occurs more markedly in certain social contexts than others. A wide range of data is drawn on in this chapter, including business meetings, intimate family exchanges, professional colleagues socialising, journalists at work and informal conversations in general.

Chapter 6 returns to theories of verbal play, to notions of literary language and to sociopsychological formulations, but the emphasis is on creativity in a range of social and cultural practices, including workplace discourse involving professional and client relations. The main argument is repeated here that creativity in spoken language involves both the creation of alternative realities and the reinforcement of existing realities, and involves some revision of the standard ways of seeing creativity. Examples in this chapter extend beyond those drawn from the CANCODE corpus to include examples of email and Internet communication, counselling and therapeutic discourse, the discourse of adolescents and of university tutorials, reinforcing throughout the importance of a view of creativity as a sociocultural process.

This chapter also looks at the kinds of blends which occur in many contemporary discoursal forms such as email, chat-lines and media 'performances', pointing out that many are more speech-based than has been assumed and that much of the pervasive creativity in such contexts is due to a blending of discourses. Monolingual, bi- and multilingual exchanges are examined. Chapter 6 also contains data in which speakers cross over between languages, exploiting patterns in more than one language, sometimes simultaneously, for creative effect. The main conclusion drawn in chapters 5 and 6 is that, while psychological explanations are helpful and necessary, spoken creativity also needs to be understood, with evidence from a wide range of texts and practices, as a fundamentally social phenomenon and as socioculturally mediated. It is important to engage not simply with creativity as an individual, decontextualised phenomenon but with creativity in context and as an emergent function of dialogue.

The epilogue, embedded within chapter 6, raises questions for further research in the area of pedagogies for language, literature and discourse study, the fostering of creativity, and the interfaces between linguistic, literary and social theory, all areas in which I have invested much thinking over the years and which are now being challenged by engagement with corpus linguistics and with the theory and practice of creativity. The chapter argues for closer links between theories of creativity, the classroom and the nature of pedagogy as pattern forming and pattern-transforming linguistic practice.

Throughout the book the data cited include two- and multiparty talk and exhibit a range of relationships ranging from informal to formal contexts, from symmetrical to asymmetrical encounters and from transactional to non-transactional exchanges. Throughout the book the ubiquity of creative language is underlined. In highlighting its uniqueness, however, the book demonstrates, perhaps paradoxically, the normality and commonality of creativity in everyday communication.

So the main theme of the book is that creativity is an all-pervasive feature of everyday language. And, as I shall say more than once, linguistic creativity is not simply a property of exceptional people but an exceptional property of all people.

Part I

Backgrounds and theories

1   Approaches to creativity

Prologue

NOW IS THE DISCOUNT OF OUR WINTER TENTS!!
(sign displayed outside a camping shop in a small town
in the English Midlands)

Cut 'n' Dried; Headlines; Making Waves; Kutz; Shampers; Klippers; Headstart; Hair Comes Linda; Way Ahead
(all names of UK hairdressing salons)

Common language expressing common thought is anything but simple, and its workings are not obvious. Special language expressing special thought is an exploitation of the common and to be analyzed only in respect to it.
(Turner, 1991: 14)

Common words, commons values and common talk

This prologue opens up further questions of the kind raised in the Introduction, underlining that the main focus for the book is on ordinary, everyday talk and on the features of creative language use to be found within such contexts. It provides a range of concrete examples while at the same time asking about the values which surround both the examples and the words we use to talk about the examples. Yet more questions are asked about the examples, and the chapter as a whole thus provides a basis from which to introduce, in chapter 2, some key theoretical paradigms from different academic disciplines which are then employed further to return to the data.

Keywords: ordinary, common, art

Ordinary people, ordinary life, ordinary language. *Ordinary* is one of those common-sense words which appear to refer unproblematically to things. But like many of the words used in the argument in this book it has a cultural history. 'Ordinary' originally had a meaning derived from the Latin *ordo* = order (with the suffix *-arius*), and referred to the designation or formal appointment of people to positions in society; hence the 'ordination' of a priest. It is not until the eighteenth century that, when referring to people, it acquires a more pejorative and dismissive sense of judgement on the grounds of their being socially inferior. More generally, the word *ordinary* has come to refer to the prosaic, unexceptional, common uses against which more exceptional or extra-ordinary uses can be measured.

Likewise, the word *common* is derived from the Latin *com* (together) and *unus* (one) and thus has etymological links with 'communal' and 'community' and 'commonwealth', that is, something which is valued on account of its being part of or belonging to a group. In the case of *common*, Williams (1983: 71) points out that it is in the sixteenth century that a reverse semantics, not dissimilar to the changes to the meaning of *ordinary*, takes place and one specialised meaning which the word acquires is that of 'vulgar' and 'unrefined'. This pejorative and derogatory sense gets extended in the late nineteenth century to refer to people (e.g. 'her speech was very common' or 'he's just so common'), though it at the same time retained the original source meaning in phrases such as 'common' ground or the 'common' good. References to language as 'common' or 'ordinary' thus often carry a sense which is both derogatory and dismissive.

The keyword *art* is used in the subtitle to this book *the art of common talk*. It is, similarly to the word *literature* which originally referred to all types of writing (see p. 55 below), also used to refer inclusively to a range of skills and competencies. For example, in the medieval university curriculum the study of the 'arts' embraced grammar, rhetoric, logic, arithmetic, geometry, music and astronomy. By the late eighteenth century the word had acquired different specialisations so that the word *artisan* came to be associated with more scientific, technological and also manual skills, while *artist* came to be associated with imaginative, intellectual and creative purposes, developing an even more abstract sense in the capitalised *Art* or its reference to the study of the humanities in a university or college Faculty of Arts. In these senses, then, the 'art of common talk' carries different inflections. 'Common talk' can refer disparagingly to the ordinary, prosaic, unimaginative talk of uneducated people which involves mechanical and non-creative techniques of communication; or it can refer positively to the universal, creative artistry of all speakers of a language.

Ordinary creativity

As discussed in the introduction, creativity is basic to a wide variety of different language uses, from everyday advertising language and slogans to the most elaborated of literary texts. Even very young children possess the capacity for telling and receiving jokes which depend for their effect on a recognition of creative play with patterns of meaning. For example, children encounter in the school playground creative exchanges such as the following:

Q: What is black and white and read all over?
A: A newspaper.

They can also give varying explanations for a newspaper headline such as the following: *Giant Waves Down Tunnel*. Both of these instances here depend on recognising dual meanings created by the phonology (*read/red*) and syntax of English (*giant* is both a noun and a modifier; *waves* can be both a verb and a noun). They tell and laugh at 'doctor doctor' and 'knock knock' jokes such as the following:

> *Patient:* Doctor, Doctor, when I close my eyes I can see spots.
> *Doctor:* Well, keep your eyes open.

> *A:* Knock, knock
> *B:* Who's there?
> *A:* Ivor
> *B:* Ivor who?
> *A:* Ivor Surprise for you.

And they enjoy reading and themselves making up titles of books such as *Keeping Fit* by Jim Nastics, *Hospitality* by Colin Anytime, or *Victorian Transport* by Orson Cart.

Advertising language also depends crucially on creative play with language and on the cultural discourses of society within which the language is embedded (see, in particular, Cook, 2002; also Moeran, 1984; Myers, 1994). For example, an advertisement for a motor car in 1992, which states that it is *A Car for the 90's*, suggests simultaneously the possibility that it is a car in which you can travel at great speeds (90 mph), that it is particularly suited to very hot weather (90° – the temperature reaches the nineties Fahrenheit), and that it is ultramodern and in tune with expectations for the decade (the 1990s). It might even suggest a car that can be put through its paces in a ninety degree right-angle turn. We might note that such texts are designed to require some engagement and interaction on the part of the reader/interpreter. The reader has been positioned in a creative conversational duetting or dialogue with a text; the text resonates with multiple meanings but they only resonate if they are interpreted as such by an audience.

Humour, creativity and everyday language

> *Airline Stewardess:* The pilot is going to have to make an emergency
>   landing. There's a problem in the cabin.
> *Passenger:* What is it?
> *Stewardess:* It's a small room at the front of the plane where the pilot sits
>   but don't worry about that now.
>
>   (adapted from the movie *Airplane*)

Everyday exchanges between people are replete with wordplay, puns and formulaic jokes. Tabloid newspapers are characterised by verbal ambiguities, often containing sexual innuendo, as in the case of the *Daily Mirror* newspaper front-page story concerning the gay international pop star George Michael who had been arrested by police in the United States on a charge of indecent behaviour in a public place. The headline made intertextual reference to a previous hit song of Michael ('Call me up before you go'): *ZIP ME UP BEFORE YOU GO, GO!!!*

Graffiti are also a not uncommon feature of everyday life, with the term 'graffiti art' sometimes reserved for the paint display often surrounding the verbal display. The medium can also be a resource for humour, as in the case of the white van, completely covered in dust and dirt, on which someone had written the words 'Also available in white'. Or the British Rail train window, similarly to wordplay reported in Chiaro (1992: 12), which had the following finger-written into the dust: *British Rail Coffee: Only £1 a slice.* The reference here is to both the expense and the consistency of the coffee served on British Rail trains. The coffee is judged to be so undrinkable that it has almost the consistency of a slice of cake or bread.

It is worth noting too that such wordplay does not exist wholly for purposes of entertainment or simply for the intrinsic pleasure obtained from the re-creation of new words and meanings from familiar patterns. As in the case of the British Rail graffiti, there can also be a social and critical purpose to the language. For example, recent problems with reliability and punctuality of trains in Britain, especially around London, led to wordplay, often written publicly and directly onto notices on stations, such as the following: *NOTwork South East*; *SNAILtrack*; *BEYONDTHEPAIL Track*. Here the phrases are critically amended from the name of the rail company 'Network South East' and the name of the track company 'Rail Track', but the humour and wordplay are directed towards the company in an adversarial response to the circumstances.

Of course, such verbal play involves varying degrees of sophistication and knowledge on the part of the consumer and the knowledge may sometimes, as here, be specific to a particular cultural context. Indeed, some even more sophisticated instances of jokes and wordplay cross linguistic boundaries, requiring knowledge of different languages or of words drawn from different languages. For example, jokes such as:

> *What do the French eat at eight o'clock for breakfast?*
> *Huit-heures-bix* [echoes Weetabix – an internationally marketed breakfast cereal]

Or

> *A: Je t'adore.* [echoes 'shut the door']
> *B: Shut it yourself.*

Or the name of a recently opened Moroccan restaurant called *So.uk*, which plays on the Arabic word 'souk' and the fact that it is at the same time very British ('so UK'), and with its spoof email address suggests that it is also very much of its time.

Cultural knowledge is needed for the impact of wordplay and humour to be at its most effective. For example, a petrol company in Ireland goes by the name of *Emerald Oil*. Interpretation of the effects of this name require a knowledge that green (emerald) is the colour associated with Ireland and that Ireland is often referred to as the 'Emerald Isle', but most particularly that an Irish accent renders the word 'isle' as 'oil', thus securing a multiple layering of effects involving cultural allusion, phonetic play and lexical ambiguity. In a related way, too, the Irish are stereotypically thought to be a group of people of inferior intellect and 'common' sense and are thus regularly the butt of jokes in which a person's lack of intelligence is at the root of the joke. In the case of the following joke, involving a public announcement at an airport, this kind of cultural knowledge is a prerequisite:

> *British Airways flight 218 departing Gate no. 10 at 13.35.*
> *Aer Lingus Flight 931 departing when the little hand is on number four and the big hand is on two.* [Aer Lingus is the national airline of Ireland.]

Creative language and shop fronts: a prototypical example

Examples cited in the introduction and in this prologue illustrate how so-called ordinary, everyday discourse is frequently patterned creatively in ways which make it memorable and striking, displaying a play with the more stable forms of language in ways which make them less stable. In the process, the limits of idioms, fixed expressions and other pre-patterned regularities are stretched and creatively de-formed and re-formed. The names of shop fronts are a good example of this creative design, playing with common collocations and idioms in order to make the language used to describe the products they offer part of the presentation. Continuing the Irish theme for a little longer, here are examples of a range of different health food shops in southern Ireland: *Nature's Way*; *Mother Nature*; *Back to Nature*; *Open Sesame*; *In a Nutshell*; *Wholesome Foods*; *The Whole Story*; *Fruit and Nut Case*; *Naturally Yours*; *Grain of Truth*; *Simple Simon*; *Nature's Store*; *Just Natural*. Most of these words and phrases (many of them fixed expressions or idioms) are connected with nature and a simple way of life and are creatively exploited to promote the sale of food which is either organically grown or which is defined as having particularly health-giving properties. For example, words like 'grain', 'nut', 'nutshell', 'store', 'whole' and 'wholesome', 'sesame (seeds)' are all words used to describe specific foods or specific qualities associated with such food; and they are then combined into fixed expressions such as 'In a Nutshell' or 'Grain of Truth', which draw attention to themselves as expressions and are made memorable by their unusual association with the sale of health food products. In other words, creativity and cultural embedding are not the exclusive preserve of canonical texts but are pervasive throughout the most everyday uses of language.

Such uses also imply dialogue and conversation. Some are more obvious, such as 'Naturally Yours' (with its echoes of 'sincerely yours/yours sincerely'; but other idiomatic phrases function at boundaries of a conversation to sum up feelings or to comment or to evaluate, so that 'In a Nutshell' or 'that's not the whole story' function in a hybrid way, depending both on our recognition that the texts are written but also on a recognition that they possess a dialogic character. As you read them, it sounds as if you are involved in conversation.

Creative purposes and functions

In a recent paper Toolan (2000a) has taken this discussion further, focusing in particular on the kinds of social attitudes conveyed by creative language play with the names of shops. Toolan points out that such verbal practices normally accompany the provision of a particular type of service or the sales of particular products. The shops are not, for example, operating in a highly serious business of chain store merchandise (they are more likely to be privately owned businesses); and they are not engaged in selling a range of products (they are more likely to be promoting a single product or service such as unblocking a drain or selling videos or cutting hair). They are not providing a service of high seriousness. Undertakers do not play with language and nor do *haute couture* hairdressers. (It is thus difficult to conceive of an undertakers called *Journey's End* or a similar all-female company called *Hearse Sincerely*!)

The shops involved in such creative play are typically places where window-shopping is not invited or is routinely uninspiring, and where the goods and services do not normally involve large sums of money; and also, perhaps paradoxically, where the service itself is not verbal (bookshops or marriage guidance counsellors or speech therapists do not normally display their 'product' in this way). Thus language play will occur with the names of independent hardware stores, photographers, plumbers, TV services, sandwich bars and cafés, hairdressers and health food shops, but normally not with the names of Michelin star restaurants, petrol stations, electrical chain stores, butchers, solicitors, estate agents and insurance companies.

An interesting exception here lies with companies which exploit the interpersonal nature of joke names or names which deviate from the expected. In Britain, new, independent, low-cost, 'no-frills' airlines which have expanded in the past few years have developed striking names such as *Go!* or *Buzz*. The motivation for creativity in name selection is a little opaque but may have something to do with making the product informal, individualised and thus unlike the more impersonal, standard, mass airlines.

Such a linguistic practice may also not be unconnected with what Fairclough (1995) has termed the 'conversationalisation' of discourse. Such a term refers to an increasing use of colloquial and personal pronoun styles of language in everyday public life. Examples abound in everything from Internet companies such as *Getmeaticket.com* which is a travel and event booking company, to products such as *I Can't Believe It's Not Butter* (a margarine), to television programmes such as *I'm a Celebrity. Get Me Out of Here!* (a 'reality' TV show).

An important function of such a practice, Toolan argues, is to individualise the supplier of the goods. The humour establishes a degree of interpersonal rapport, a kind of phatic communication, but it also establishes a kind of contract with the potential customer, revealing shop owners to be people who know that they provide a more or less one-dimensional service but that they are not to be socially so categorised themselves. As Toolan points out, 'A jokey name and shop sign becomes one small and perhaps memorable way in which the service-provider resists the consignment to invisibility. There is a situated rationale for making the shop name interesting, and attention-holding.' In other words, they know that they operate in a literal world but want to fictionalise and non-literalise a little. Searches in any local *Yellow Pages* telephone directory will disclose the differences and distinctions between jokiness and the various services, but at the same time reveal the very considerable extent of such creative practice and its sociocultural parameters. As we have seen, a key question in such exploration is, of course, the extent to which value (whose values and what kind of value?) may be ascribed to examples of everyday, demotic creativity.

Next steps

In the CANCODE corpus there is a short stretch of dialogue in which two friends are talking. One friend (*A* below) refers to a mutual colleague who has a bad track record in repaying debts. This colleague has borrowed money from him and has promised to repay the money within a few days. This is related to the friend (*B*) who replies as follows:

> *A:* He won't forget this time.
> *B:* Brian, can you see those pigs over my left shoulder moving slowly
>   across the sky?
> [*A* and *B* both burst into laughter]

The laughter results from both *A* and *B* recognising a piece of creative language use. The creativity results from a common starting point in an everyday idiom 'Pigs might fly' which is used to describe an impossible or at least unlikely event, in this case the repayment of a debt. The creative paraphrase of the idiom forces *B* to infer the original form of the idiom and *A* to interpret accordingly the intended meaning of *B* in this new context.

Several times in the corpus there are instances in which remarks about bad weather are given an ironic preface such as: *Lovely day, isn't it? Warm enough for you? Just right for a day on the beach. Lovely weather for ducks*, all of which refer to weather which is cold, wet and generally inclement and which require a listener to work out that the word meanings do not apply directly or literally. The listener furthermore interprets the speaker as making a critical, evaluative comment on current meteorological conditions.

These examples belong within a range of contextually generated effects such as irony, sarcasm, satire, understatement and hyperbole producing meanings which are non-literal and which require listeners to make indirect, interpretative inferences. That such communicative features are common in conversations (particularly in informal casual discourse) reinforces the view that ordinary language can be routine and formulaic or pervasively unordinary and can involve, as we have seen throughout this prologue, the creation and interpretation of patterns which enjoy a family resemblance with those more usually designated literary. The examples here are pieces of everyday linguistic interchange, unremarkable in their way in that such exchanges occur routinely, but remarkable in that such everyday exchanges are far from mundane and illustrate a pervasive creativity in common thought. It is the relationship between this kind of spoken language and creativity which forms the main focus in this book.

This prologue has further underlined the significance of ordinary, common creativity. I have begun to show that it takes many different forms, that it is specific to social context, that it is monologic but also fundamentally dialogic, that it is all around us, that interaction is basic to creativity and that creative acts have variable values depending on the language used to describe such values.

In this chapter and in chapter 2 these topics are pursued further; and, as in this prologue, we return many times, in relation to the term 'creative', to the definitions and social values of words such as *ordinary*, *art*, *common* and *literary*. Indeed, it is with the sociocultural history of words that the chapter proper begins.

Introduction

> Creativity is a puzzle, a paradox, some say a mystery. Inventors, scientists, and artists rarely know how their ideas arise. They mention intuition, but cannot say how it works. Most psychologists cannot tell us much about it either. What's more, many people assume that there will never be a scientific theory of creativity – for how could science possibly explain fundamental novelties? As if all this were not daunting enough, the apparent unpredictability of creativity seems to outlaw any systematic explanation, whether scientific or historical.
>
> (Margaret Boden in Boden, 1994)

The main orientation of this book is applied linguistic with a particular focus on social and cultural perspectives. This chapter begins by investigating the cultural history of the word *creativity* and by examining changes to the meaning of some keywords connected with creativity. Exploring the main lexical partners of the word *creative* such as *individual*, *genius* and *originality* reveals that views of creativity change over time and that our understandings vary according to different sociohistorical and cultural positions.

However, the most dominant recent research paradigms for investigations of creativity have been within the discipline of psychology, and these perspectives are investigated on pp. 30–42 below. On pp. 42 ff. I argue that linguistic, social and cultural factors also need to be more fully considered. A sociolinguistic, socioanthropological and sociocultural perspective on creativity underlines how creativity is both differently accented and socially constructed in different times and places. Such a perspective also shows how contemporary societies place different values on different forms of creativity. Throughout the chapter it is argued that understanding the semantic history of keywords is an important part of this perspective.

Keywords and cultural histories

> O art thou but
> A Dagger of the Mind, a false Creation,
> Proceeding from the heat-oppressed Brain?
>
> (William Shakespeare, *Macbeth*)

As we have already seen from the introduction, creativity is difficult to define. It has been studied within a number of different research paradigms and traditions. In fact, research to date has posed more questions than it has answered. One of the reasons for the general lack of research into creativity has been a widespread assumption that it is an essentially spiritual or transcendent process which is inaccessible to scientific investigation or analysis and which is certainly resistant to linguistic analysis. This assumption is reinforced by many creative artists, such as the poet Robert Graves, paying homage to a 'muse' of external influence and spontaneous inspiration (Graves, 1966). The notion of inspiration (with its derivations of 'breathing in'), suggesting the influence of natural but unaccountable outside forces, can be traced back to the time of Plato and has been dominant in much Western thinking about the subject. Sternberg and Lubart (1999: 5) comment that 'The creative person was seen as an empty vessel that a divine being would fill with inspiration. The individual would then pour out the inspired ideas, forming an otherworldly product.'

Create and creation: what is created, what is divine?

The connection between creativity and divinity is, of course, found in the word *create* itself, which is the past participle form of the Latin *creare*, meaning 'to make' or 'to produce'. The basic word form is used in Latin mainly in the sense of an original 'divine' creation of the world. The words *creation* and *creature* are semantically interconnected too, in that according to many established accounts it was a divine act of inspiration that resulted in the creation of living creatures.

In his valuable semantic and cultural history *Keywords* (1983: 82) Raymond Williams points out that creation has not, at least until the Renaissance, been seen as a human act. From the Renaissance period, Williams argues, the meaning of the word changes to embrace the idea that human beings are capable of creative acts, notably acts of the imagination, which allow the creation of alternative worlds. This liberation from creation as an exclusively divine act was, however, by no means a smooth process and uncertainties continue to surround processes of human creation. Williams points out how in Elizabethan literature the use of the word *creation* for human acts was never far away from a sense of imitation or counterfeit creation, a process that could be seen as having potentially unpleasant and even dangerous implications, as the quotation from *Macbeth* at the heading of this section neatly illustrates. The residual view of creation as associated with the supernatural and of creation as essentially the prerogative of those with a special power(s) remains highly significant through to the present day.

The modern sense of creation as a human and aesthetic act only becomes more firmly established in the eighteenth century. The link between creation and art led to the notion of the artist as creator, although the values which attach to the word still carry the sense of this act being a special or divine calling, as Williams (1983: 83) illustrates with a revealing quotation from the Romantic poet Wordsworth, in which he writes to the painter Haydon, 'High is our calling, Friend, Creative Art.' Although the equation between creativity and artistic production is now firmly established, the semantic history of the word *creation* continues to exercise influence in that the collocation of any activity with the word *creative* almost immediately confers a sense of high seriousness, value and transcendent significance.

The 'novel'

It was also in eighteenth-century English literature that a new art form, the novel, came to prominence. Within this context of cultural expectations the form was of course resisted for its centred depiction of individual personal experience, and was initially distrusted because of its depiction of fictionalised events. Historically, too, the form of the novel was closely connected with the growth of Protestantism, the rise of capitalism and the cultural significance of a growing individualism in society (see Watt, 1948). The word *novel* itself, suggesting something new and possibly original, and the broader conception that *fiction*, something made up and invented as opposed to something factual and real, can creatively represent individual human experience is an important development in the cultural history of creativity. The complex relationship between creativity and the creation of alternative and fictionalised worlds is a significant one and is explored at several points in this book.

Creativity and originality

Another important semantic connection exists between the words *creative* and *original*. It is a link which goes some way towards explaining why the creative act is always seen, at least in many modern industrialised cultures, in terms of making something novel, i.e. new or innovative. The meaning of *original* here is of something new and unexpected (e.g. *He's such an original thinker. That's a really original idea*). However, the word *original* also has a meaning of 'origins', or original sources (as in 'the original walls of the city' or 'the original inhabitants of the town'). The word derives from Latin *origo*, meaning a rise or beginning or source, and this meaning links it with the sense of a basic source from which everything organically grows. In terms of etymology, therefore, there is no sense of anything 'new'; the most salient etymological meaning of 'original' is of going back to an original, perhaps divine, creative beginning.

It is in the eighteenth century and in the early nineteenth-century Romantic periods of art and literature, Williams points out, that the word *creative* comes to be linked with a sense of something singular and rare and comes to be used to describe works of art. He revealingly cites the writer and critic George Young, who wrote in 1759: 'an Original . . . rises spontaneously from the vital root of genius; it grows, it is not made; Imitations are often a sort of Manufacture, wrought up by those mechanics, art and labour out of pre-existent materials not their own' (*Conjectures on Original Composition*, 12, cited in Williams, 1983: 230). Such a position, stressing as it does both a return to origins and the establishment of the new, reveals a point of transition from Classical to more Romantic and thus modern conceptions of creativity, illustrating how contemporary views of creativity are connected with an individual act, and how creativity is associated with the properties of the individual human mind; and how the stress on the creative individual and on the link between creativity and human originality is a relatively recent historical development.

Genius and individuality

Genius is the crucial middle term developed mainly in the eighteenth century, in the millenial transition from theories which view the source of poetic originality and creation as external – i.e. concepts of divine inspiration and poetic madness – to theories which posit them as internal i.e. as processes of imagination or of the subconscious.

(Preminger and Brogan, 1993: 455–6)

The Romantic conception of the individual creative author-artist develops gradually from this mid-eighteenth-century view. But it also evolves from a view of the writer-artisan as collaborator, a view which was securely established before and during the Renaissance. In the case of Shakespeare, for example, many Romantic and post-Romantic accounts stress his individual and universal genius – accounts which are the most pervasively ingrained within popular cultural reproductions of Shakespeare (ranging from souvenir T-shirts to the names of theatrical companies). But these accounts conflict with alternative representations of the complex of collaborative, creative roles taken on by Shakespeare himself in what we know to be his daily cultural practices as actor/writer/director/theatrical financier/playwright and collaborator in a dramaturgical company.

The Romantic and post-Romantic notion of creative artist as individual is thus a relatively recent phenomenon. It is reinforced by stereotypical images of the lone artist suffering in isolation for his art or the individual (and often mad) scientist with a shock of vertically pointing white hair, persisting against all the odds with his singular vision in a remote laboratory. In many ways the images run seriously counter to some contemporary practices such as the collaborative creative practices invoked in the production of many modern media. It would be a mistake therefore to view creation as a wholly individual act. In many way creation also involves co-creation.

The equation of acts of creativity with *genius* and of works of art with the artistic creations of a genius also has semantic roots. For example, the word *genius* in Latin carries a sense of a 'guardian spirit' which links it firmly, in an association not dissimilar to that of *creation*, with a spiritual process. The core meaning of the related Latin word *gens* is, however, of a group or a collective spirit, a sense of (spiritual) belonging which is retained in the phrase 'genius of place' or 'the genius of the age'. Paradoxically, therefore, there is no etymological link to the idea of a genius as an individual, and between the fourteenth and eighteenth centuries the word carries a main meaning of characteristic traits or abilities which can be applied to periods of time and to places as much as to individuals. Once again it is during the eighteenth century, according to Williams (1983: 143), that the word *genius* comes to be much more unambiguously associated with exceptional individual ability and to be collocated with words such as *individual* and *creative*. The semantic connection of the word genius with the word 'ingenious' and thus with novelty and innovation also becomes more transparent at this time. Such a view is reinforced further by several recent studies of creativity which are based on studies of individual creative geniuses; for example, Gardner's anatomy of creativity through a study of Freud, Einstein, Picasso, Stravinsky, Eliot, Graham and Gandhi (Gardner, 1993c) (see below, pp. 33–5).

The connection between creativity and individuality or individual genius is thus not a natural and universal feature of creativity. The assumption that creativity is mainly an individual act is a concept which derives its particular strength from a late eighteenth-century sense of the individual which in turn is inseparable from the break up of a medieval social, economic and religious order with its developing emphasis on the individual's personal existence over and above his or her anonymous place within a social and religious hierarchy. It is a way of thinking reinforced by Charles Darwin's evolutionary biology of the mid-nineteenth century as developed in *On the Origin of Species*, published in 1859, where the word *origin* in the title captures both a return to origins and the uniqueness of the human species.

Art and the creative artist

These various ways of conceptualising the individual lead to the post-Romantic view of the (almost always male) artist/genius as an isolated individual struggling to convey a unique, personalised vision. Post-Romantic conceptions hold therefore that creativity is of necessity an isolated act, in which the individual withdraws into his or her writing (or music or art) in order to preserve a unique vision, a vision which goes beyond ordinary communal experience and one of which only a special and presciently inspired individual may be possessed. The writer may well seek to adopt communal forms (e.g. ballads) or, as in the case of the manifesto to *Lyrical Ballads* (1798) written by the English Romantic poets Wordsworth and Coleridge, argue that the language of poetry should be the language of ordinary people ('the language of men'). These practices are undertaken in order democratically to encode such a vision, but it is the uniqueness and individuality of such self-expression that is commemorated and valued.

Creativity and inventiveness

The word *creative* is also closely connected with *invention* (at the present time, especially technological invention) and of inventing or spontaneously discovering something new. The word derives from the Latin *in-venire* (to 'come in' or to 'enter into'), and encodes a sense of finding or discovering something new or of bringing about something that never previously existed. An invention is always to some degree an intervention (from *inter-venire* – to 'come between'). That is, a 'discovery' is often best seen as an 'uncovering' of what is already there, not simply or exclusively a making up from the beginning. For example, the invention of something like the light bulb or the steam-engine or the computer microchip involved building on existing knowledge (often involving teams in different places rather than a lone individual); it involved traditions of work by others in the field or in related fields; and it entailed intervening creatively to adapt to the circumstances and requirements of the present time. It is only in one particularly narrow and modern sense of the word that *invention* is seen as the work of a spontaneous, individual, creative genius.

Creativity and context: novelty and appropriacy

Already in this chapter we have seen how the meanings of the word *creativity* are variable over time and space and how in the past century the main assumptions underlying creativity have stabilised. The dominant current definition of creativity is an ability to produce work that is *novel* and *appropriate*. As we have seen above in connection with the history of the literary novel, by 'novel' is meant something that is new and unexpected and normally original in so far as it represents a departure from existing practices. By 'appropriate' is meant something that is normally fitted or adapted to the resolution of problems or difficulties existing within defined constraints. It should also have outcomes which are clearly valued as specific within a particular work or activity domain and which are approved and valued within the cultural community associated with that domain. The reference to 'ability' and 'production' also embraces creativity as a human capacity for acting on and changing perceptions of the material world.

The modern post-Romantic view of creativity, particularly its association with artistic production, is, as we have seen, a markedly time-bound, culturally located conception connected in part but not wholly with the industrialised societies of the Western world. This view has, however, been profoundly influential on thinking about and on research into creativity in the past century. It contrasts with the views of creativity developed and adopted in other cultures, and contrasts with the different values which exist within cultures and subcultures towards individual as opposed to, say, collective or group approaches to creativity. And, of course, we should not forget that common conceptions and viewpoints shift and that in the post-modernist practices of the present time, new views of the nature and definition of creativity will undoubtedly emerge.

Cultures characterised by individualism define the self as autonomous from the collective. More collectivist cultures stress the significance of the individual only in relation to the norms and expectations of a larger whole, such as the family or a social or national grouping. Creativity therefore becomes much more an expression of adherence to established norms and the emphasis is on successful achievement through reproduction of those norms.

In some cultures, the skilled creator is thus as much an *imitator* as a creator and is especially creative in the way in which imitation is undertaken. For example, Lubart (1999: 341) points out how some Eastern conceptions of creativity are less focused on innovation and originality and on working against established conventions and systems of ideas and much more focused on the re-visioning or re-membering of existing ideas. Western notions of creativity also seem to involve a linear or sequential development of thought, with creative innovations constituting a new point of departure; whereas in Eastern conceptions of creativity, notions of progression are weaker and the dominant movement is circular and restorative.

I will argue below that Eastern views of creativity to some degree provide a valuable corrective to dominant Western paradigms and also help us to recognise that creativity is closer to oral expression than is often understood. I will also argue that the kinds of creativity valued in many non-Western cultural contexts are essentially collective, and express mutuality and convergence rather than express an individual self, an argument which is especially important for an understanding of the 'demotic creativity' which is the central focus of this book. At the same time it will be argued that what is valued as creative is itself highly variable, both socially and culturally, and that creative purposes and outcomes cannot be explained or understood with reference to definitions either of culture or of value which are too exclusive or essentialist. Understanding creativity, especially in so far as it is manifested in spoken language, requires therefore a sharp sense of the relativity of cultural production over time, in context and across different societies.

Creativity: the view from psychology

Research into the phenomenon of creativity is by no means extensive and has only been actively pursued during the past fifty years or so. The subject has been seen mainly as the domain of various sub-disciplines, a process which to some degree has led to fragmentation and marginalisation of creativity as a topic for study. The position has also been compounded by it not being wholly clear whether, as an object of study, creativity belongs within more empirically based scientific approaches or within the broader qualitative investigations more usually associated with the human and social sciences. Within the broad field of the human sciences the study of creativity has been confined to the exploration of creative processes, mainly in respect of the creation of artistic texts – and to a lesser degree in respect of processes of language acquisition and development.

Research has been most active within the field of psychology, where the concern has been to identify the characteristic cast of mind and the properties of the brain associated with creative acts. The next part of this chapter examines current and recent research into creativity from within the field of psychology. Subsequent parts devote space to sociocultural and literary-linguistic approaches. This background establishes useful and developing frameworks within which the main topic of this book, the study of creativity within everyday spoken discourse, can be focused.

Psychological approaches

> How is creativity different from intelligence? How can we measure a person's creativity? Which cognitive processes are involved in creative thinking? How does a creative product happen? Which life experiences produce a creative person? What are the characteristics of a creative person? What motivates creative people? What are the biological and evolutionary bases of creativity? How do social and cultural contexts affect creativity? Is creativity the dominion of an elite few or can everyone be creative? How does creativity develop? Can people learn to become more creative?
>
> (Meyer, 1999: 449)

Practical and pragmatic approaches

Pragmatic approaches to the study of creativity and to the description of creativity in action have provided a particular public face for applications of insights into creativity. They have been assimilated within corporations and businesses as a framework for training of personnel and as a focus for determining the problem-solving character of a group of people or of the people who make up a team or an institution. As a result, problem-solving activities such as 'brainstorming' (Osborn, 1953) or de Bono's 'lateral thinking' programme (de Bono, 1992) have become established as common practices and are used in a wide range of activities. The underlying value attached to such activities is that the stimulus that they provide to the establishment of habits of 'lateral' or innovative, creative thought enhances a capacity for problem-solving. The outcomes of pragmatic approaches have had and continue to have an enduring popular appeal, although they lack any clear basis in empirical research and the 'results' have in general not been given any external validity.

Psychometric approaches

In contrast with pragmatic approaches, psychometric approaches to the study of creativity emphasise controlled experimentation, quantitative measures and highly specific analyses of mental traits, mainly those of divergent thinking and of problem-solving ability. Psychometric approaches have also developed specific tests in order to assess the degrees of creative thinking engaged in by individuals and to compare the degrees of creative ability possessed by different subjects. One of the best known is the IQ (intelligence quotient) test which was developed in the mid-twentieth century in the United States by Ternan and Cox and Torrance and others. Such tests use simple paper-and-pencil assessments of basic verbal and figural abilities.

The scores from these easily administered tests certainly provide more objective results than measures hitherto, and there are certain benefits too in tests which can be undertaken with ordinary people from different walks of life. Researchers in the non-psychometric tradition have, however, criticised the methodology for being oversimplified and for reducing the scope of the definition of creativity, questioning in the process whether intelligence and its relation to creativity can be easily assessed. For example, where they are used as an index of creative thinking such tests are limited because they tend to measure only logical or analytical competences, neglecting any more inclusive measure of creative response. Others question whether creativity can be isolated by an approach which simply takes a rarity of responses in certain categories as evidence of originality. And others question whether insights into ordinary subjects, however revealing, shed any light at all on the creativity possessed by people who are socially and historically valued as creators. In such cases, it is argued that a more flexible and inclusive measure of *multiple* intelligence (including, as well as more cognitive dispositions, kinetic, tactile, emotional and interpersonal factors) is adopted (see Amabile, 1983; and several papers in Sternberg, 1999).[1]

Psychodynamic approaches

Psychodynamic approaches are different again from pragmatic and psychometric ones, lacking the popular appeal of the pragmatic view and avoiding the limited scientificity of the psychometric tradition. They originate to a considerable degree in the work of Sigmund Freud, who was particularly fascinated by the work of eminent creators. Freud established a case-study approach which was built on better understanding of the work of figures such as Leonardo da Vinci, and from these studies he elaborated a theory that the creative impulse is an inflection of unconscious wishes on the part of the creator, for example for love, wealth, social respectability. Later Freudians such as Kris (1952) elaborated these ideas, arguing that movement from the unconscious wish to the conscious creative product involved different stages in which unmodulated thoughts – which normally appear in sleep, daydreams or in drug-induced conditions – are controlled by ego-induced conscious thought and then creatively transformed. Kubie (1958) has pursued similar lines, arguing that the creative process consists of a *primary* and a *secondary* process and does originate in a flow of loose and unconnected thoughts (primary process) which are able to be connected and refigured by creative thinkers, and in the case of artists transformed (secondary process) into novel and original material.

The tradition of psychodynamic work has been criticised by Weisberg and others (see Weisberg, 1986, 1993). Its problems as a research method are the lack of an easily retrievable methodology and the degree of subjective assessment and interpretation associated with the investigation of a single subject. Such categories as primary and secondary creative processes, while appealing as concepts, are also not directly amenable to definition and empirical testing. The psychodynamic tradition has links, however, with more recent biographical approaches, which have in turn differentiated themselves from earlier approaches both by an avoidance of speculation on creative processes, and by a focus on multiple case studies which together provide a more secure basis from which generalisations can be drawn.

Biographical approaches

The *biographical* approach derives its strength from a rich and authentic documentation of the lives and life histories of distinguished, historically valued creators. Biographical approaches have their origins in Francis Galton's (1869) study *Hereditary Genius,* which attempted to isolate recurring features in the lives of highly accomplished individuals. More recent work within this tradition includes Wallace and Gruber's twelve case studies (Wallace and Gruber, 1989) and Gardner's longitudinal study of the lives and works of seven renowned creative individuals from different artistic, scientific and public domains (see Gardner, 1993b and c). Gardner's subjects were: Einstein (scientist), Darwin (evolutionary biologist), Picasso (artist), Stravinsky (musician), T. S. Eliot (poet), Gandhi (politician) and Martha Graham (dancer). The aim of biographical approaches is to combine a qualitative analysis with a quantitative analysis which (even if based on relatively few subjects) seeks to identify the childhood experiences, life events, personal and relationship qualities and personality traits which contribute to the development of the creative individual within the framework of a theory of 'multiple intelligences'. In this sense, 'multiple intelligences' refers to the ways in which creative capacity draws not from any single source but from many sources and has many different origins in the life experiences of an individual. Creativity is not singular, and different creators have different creative capacities.

In one particular case Policastro and Gardner (1999) are able to hypothesise that there are four main types of creators:

- *The Master:* someone who fulfils and exploits to the maximum all the genres and available modes of thought associated with a particular field or domain (Mozart; Rembrandt).
- *The Maker:* someone who challenges the genres and ways of thinking associated with a particular domain or field and in the process creates new domains or sub-domains (Beethoven; Einstein; T. S. Eliot).
- *The Introspector:* someone who directs all his or her energies to engagement with their own state of mind and to a better understanding of their own psyche (Freud, Virginia Woolf).

- *The Influencer:* someone who acts upon the outside world, effecting change in the public sphere (Gandhi, Mandela, Eleanor Roosevelt).

It should be noted that these are dominant and salient characteristics of the creators and that the characteristics are not mutually exclusive; for example, Virginia Woolf was most creative in the realm of introspection but also made many creative innovations as a maker within the genre of the modern novel.

Through biographical investigations Gardner has also explored the common features, especially in personality traits, of eminent creators. Policastro and Gardner (1999: 223) summarise their research as follows, describing, in particular, the differences of creators from others as a *fruitful asynchrony*:

> What emerges from studies of highly creative individuals is a different but related phenomenon. Creative individuals stand out not on account of their asynchrony from the society *per se*, but rather in the light of the ways in which they deal with these deviations. Rather than becoming despondent and shifting to another line of work, creative individuals are characterised by their disposition to convert differences into advantages.

The biographical research of Gardner and his associates has also succeeded in hypothesising particular types of creative behaviour which range from problem solving to theory building, to the creation of a symbolic system which can only be fully appreciated and understood several years after it has first been published or presented or performed (examples of the latter type would be T. S. Eliot's *The Waste Land* or Picasso's *Guernica*). Citing the dance creations of Martha Graham as a prototypical instance, Gardner also notes individuals whose creativity resides not so much in an enduring artefact but in real, time-bound, ritualised performance. Gardner also notes risk-taking in his typology and cites the actions of Mahatma Gandhi, who often had no opportunity to rehearse or work on his actions but had to create from responses to an immediate and evolving situation. Policastro and Gardner also underline from their findings that, 'if someone shows creative behaviour of one kind, it does not necessarily follow that he or she may be equally capable of showing creative behaviour in other kinds of activities' (1999: 221). In this connnection it should also be pointed out that creativity is not always an impulse for good. History provides many examples of the evil genius whose creativity works for destructive ends.

Although biographical approaches may appear to be primarily social and historical, the main emphasis is on the cognitive domains associated with the creator. Amabile (1983) and Gardner (1993a and c; 1995), for example, describe creativity as a confluence of intrinsic motivation, knowledge of a field and particular cognitive skills. They isolate the following creative-cognitive skills as especially relevant:

- coping with complexities and being prepared to change one's established mind set during problem solving, including being willing to try counter-intuitive approaches;

- a style of working which embraces great energy and commitment, the ability to set aside other problems and minimise external constraints, the capacity to focus for a long time to the exclusion of other concerns, including personal relationships.

How far can we go?

A focus on the individual creator and on an analysis of his or her creative disposition is always valuable but it may obscure questions about the nature of creativity as seen from the point of view of the audience or receivers for the created product. This point is developed further below but a question can be raised here about the distance a creator may sometimes need to go to express a particular vision or to represent a particular set of ideas and about how the distance travelled may mean that the 'consumers' of the work produced might not be able or willing to make that journey.

For example, paintings in the Modernist period in the first half of the twentieth century deliberately displaced these 'normal', 'realistic' ways of seeing and representing, in the process questioning where the boundaries are between real and unreal. A good example is the painting of the later Picasso, which moves conventional three-dimensional perspective into multidimensional spaces. Or the constructivist art of the Soviet Russian artist Malevich, who used black and white geometric shapes to angle new ways of seeing, finally arriving at a depiction of a white square on a white square which was then deemed by the artist to be a point which he could not go beyond. Or the American Jackson Pollock's action painting, in which traditional brushwork is supplanted by paint being distributed across a canvas by a range of different implements and actions, resulting in pictures which are more visually kinetic and which disturb the conventionally static 'framed' picture with its conventional perspective. And in the 1990s artists have used all kinds of objects in the setting of the art gallery itself to question what might properly be constituted as art: an unmade bed, a collection of bricks, an ordinary room in which a light goes on and off every few seconds.

How far the artist may go in producing art, it should be stressed at this point, is not only a matter for the artist to decide. There are limits and those limits are not entirely internal to an individual mind or rooted in a psychology of the exceptional. They involve social and cultural factors external to the individual.

But, first, back to our psychological orientation.

Cognitive approaches

In their own right, cognitive approaches come under the broad heading of 'experimental psychological' approaches to creativity and are concerned with fuller understanding of the kinds of mental operations which underpin creative thought. Recent studies, using techniques from artificial intelligence, have seen computational simulations of the creative movements of the mind in a range of activities from attempting to reproduce the processes of discovery of scientific laws to a re-creation of processes of jazz improvisation. The underlying theory for such research activities is that creativity is 'combinatorial' (Boden, 1999), that is, it involves connections between ideas and and ways of creatively applying those ideas in 'exploratory-transformational' modes. Creativity involves a search to apply such combinations to the solutions of problems within a conceptual space.

Some studies (for example, Weisberg, 1986, 1993) have claimed that the major processes involved in creative thinking, such as thinking analogically, are essentially common and shared and are not necessarily the property of unique individuals. Cognitive approaches seek to build from aspects of psychodynamic approaches and, in particular, explore how, for example, different phases of the creative process can be measured, preferably intersubjectively by a group of judges, thereby avoiding the subjective biases of individual researchers.

For cognitive researchers there are two main processing phases: a *generative* phase which includes pre-conscious and unmodulated components and an *exploratory* phase which embraces, with different inflections in different individuals undertaking different tasks, processes of retrieval, association, analogy-formation, category transformation and so on. (The two processes have similarities with the primary and secondary processes described on p. 32 above.) Finke and his associates have developed what they term the Geneplore model (see Finke, 1990), a model from which experimental tests such as the following have been developed:

> subjects will be shown parts of objects, such as a circle, a cube, a parallelogram, and a cylinder. On a given trial, three parts will be named, and subjects will be asked to imagine a tool, a weapon or a piece of furniture. The objects thus produced are then rated by judges for their practicality and originality.
>
> (Sternberg and Lubart, 1999: 8)

In an often quoted study from the early part of the last century, Poincaré (1913) comments on how approaches to problems often involve a conscious focus which in turn invokes an unconscious process of which the creator may not be fully aware. The subsequent unconscious process leads to a random combination of ideas, one of which may then emerge as an appropriate creative solution to the problem.

Biological approaches

Biological or cognitive neuroscience approaches explore the physiology of creativity, investigating the brain activities of people engaged in creative thought. Studies underline that creativity is likely to take place when there is low overall cortical arousal. For example, Martindale (1999: 139–41) summarises evidence that creative inspiration occurs in a mental state where attention is defocused, thought is associative, and a large number of mental representations are simultaneously activated . . . as shown . . . by low levels of cortical activation, more right- than left-hemisphere activation, and low levels of frontal-lobe activation.

The evidence obtained by these neuroscientific approaches contrasts with other approaches and, even though it is naive to suggest that creativity can be explained by analysis of physiological activity, the research provides alternative perspectives on the issues which can be used in conjunction with other approaches.

Social-personality approaches

Social-personality research approaches have concentrated on determining some of the relevant personality factors and environmental variables affecting creative thought and creative production. One such factor is motivation, and Amabile and her associates (Amabile, 1983; Collins and Amabile, 1999) have undertaken detailed studies of the effects of intrinsic motivation on creativity. These studies illustrate the extent to which motivational training can help, as well as the extent to which a supportive social environment for creativity can in itself generate motivation, especially in educational contexts. Such studies also underline that individual differences between creators are not simply a matter of cognitive style but also involve a complex of individual and situational interactions. Studies of the social environment, in particular extensive historiometric case studies by Simonton (1984, 1994), have also underlined the part played by resources, including financial resources, peer group support and/or peer competition, political stability, densities of population of others working in the same field and so on. Studies by Lubart (1999) also show the importance of variability in the estimation of creative output and creative thinking from a more social and cross-cultural dimension. It is, however, notable that there is no real integration of the cognitive and social traditions so that styles of thinking and cognitive measures have not been conjoined in any systematic way to studies of environmental variables and cultural determinants on creativity.

Multiple components of creativity: the value of a 'systems' approach

What we call creativity is a phenomenon that is constructed through an interaction between producers and audience. Creativity is not the product of single individuals, but of social systems making judgements about individuals' products.

(Csikszentmihalyi, 1999: 313)

This brief survey of dominant paradigms in the psychological approach to the study of creativity has illustrated the diversity of work but has also pointed to the fragmentation of the field. Approaches have tended to view a part of the phenomenon and to treat it as if it represented the whole, with the result that some theorists have criticised the respective traditions and approaches for their reductiveness. More recently, what have been termed 'systems' approaches have sought to correct such tendencies.

The Russian psychologist Mihaly Csikszentmihalyi (1988, 1996, 1999) has, for example, taken a 'systems' approach to the study of creativity by investigating the interaction of the individual creator (including personality traits, dominant motivating factors and creator typology), the particular field in which he or she works (including the influence and reaction of those who control the flow of creative products, e.g. publishers, critical reviewers, etc.) and the domain of their creations (the culturally accepted forms and styles available). Mastery of domain is seen in a number of studies to be crucial to successful creativity; in some cases, mastery may take several years (Darwin's *On the Origin of Species* was the result of over thirty years' research) but it is a necessary prelude to ground-breaking output or innovative solution to problems. Czikszentmihalyi comments (1999: 315–16) that the creativity makes no sense unless it is accepted by others in the domain and can be adapted to a changing environment:

> Creativity occurs when a person makes a change in a domain, a change that will be transmitted through time. Some individuals are more likely to make such changes, either because of personal qualities or because they have the good fortune to be well positioned with respect to the domain . . . To be creative, a variation has to be adapted to its social environment, and it has to be capable of being passed on through time. What we call creativity always involves a change in a symbolic system, a change that in turn will affect the thoughts and feelings of the members of the culture. A change that does not affect the way we think, feel, or act will not be creative.

In other words, creativity must not go too far, and must not deviate too far from accepted norms. The creative artist or thinker must respect though not necessarily conform to the norms, the canons or the received views which operate at any one time within the communities which respond to or are affected by the creative output.

The modelling of such systems can be illustrated in Figure 1.1. The crucial underlying organisation is one of interrelationship of structures. No single factor can be isolated as primarily significant, as it can only be significant in relation to other factors which make up the whole. Most important, however, is that, according to Czikszentmihalyi, the evaluation of what is creative is neither global nor universal but varies from one domain or context to another and can only be fully appraised according to the criteria of a particular field of activity or 'domain'. It leads to a recognition of the importance of different social and cultural mechanisms in the recognition of what is creative.[2] In other words, 'systems' need not only be psychological.

There are some limitations to this account of creative processes. For example, there is little attention given to how and why different domain-specific values

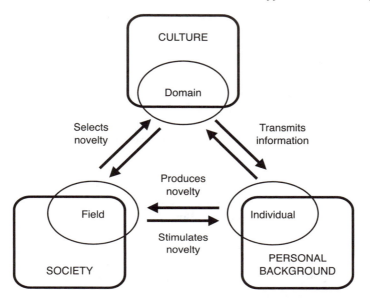

Figure 1.1 A systems view of creativity (reproduced from Sternberg, 1999: 316).

come to be formed and then culturally established or how such systems cope with creative activity which resists or works against the community's values and criteria for what is creative. There is also perhaps too overt an assumption that creativity is necessarily the product of a single individual. But the approach has possibilities. It is a view of creativity as *socially* and *culturally constituted*, and raises valuable questions about reception and evaluation. It suggests that there are creativities rather than a single and unitary creativity.

Chairs, interviews and Mrs Merton: heavy relief or light relief

> So what does an attractive, 25-year-old girl like yourself see in an 80-year-old man with immense personal wealth?

Creativity is not simply a matter of words and phrases. It is not simply definable in terms of different times and cultures. It is not simply measurable as a psychological entity. And it cannot be simply located with reference to the product which is created, whether that be by an individual or a group. In the book so far there has been an understandable temptation to deal with a product as it is found on the page or in the conversational transcript. In this short section, it is pointed out that an understanding of processes may also contribute to our understanding.

When we try to take some account of the processes by which creativity comes to be recognised and valued, there is a need to focus not so much on the producer or on the product but also, as noted above, on those who are the receivers or consumers of a creative act or artefact. Crucial to this act of reception is an expectation of form and convention in the use of material, whether that material is a painting, a poem, a TV comedy programme or a piece of domestic furniture such as a living-room chair.

The importance of understanding such processes is underlined by the example of a chair created by the Hungarian-born architect and designer Marcel Breuer which first appeared in 1928. The chair was a cantilevered tubular steel chair and was designed for domestic use. Breuer's creativity can only be understood by recognising the position of the 'audience' for his product, an audience who at that time would have associated a metal chair with garden and café furniture, with prison beds and dentists' chairs or with furniture for domestic staff. Without further empirical research it is not clear what the precise horizon of expectation was of those who bought the chair or those who chose not to buy such a product. But Breuer's consumers would be likely to be shocked to some degree.

The fact is, however, that today stores throughout the world such as IKEA and Habitat sell metal chairs as living-room furniture and the genre has evolved to include further material combinations of wood and metal, of leather and metal and of metal and plastic. It is a genuinely popular piece of art that is now naturalised and domesticated, so to speak. But at the time, Breuer's chair would have impacted greatly on conventions of seeing and thinking, and to different degrees for different consumers, challenged expectations. Within the context of Breuer's own work too, this chair evolved from his famous Wassily chair in 1925, and evolved further into his work with MARS (Modern Architectual Research Group) in London in the 1930s which led to his design of a range of domestic furniture which included tubular metal tables and chairs made from a frame of moulded plywood of the kind normally seen in deck chairs for outside sunbathing (see Bayer, 1997 and Pile, 2000 for historical accounts). The points to stress here are the historical and social processes which both production *and* reception entail. It is also worth underlining that the creative act always requires a background or some relief against which to operate.[3]

An example drawn from the world of British television comedy programmes provides a related context. In the case of much comedy, the light relief is set against something more serious or established or conventionally accepted. On the surface the programme *Mrs Merton* conforms to the genre of a typical TV chat show in which an interviewer has celebrity guests who answer questions about their lives and future plans, at the same time taking an opportunity to promote a product with which they are associated. In *Mrs Merton* there is a subtly different formatting of the genre. The interviewer (the actress and script-writer Caroline Aherne) plays a woman in her sixties who is deliberately dressed down in very ordinary day clothes of the kind which might be worn in a living room for watching television. The invited audience for the programme consists entirely of senior citizens like herself and, in a break from expectation, members of the audience are frequently asked for their reactions to what the guest has just said, as if the talk were taking place in an altogether different setting such as a pub or street corner after the show. The questions from the interviewer are also differently formatted, being designed not so much to allow the guest to present him or herself in a good light and to promote their product but rather to expose, embarrass and generally make the guest feel uncomfortable. The interviewer's questions can be seemingly light and everyday but can also be directly personal. A typical question directed to a guest, a soap opera actress, who had just married an older man might be:

> *So what does an attractive, 25-year-old girl like yourself see in an 80-year-old man with immense personal wealth?*

The creativity of the comedy in the programme inheres in the formation of new patterns which then become assimilated into an accepted style. The programme would fail if the break with expectation were too radical and an unfamiliar genre were created to which a television audience could not relate. The displacement of expectation and convention here is less challenging and disturbing than Marcel Breuer's chair which, it can be imagined, some communities might have taken longer to accept. In the case of the programme *Mrs Merton*, however, we have a new pattern formed from a previous pattern with a distinctly creative play, and humour residing in the gap between the old and the new.

Psychological approaches: initial conclusions

- Creativity is a complex phenomenon and difficult to measure. Psychological approaches are diverse and vary in research methodology, though they inevitably converge in regarding creativity as a mentalistic operation and as mainly a matter of individual creative thought.
- In spite of individual differences between creators, progress has been made in isolating common characteristics of creative individuals and of recurring processes in the creative act.
- Creative thought can be defined by an ability to think laterally and innovatively, especially for purposes of problem-solving and of changing accepted ways of seeing and understanding. Creativity can also involve problem-posing as well as problem-solving.
- In order to be creative, creative processes and creative thought have to be adaptive and to be fitted to a changing environment and existing social conventions.
- Creativity is best understood with reference to a confluence of different systems involving both mentalistic predisposition and sociocultural domains such as community reception and acceptance within a particular domain. The systems approach proposed by Czikszentmihalyi is particularly helpful in taking such factors into account. It is dynamic rather than static. Rather than an unchanging, essentialist and one-size-fits-all version, it suggests a variational, relative and emergent view of creativity.
- 'Systems' are social and cultural as well as psychological.
- Creativity is monologic and involves individuals; but it is also dialogic and involves interaction with other individuals.

Sociocultural approaches

> The Eastern conception of creativity seems less focused on innovative pro-
> ducers. Instead, creativity involves a state of personal fulfilment, a
> connection to a primordial realm, or the expression of an inner essence or
> ultimate reality. Creativity is related to meditation.
>
> (Lubart, 1999: 340)

The above approaches all assume a particular definition of creativity; even the
more historiometric accounts (Simonton, 1984, 1994) appear not to recognise
that such definitions might be time- or culture-bound. In a valuable overview
of creativity across different cultural boundaries, Lubart (1999) points to some
of the characteristics of creativity assumed within other cultures, and in particular offers insights into what he argues to be differences between Eastern and
Western conceptions. Such accounts underscore that creativity does not exist
in a vacuum and cannot be fully understood if its study and the research associated with it are decontextualised. Case studies of cultural production in Eastern
cultures provide revealing differences when compared with those generally
accepted within Western societies. One major difference is that notions of creativity within many Eastern cultures are more process-orientated. That is, one
of the main purposes for creativity is for self-realisation. The creative process
may be an essentially circular process leading nowhere other than fuller understanding and recognition of inner realities. Because of the different values which
attach to conformity and the different degrees of respect for different traditions, the creative act in Eastern cultures is often best seen as essentially
reproductive. If there is change or innovation, then the outcome will be likely
to be minor and may involve no more than a different perspective on or re-
interpretation of enduring truths. Eastern models of creating describe creative
realisations as a 'being' or a 'becoming' rather than as a 'doing' or a 'making'.
For example, in Hinduism, creativity is regarded more in spiritual terms rather
than in terms of an original solution to a problem. Indeed, Hallman (1970)
considers the lower value attached to originality and innovation to be the single
main difference between Hindu and Western definitions of creativity. Chaud-
huri (quoted in Chu, 1970) describes the Eastern creative process as 'a flash of
aesthetic insight into the heart of the object' . . . 'The artist experiences intimate oneness, the spirit of the object.'

This more personal, process-orientated and reproductive sense of creativity
contrasts with the greater product-centredness of industrialised Western societies, in which positive outcomes are expected which refresh and renew ways
of seeing or in which original approaches to problems are established. The
Western concept is more closely connected with prototypical creation-myths
and with the view that something positive and tangible should be achieved.
Many Western conceptions also assume a linear sequence rather than a cyclical
or reproductive creative emergence.

The Eastern artist and 'the new'

The very materials which are worked on or with or the very domain in which the artist works are also differently conceived in some Eastern cultures. It is not seen as the responsibility of the artist to produce major change in artistic form or structure. For example, the American anthropologist Margaret Mead's studies of art in Bali, Indonesia, underline that the more serious the art form, such as sculptures of gods or ritual dances, the more likely it is that change will not be permitted or expected. In less societally valued forms such as domestic carvings of kitchen gods or the weaving of containers greater variation is the norm; although basic aspects or design are culturally stipulated, decoration is more open to invention or individual style. In a study of Samoan dance routines Colligan (1983: 42) makes the following related observations:

> Each Samoan is expected to create his or her individual style within the basic framework . . . a dancer, no matter how original, does not compose new steps; nor does the overall order of the positions change . . . There are no fundamental structural changes in the dance in Samoan culture. Creativity occurs [in minute changes] on the surface level because the culture [allows and rewards it on that level].

It should, of course, once again not be forgotten that such conceptions of artistic production were also dominant paradigms at particular points in the cultural history of several industrialised literate societies. For example, in the seventeenth and eighteenth centuries, literary imitation of classical models in drama and poetry were highly valued and artists were valued because they were able to reproduce, with minor variations, more than they were valued because they were able to innovate. Imitation was seen as a compliment or homage to a cultural heritage with its largely unchanging values.

The basic point to stress here once again is the cultural and historical variability of creative production. Taken from a culturally relative position, creativity is also not always to be seen or defined in respect of individual performance or in terms of what is new or 'novel'. For example, in Bali, musical innovation, where it is allowed, is regarded as group practice, with individual musicians subsumed to the collective endeavour. Many examples of creativity in non-industrialised cultures involve practices which are not written or text-bound, which do not assume conventional practices of recording and preserving creative products over time, and in which there is an important link between the text and the social context. Such practices demand rather different conceptualisation and theorisation of creativity.

East and West: a note of caution

The research reported above may, of course, be in danger of overgeneralising differences and distinctions between 'East' and 'West' and of oversimplifying where the cultural, geographical and historical lines are drawn between Eastern and Western conceptions. Indeed, several of the examples cited and drawn on for illustration in this section are taken from African or South American societies. There are Indian and Chinese artists who operate unambiguously as individuals. It is necessary, therefore, to regard some of these more overt and obvious contrasts with some caution. Although the generalisations and observations of differences are insightful and are clearly a matter of cultural difference, it may be both preferable and more accurate sometimes to speak in terms of modern, literate, industrialised cultures on the one hand and traditional, non-literate and predominantly oral cultures on the other, though in such descriptions yet further questions are begged about dividing lines and contrasts. If the term 'Western' or 'Eastern' is used, therefore, it is as a kind of pragmatic shorthand which I will try suitably to hedge or qualify in what follows.

Performance and creativity

The practice of performance is standard in many cultures, especially in certain non-industrialised cultures. In many different cultural contexts performance entails a particular, culturally sanctioned way of speaking. Performers produce the 'text' live within a 'stage' setting and are judged in terms of how well they conform to and reproduce a way of speaking within the context of an agreed framework or 'contract' between speaker and audience, a contract often established by cultural tradition. Linguistic and other formal features of the speaking performance are highlighted, but they are not the only or even the main index of creativity; the performance also depends on the quality of the interaction between the performer and the audience. The performance may involve a range of different framing features which are in part expected by the audience and which may signal key points in the performance which demand responses from the audience. These include fixed phrases and formulae, particular gestures or postures, variable sound pitch and loudness, densities of repetitions and related patterning, and may even include a particular setting to which attention is drawn during the performance. In some cases the performance may be explicitly linked to a key social event; see for example Keenan's account (1973) of the *kabary* ways of speaking in the context of marriage ceremonies in Malagasy. Performances may also be joint performances, as King (1981) illustrates with examples from Nigeria from the Hausa genre of *waka* or 'professional song' which includes primary and secondary performers, the latter here in the form of a chorus. And the correlation between creative performance and public event is significant too, adding both permanence and a cycle of expectation and ritualism to the event. Kaivola-Bregenhoj (1996) notes how in many societies the setting of riddles can be part of a process of courtship, greeting or formal educational initiation.[4]

Within such practices, creativity is seen as a social and interactional act as much as it is a distinctive individual act. In many cultures, texts which are not performed are paradoxically not considered to be enduring cultural products. Although each performance is transient, its permanence resides in the immutability of the basic framework of the specific rules. In the context of performance it is important not to neglect such practices within Western cultures too, even if they may sometimes involve more culturally marginalised forms. For example, the classical concerto is a co-produced performance. It does not exist except as performance, though particular recordings may be made. Performance poetry and rehearsed and semi-rehearsed dramatic productions (including the more overtly 'Western' forms of improvisation) are accepted cultural forms, and Wolfson (1979) offers illuminating discussion and structural analysis of a story told jointly by a husband and a wife. (For a more detailed survey, see Fabb, 1997: chapter 9.) Chapter 6 of this book also picks up issues of multimodal creativity which involve a confluence and juxtaposition of the verbal and the visual, movement and music, the physical body and the human voice.

Poetic duels and performance practice

> *We're plumbing shallows here we didn't know existed.*
> (BBC 2 TV quiz *University Challenge*, 6 September 1998)

Not all performances are produced by individuals; some are more dialogic in form and are evaluated by audiences accordingly. One such example is the cultural practice of *poetic duelling*. The poetic duel is explored in detail in Bowen's study of the Gayo culture of Indonesia (Bowen, 1989). In one sense the poetic duel is a contest and in another sense it can be seen as a collaborative performance, embracing 'canonical' instances such as the collaborative story-telling basis of Chaucer's *The Canterbury Tales*. In Gayo culture, performances are regularly enacted as dialogue and involve primary and secondary performers. The particular context for the poetic duel is a wedding ceremony in which around the fabric of a set of ritualised songs and dances and ways of speaking riddles are set and answered, until a winner emerges when a particular riddle cannot be answered. In almost all cases the performers display their skills in a range of ways, including cultural allusion, intertextual reference and poetic parallelisms. The particular aesthetic value of the performance and the particular enhancement conferred on the wedding reside in the continuities with the past, the essentially cooperative spirit of the interaction, the mutuality of the performances, together with the fact that the performers are channels for the culture rather than innovators within the culture. Bowen suggests that the dialogic nature of the duelling presents 'an idealized and socially salient image of social interactions'.

Interestingly, Bowen's study concludes with reflections on changes to the cultural institution of poetic duelling emerging as part of political and social change within contemporary Indonesia. Bowen notes that duelling can be politically sponsored and can involve duelling groups. The emphasis in such state-sponsored duels is on effective rhyming, with the change in the form in a way sanctioning an insertion of different, more contemporary and often politicised content. It is worth noting, too, that, verbal duels in particular transfer across cultures, though sometimes with different inflections and for different social purposes. The connection with ritualised verbal performance, the dialogic and interactional nature of the creativity, the culturally rooted nature of the content are, however, all shared components of these oral 'texts'.

Research in the fields of sociolinguistics and anthropological linguistics has described a number of examples of verbal duelling, often involving teenage boys. Established studies include accounts of 'playing the dozens' (Abrahams, 1962) and of 'ritual insults' (Labov, 1972), in which teenage Afro-American gangs verbally insult each other through shared conventions in which boasts, insults and abuse can be a prelude to gang fights. Dundes *et al.* (1970) describe not dissimilar practices among young Turkish males. And Shippey (1993) establishes the continuities of such practices by examining the pre-battle chants of Anglo-Saxon warriors, as represented in poetry. Gossen's (1976) research in the Chamulan community in southern Mexico reveals the extent to which insults are performed by young men, by means of linguistically intricate rules for insults. With the relative competence of the individual duellers often being evaluated by an audience, Gossen observes that the duelling has a primary social function of establishing collaboration and solidarity among the performers, who use the often sexually explicit character of the insult as an outlet for aggression (the society does not sanction pre-nuptial sex). In a number of instances, although the duelling is combative, the actual contests are more often than not purely displays of verbal artistry and described by researchers as 'play'. The content of the insults is less important than the skills with which they are delivered and reformulated, and the content itself is often designed, often playfully, to represent an alternative fictionalised reality rather than to refer directly to any real-world events.

Some limitations of sociocultural approaches

There are dangers in the research accounts of creativity as a sociocultural practice. There is a danger, first of all, that the acts will be marginalised or seen to be the preserve of marginalised, 'exotic' social and cultural groups. The social and cultural purposes of such activity may be circumscribed in such a way that, for example, verbal play is merely seen to take place for its own sake. There is a danger, too, that the formally rule-bound and ritualised nature of the event will obscure its creativity, not least, as we have seen above, because currently dominant paradigms of creativity are built around assumptions of making new or breaking down forms and conventions. The more insular view is challenged by Cook (2000: 67), who comments how, in general, this kind of verbal play is by no means exclusive to such groups and cultures and argues that similar, publicly verbal activities such as chants and cheer leading involving rival supporters at football matches, media marketing campaigns and parliamentary debates are all more common examples of duelling in the more industrialised societies than is generally assumed. 'Western' views of creativity remain none the less more individualist than collaborative.

The existence of verbal and poetic duelling underlines the importance of not taking a monocultural or ethnocentric stance towards creativity, of recognising the powerful oral basis of creativity, of seeing creative verbal play as having traditional rule-based roots and of regarding creativity as refashioning what exists as well as fashioning something new.

Critical creativity and creating identities: a brief note

The notion of *critical creativity* underlines that creative output is never simply consensual and integrative. Even when it involves imitation of existing models, the creative output is usually more than mere copying or reproduction. In modern 'Western' conceptions of creativity the purpose is often to offer an alternative point of view and to create an alternative world or reality, and often this can involve a critique of what is already in place.

The presence of creativity in language also raises questions of identity and self-expression. And, indeed, a critical creative stance allows an individual creator's identities to be established as part of the expression of alternative viewpoints. In some contexts creativity is used for purposes of marking out and constructing individual identities; in other contexts the identity of the individual (though the assumption that each individual has a single self or identity is questionable) will be found in a sense of collaborative belonging to a group, with identities more likely to be submerged within a collective co-created whole. There is thus also a close connection between language, critical creativity and identities – a set of links and traces to be fully explored in subsequent chapters, especially chapter 6.

Conclusion: what is creativity? The story so far

Creativity is the ability to produce work that is both novel (i.e. original, unexpected) and appropriate (i.e. adaptive concerning task constraints).

(Sternberg, 1999: 3)

- Examining the cultural and semantic history of words such as *common*, *ordinary*, *genius*, *art*, *inventive* and *original* as well as the word *creative* itself underlines that many contemporary statements impart an essentialist and universalist character to creativity, without recognising that the creativity is time-bound and is constructed differently at different moments in history and in different contexts.
- At the same time it is clear that creativity is not wholly time-bound; otherwise, there would not be the many references that there are in this chapter to artefacts which have endured and which transcend particular times and places. It is important to underline that some creative art can be of its time and some art beyond its time; some creative art can be socio-culturally relative and some art universal; and some creative art can be valued by specific groups and some art valued by a wide range of groups from different human communities.
- Creativity is commonly assumed to involve novel analogies or combinations between conceptual elements which have been previously unassociated.

Creativity is commonly regarded as a process which can result in the solution or identification of problems, normally as a result of a process of divergent and innovative thinking.

• Within 'Western' traditions of thought, creativity is closely connected with originality but originality becomes *bona fide* creativity only when it is made to fit and is recognised, accepted and valued as such both by the community peers of the creative individual and by the guardians of the particular artistic or scientific domain in or with which the creator works.

• Creativity results in changes to domains or in the establishment of new domains. Detailed knowledge of a particular domain or activity is a necessary but not sufficient condition for creativity.

• Historiometric measures and biographical accounts of eminent creators have enabled researchers to identify recurring personality features associated with creative acts. None of the personality traits which research has shown to be intrinsic to creativity is rare in itself, but it is rare to find them constellated within the same individual.

• The dominant paradigm of research into creativity is based on the discipline of psychology, and views creativity as a mentalistic phenomenon. Yet the phenomenon cannot be decontextualised or studied in a disciplinary vacuum or seen as an exclusively mental process. Creativity is a social, cultural and environmental phenomenon as well as a psychological process.

• Creativity is culturally variable. An original or creative act in one culture may not be so valued or may be thought trivial in another culture. Not all cultures regard creativity as an individualised response, some preferring to see it as a collective, collaborative phenomenon and as an event which may be publicly performed and evaluated. Creativity has roots in oral traditions. Written creativity is a more recent phenomenon which is more specifically associated with industrialised societies.

• Identities can be created through creative acts. Creativity inheres in responsive, dialogic, interpersonal acts of mutuality as well as in individual acts of self-expression.

• The variability of cultural assumptions concerning creativity is borne out by the semantic histories of keywords such as *genius* and *original* which underline that the view of creativity as making new is a post-Romantic and Modernist conception and that creativity can also be concerned with re-interpretation of origins and of enduring values. It can be a matter of re-vision as well as vision, of re-membering as well as dis-membering and of re-creation as well as creation. Creativity should not be seen as a matter of creation out of nothing. And the word *re-creation* reminds us that creativity is closely linked with notions of play in its various forms within society.

• Creativity is not neutral and can have sociopolitical and ideological implications. Creativity can be critical. That is, it can be used for non-consensual purposes of critiquing people, places, ideas. Creativity is not always a force for good.

- Creativity is demotic and endemic to everyday discourses.
- The variability of creativity suggests that the plural term *creativities* may be preferable.

Where next?

The human mind is a remarkably creative instrument and it may well be that it is a capacity for imaginative, generative thought which differentiates humans from other species. It might be argued that the focus in this book on everyday, demotic creativity reveals little that will help unravel the complex relationship between language and creative conceptualisation at the highest levels of human achievement.

The argument presumes, however, that different processes are entailed. The examples cited so far illustrate that people use spoken language creatively for a wide range of purposes and that it is a mistake to look the other way and only towards gifted individuals. To say that some people are more creative than others is not to say that creativity is limited to a few; it is to say that there are continua of creativity and that it is important to study different points along these clines and continua and not to pre-judge or pre-value. To focus on common talk is not to devalue other forms of creative language use or to deny the universal achievements of artists whose language use has stood the test of time. To focus on common talk is instead to enhance the ordinary, everyday culture-specific achievements of each of us. To focus in this way in this book is a step, admittedly a small step, in a democratic endeavour to restore and revalue creativity as a common property of virtually all human beings.

Chapter 2 pursues these and related questions further, with particular reference to clines and continua for creativity and to the ways in which spoken language highlights the collective, dialogic nature of creativity.

Notes

1   Cattell (1971: 408–9) comments, 'the verdict that a test measures creativity is only a projection of the test constructor's personal view about what creativity is. Thus in the intellectual tests developed by Guilford's students and many others, who have worked on creativity in this decade, creativity has finished up by being evaluated simply as oddity or bizarreness of response . . . This indeed comes close to mistaking the shadow for the substance.'

2   It is important, therefore, to see creativity itself in variational terms. For example, some scientists depend less on inspirational insights and more on a creative isolation of problems for investigation from a wide range of knowledge of the field. And Sternberg and Lubart (1991) have developed an 'investment theory' of creativity which defines creativity as 'buying low and selling high': that is, the creative individual typically pursues ideas which are not in fashion or which have been discarded by others and, often in the face of criticism and resistance, accepting the risk that they will eventually pay off. The approach integrates different research traditions by showing the confluence of personality

and cognitive styles, knowledge of a field, motivation and environmental determinants.

3   I am grateful to Chris Candlin for drawing my attention to this example.
4   It should not be supposed either that different types of creativity are uncon-nected to differences in social, sub-cultural or gender formations. For example, Mar'i and Karayanni (1983) have discussed how Arab males tend to perform better than females on creativity tasks and argue that different performance may be due to the submissive social roles expected of women in many Arab cultures. Babcock (1993) reports how story telling is a male activity and pottery making a female activity among Pueblo Indians in the American South-west. Lubart (1999: 343) offers the following description of the musical creativity of the Kaluli of Papua New Guinea: 'the focus is on gender-based groups. Men and women can both be creative but in different musical genres. For women songs that express the personal emotions of the singer are valued . . . For men, songs that provoke a collective emotional response are valued, such as those that incite the audience to cry or even to attack the singer.'

Exploring further

For further discussion of keywords in relation to creativity see discussions of *imag-ination* by Richard Kearney (1998) and of *inspiration* by Timothy Clark (1997), studies which explore the contemporary meanings of these slippery words in the light of post-Romantic accounts of the position of the creative artist, theories of subjectivity and self-transcendence and recent work in phenomenology, hermeneu-tics and deconstruction. Kearney, in particular, sees a post-modern world of technological innovation in which the powers of human imagination are radically reduced, displaced by a more anonymous system of reproduction.

On the meanings of *creation* in aesthetics, theology, philosophy and scientific theory, George Steiner's *Grammars of Creation* (2002) is a monumental study, explor-ing ways of reconciling divine and secular models of creation and of accounting for the relations between the exceptional and the unexceptional. The book contains extensive deliberations on the meanings of words such as *originality* in art and *genius* across a range of creative outputs. Steiner is constantly pushing at etymological and semantic frontiers as, for example, in extended deliberations on the links between creation and giving birth (links between *genius*, en*gender*, *genetics*, ori*ginality*) founded on the roots of the words in the Greek *gennaein*/Latin *gignere* (to 'be born' or to 'beget/give birth to'). Note, too, that Steiner prefers the word *creation* to cre-*ativity*, underlining the relative modernity of the latter word and his concern to take a historical perspective, although Steiner neglects feminist theories in relation to such perspectives.

The word *genius* and its cultural and literary theoretical resonances are extensively explored in Harold Bloom's *Genius* (2002), a study complemented on several levels by earlier studies of excellence and exceptionality in the creative arts by Ochse (1990), Simonton (1984, 1994), Gardner (see above pp. 33–5) and others in that tradition. Francis Galton's *Hereditary Genius* (1869) still remains a foundation study. See, however, Weisberg (1993) for arguments which to some degree run counter to the 'extraordinary' view of creativity. Arthur Koestler's *The Act of Creation* (1964) is a classic study of creativity across the span of both arts and humanities and sciences. Finke (1990) looks in particular at creativity and the visual. For a study of gender in relation to creativity see Nicole Ward Jouve's *The Female Genesis* (1997). Jenny Uglow's *The Lunar Men* (2002) is a fascinating study of eighteenth-century creative achievers. Burke (1993) examines eighteenth-century (and earlier) manuals which provide rules for and guidance in the 'art' of polite conversation.

An important reworking of aesthetic accounts of 'creative and cognitive life' is Isobel Armstrong's *The Radical Aesthetic* (2000), in which, in place of aesthetic experiences associated with a trained or specially privileged elite, an argument is made for a democratic base for aesthetic experience rooted in experiences common to everyone. For an outstanding general survey containing numerous insights across a wide range of fields, including literature, critical theory, social theory and accounts of creativity in processes of scientific investigation, see Pope's *Creativity* (forthcoming).

The study of creativity within psychology is well charted in a number of key studies, compendia and collections of papers. In addition to the collection by Sternberg (1999) which is extensively drawn on for the main part of this chapter, other seminal studies include: Vernon (1970); Sternberg (1988) (an earlier collection); Glover *et al.*'s (1989) collection; Boden's *Dimensions of Creativity* (1994); Rothenberg's study of the creative process in art, science and other fields (1979).

Cohen's *Creativity* (1977) is a pioneering question-raising study of the place of creativity within different academic traditions, including chapters on creativity and evolution, creativity and illness, creativity and intelligence (see also Cohen, 1974), the nature versus nurture debate, and creativity in terms of particular activities of the right hemisphere of the brain. An earlier study by the psychologist Anthony Storr, *The Dynamics of Creation* (1972) takes a primarily biological view, subsequently extended by contemporary biologists such as Richard Dawkins and Matthew Ridley by seeing creativity as an evolutionary process of adaptation, the 'survival of the fittest' being those with the greatest capacity to compete and collaborate and thus adapt within an environment.

Sigmund Freud's view of creativity as a kind of pathological sickness represents an extreme view of the isolated, creative individual struggling to overcome and work through neuroses. Freud's position is balanced by positions taken up later in the twentieth century by Weisberg, Rogers and others that creativity is crucial to the survival of the human race in a nuclear age. It is therefore a practical necessity, a basis for continuing technological innovation and development, but also needs to be rigorously promoted in educational contexts as a sign of communal health and well-being. Carl Rogers (1990), as a pioneer of client-centred psychotherapy, offers a more distinctly social agenda for creativity rooted in individual self-realisation as a compensation for an increasingly anonymous and impersonal society. Accounts of creativity as a kind of salvation for an ever more threatened human species in a modern world engaged in a technological race have their origins in the work of one of the founding fathers of creativity studies J. P. Guilford (see Guilford, 1950 for a foundational view). Guilford's position is that creative problem-solving is needed as the main response to social and global change. Rather than a more radically transformative view of creativity, his position is an essentially conservative one, concerned to sustain the social and political status quo.

The place of creativity in the field of management studies, organisation theory, education and training is seen as a matter of delicate balance between innovation and adaptation. Indeed, the title of a key book in the field by Michael Kirton, *Adaptors and Innovators* (1994), prototypically applies this perspective to questions of *problem-solving* in relation to organisational change (and resistance to change), to the relationships between the individual and the team and to issues of restructuring in the workplace. De Bono's *Serious Creativity* (1992) brings many of his influental ideas in this domain together.

Among the scientists writing on creativity, David Bohm (Bohm and Nichol, 1998; Bohm and Peat, 2000) comes closest to the ideas explored in this chapter in his concern that creative thought and related scientific developments can only be truly creative if they are *fitting*. That is, to be truly creative, the outputs need to be in harmony with and in proper ratio or proportion to the contexts in which they are produced, and the creative individual is one who perceives order and continuity and proportion where there is otherwise only chaos and disorder.

A valuable recent collection of papers edited by Thomas Ward, Steven Smith and Jyotsna Vaid is *Creative Thought: An Investigation of Conceptual Structures and Processes* (1997). It is a study of the role of creative thought in a wide variety of different activities, including those not typically thought of as creative. The contributors to the book place a special emphasis on conceptual combination and expansion in analogical thinking, finding evidence for these features along continua from everyday metaphors to the scientific inventions of the seventeenth-century physicist Johannes Kepler. The editors conclude their introduction to the papers with an argument which, though grounded in psychological research, is none the less not dissimilar from the conclusion reached and the focus proposed at the end of chapter 1:

> it is also useful to consider the possibility that the mundane and the exotic represent endpoints on a continuum of human creativity. Underlying those differing manifestations of generative thought are the same sets of mental processes. The processes may be deployed to different degrees of complexity, flexibility and richness, but they are nevertheless the same processes in principle. That is, in the creative cognition view, the differences between mundane creativity and genius are quantitative rather than qualitative . . . Examining in detail the basic mental processes that seem to be associated with the development of novel ideas therefore can shed light on both types of outcome.
>
> (Ward *et al.*, 1997: 5)

2 Lines and clines

Linguistic approaches

Introduction

Neither psychological nor sociocultural approaches to creativity have paid detailed, systematic attention to language and language use. For this perspective we turn in this chapter to the field of linguistics, and in particular to frameworks for discussion which are applied linguistic in orientation. As in chapter 1, the initial focus is on the semantic history of core words such as *literate* and *literary* and the particular values they carry concerning the central social and cultural significance of written language and creativity in writing. The reason for this is to explain the relative lack of attention to speech in both linguistic theory and descriptions of language. Developments in the linguistic description of creativity and literariness have also privileged writing, and a central section of the chapter explores the ways in which written literary language has been defined and described. At the same time, however, the word *literary* is itself questioned and problematised. Working, as indicated, with broad rather than narrow research questions, the aim is to create space for a focused study of creativity in spoken language in the remaining chapters. Running through the chapter are basic questions.

- Why is creativity in language associated with written language and with literary texts?
- Is there such a thing as literary language or is all language literary?
- Is creativity in language extraordinary or ordinary?
- What is language play and how does it relate to creativity in language?
- Are figures of speech special or normal?
- Is language primarily literal or non-literal?

Connected with these questions are others which set up frameworks for subsequent examination of creativity in spoken language.

- Do definitions of creative language depend primarily on identification of forms or of functions?
- What is the significance of playing with words and is it specially a written phenomenon?

- To what extent are creative uses of language connected to identity and self-expression?
- What is the part played by the creation of fictional and alternative worlds?
- Is creative language universal or relative to context?
- How is it judged and evaluated?

By the end of the chapter provisional answers to these questions are offered. I argue that creativity is best understood by means of clines and with reference to social contexts. The argument builds on and develops Csikszentmihalyi's 'systems' theory of creativity discussed in the previous chapter (p. 39). That is, what is deemed to be literary or what is valued as creative or what is seen to be *ordinary* or *extraordinary* is relative to the contexts in which it is used and to the values of those who share in its use as both producers and consumers. By also utilising the notion of clines, relative degrees of creativity in language can be measured in relation to different goals, different uses and different values. The argument leads to a conclusion that it may be preferable to speak of creativity in terms of *creativities*.

At the end of this chapter I begin to illustrate more fully the topic of *the art of common talk* which forms the main basis of example and argument in this book. By looking at a range of contexts of use, it is argued that creative language use is ubiquitous and should be valued as such. In particular, I argue that creativity is pervasive in many contexts of *everyday* language, especially interactions in common speech. Although the main contexts of use discussed in this chapter are contexts of written language, there is an an increasing focus on spoken language towards the end of this chapter. More detailed investigation is undertaken in chapter 3, but I argue here that spoken language is also best understood as operating along clines of 'spokenness' and 'writtenness', and this also underlines the importance of clines and contextual variations in the analysis of creativity in common speech. This chapter establishes frameworks for subsequent discussion.

Creativity, writing and the individual

There is a culturally shaped tendency to regard writing as the basic form of language. There are numerous reasons for this tendency, not least the promotion of the word 'basic' in connection with literacy, for example in societal campaigns for basic skills, for 'back to basics' reading and writing schemes, and in the classroom use of simplified 'basal' readers. There is a corresponding tendency to value written language highly, especially in comparison with spoken language.

The fact that writing has to be learned and that spoken language is for the most part spontaneous, automatic and unconscious is underlined by the positive associations of the words 'literate' and the negative connotations, even to the extent of a construal of lack of intelligence, accorded to words such as 'illiterate' (see Williams, 1983; Carter, 1995). In educational contexts too, examinations, even examinations in foreign languages and driving theory tests, are almost always weighted in favour of written performance. For many centuries dictionaries and grammars of the English language have taken the written language as a benchmark for what is proper and standard in the language, and have incorporated written and often 'literary' examples to illustrate the best usage. What is written and what is literate are accorded high cultural status and what is spoken is accordingly not privileged.

What is valuable lasts and many societies value what is permanent. The capacity of the written language to generate enduring records, and most markedly records of human achievement or of sacred significance, even when these records may have originated in oral discourse, is central to its value. At least until the advent of the tape-recorder and of sound and visual recordings, speech is seen in social and cultural terms as much more temporally bound and is only 'recordable' as part of individual or folk memory. In a related way, good writers have been identified for centuries and exemplars of excellence held up for imitation and, similarly, classical rhetorical models have been available to demonstrate highly formal, often pre-planned and often public oratorical and debating skills.

By contrast, there are few similarly canonical models of the good conversationalist or of what is agreed to be successful practice in less formal conversational exchanges. Speech is generally represented in terms of written performances such as the wartime speeches of Winston Churchill. There is no *Palgrave's Golden Treasury* of Spoken Language. Some ceremonial functions of language such as marriage vows remain oral, but when spoken language is preserved, it is normally in the form of a transcribed 'text' which provides its own distortion of the communicative complexity of the original source. (Note also how spoken performance is influenced nowadays by new informal modes of performance such as chat-shows, stand-up comics and rap.) And note too how, in contrast with written models, spoken language can be easily discredited and devalued by writing examples out in such a way as to illustrate its 'formless' nature. In this particular sense, the comments of Ong (1982: 12) are especially apposite:

> Writing . . . is a particularly pre-emptive and imperialist activity that tends to assimilate other things to itself even without the aid of etymologies . . . In view of this pre-emptiveness . . . it appears quite impossible to use the term 'literature' to include oral tradition and performance without subtly but irredeemably reducing these somehow to variants of writing.

The semantic connection between *literacy*, *letters*, *literature* reinforces such social values and attitudes, with the term *literature* (Williams, 1983) used, more or less exclusively, to refer to highly valued and imaginative written material. Williams points out that in the eighteenth century the word 'literature' was used to refer in general to a range of written texts such as letters, diaries and reports (the meaning is preserved in terms such as 'travel literature' or 'insurance literature') and that the more specialised sense of literature to mean original, imaginative writing is a post-Romantic development. Even dramatic performances are conventionally valued and studied only when seen as written text.

The relative isolation and detachment of written language and of processes of written composition have also come to acquire value, especially when compared with the relative communality of most spoken language. In turn, writing is valued as an activity in which the unique 'voice' of an individual can be marked. And the distinction between speech and writing is complicated further by the fact that reading a novel or a poem can also be affected by the ways in which the writing may be designed to be sounded in the head as if it were being spoken and heard.

As we have seen in the first chapter, this notion of creativity is not unconnected with the idea of creativity as a divine act and with the idea of the creative writer as genius, a paradigm which gives to the literary writer an even more mystical, transcendental status and which in the process affords to such individuals an even richer, cultural capital. And notice how the word *creative* slips into easy company with the word *writer* whereas it may be a less familiar guest to the word *speaker*. Once again we see that the semantic history or at least a historical prosody of words is very telling.

Writing and speaking

> Perhaps the greatest single event in the history of linguistics was the invention of the tape recorder, which for the first time has captured natural conversation and made it accessible to systematic study.
> (Michael Halliday, 'Introduction' to Halliday, 1994: xxiii)

The spoken language has also been largely underdescribed and undertheorised within linguistic science. The easy availability of written language sources and, until the advent of sound recordings, the difficulty of access to authentic spoken material have meant that the analysis and description of written language has always been privileged and prioritised for analysis. The history of linguistics in the twentieth century has mainly been a history of the study of detached written examples, with all the characteristic features of spoken discourse dismissed as peripheral to the enquiry. The influence of two major figures in twentieth-century linguistics, Ferdinand de Saussure and Noam Chomsky, is found in the way in which for Saussure the focus should be on *langue*, the abstract system, rather than on *parole*, the particularities of real speech events and of the people producing such events. The parallel influence of the work of Chomsky on language description has also served to shift attention away from particular spoken performances in favour of accounts of the underlying system, often described not even in terms of extended written examples but rather by means of example sentences invented by the analyst to test the limits of the system (see also pp. 77–8 below for Chomsky's stance on creativity and language). According to these theoretical paradigms, such features as literary uses of language, metaphor and ordinary day-to-day conversational exchanges are dismissed as marginal and peripheral.

Linguists working within alternative traditions have taken a different path, especially in the past twenty years or so, and there has been a growing recognition of the importance of spoken language. For example, Bloomfield (1935: 21) dismissed writing as being not real language but merely a way of rendering and recording the more 'real' spoken language; and Prague School linguists such as Havranek (1932) tried to give a balanced account of both spoken and written forms when attempting to produce their theoretically influential descriptions of literary Czech. Ancient Hindu grammarians were as interested in the grammar in speech as in writing.

In much of his work Halliday argues that the potential of the language system is much more richly realised in spoken than in written discourse. For Halliday it is the essentially unconscious, often unplanned, nature of speech, the fact that the system is so mobile and in a constant state of flux, alert to context, responsive to the smallest and most subtle changes in its contextual environment, that makes it so fascinating (1994: xxiii). Spoken language thus represents *language at full stretch*, so much so that even the most detailed, faithful and sympathetic transcription cannot hope to capture it. On account of these values, Halliday argues that it merits special attention. This perspective is carried forward in work in the fields of conversation analysis and ethnographies of speaking which are discussed on pp. 78–80 below.

The spoken–written continuum

There are of course many links between speech and writing. There are many written messages such as text messages on mobile phones, emails or communications on computer chat-lines which work like spoken language. The following fax contains features of language which are close to spoken communication.

> *Could you email Kyle Barber and ask him for a quote for a laptop? Said we'd let Tatchell have one for himself as part of the deal. Compaq or Toshiba. At least 420Mb hard disk and 16Mb RAM. Good deal, tell David. Worth the laptop. More in the pipeline.*
>
> (Inter-company fax, 1997)

For example, in the structure *Good deal, tell David* the absence of *that* together with ellipsis of a subject and verb and the indefinite article *a* (*Tell David that it is a good deal*) is a grammatical feature which is much more common in speech than in writing but is becoming standardised in many written communications.

And most political speeches, for example, are written to be spoken, and are carefully crafted texts, even if they are written to sound spontaneous and natural. Generally, different models have grown up for analysing spoken and written language and it is widely agreed that there is no simple, single difference between speech and writing. McCarthy (2001b: 49) has put things clearly:

> The most useful way to conceive of the differences is to see them as scales along which individual texts can be plotted. For example, casual conversations tend to be highly involved interpersonally (detachment or distancing oneself by one speaker or another is often seen as socially problematic).

Public notices, on the other hand, tend to be detached, for example, stating regulations or giving warnings. But note we have to say *tend*; we cannot speak in absolutes, only about what is most typical. Speech is most typically created 'on-line' and received in real time. Writing most typically is created 'off-line', i.e. composed at one time and read at another, and there is usually time for reflection and revision (an exception would be real-time e-mailing by two computer users simultaneously online to each other, one of the reasons why e-mail is often felt to be more like talk than writing). What is more, written discourses tend to display more obvious degrees of structure and organisation whereas talk can appear rather loose and frag- mented, though this may be merely a perception of the researcher, and probably does not correspond at all to how the 'insiders' to a conversation experience things. These and other possible features of variation enable us to plot the characteristics of different types of discourse as 'more or less' typically written or typically spoken.

Explorations of language in use indicate the extent to which speakers and writers make choices from the underlying system for purposes of communi- cating meanings. Sometimes these choices can alter perceptions and create new meanings; sometimes they serve to reinforce existing meanings; sometimes new blends can be made from the resources of spoken and written forms. Such choices will often be specific to a particular context, and meanings will there- fore often be emergent. Examples of such language use would be the recent phenomenon of email, as indicated above, or texting, in which, on account of the informality and speed of composition associated with the medium, the character of written language is made more closely to approximate the spoken language in form and function. Our understanding of such language use is more likely to be assisted by the kinds of clines and gradations of meaning described within the more social semiotic frameworks developed by Halliday and his asso- ciates. This is the main applied linguistic direction taken in this chapter.

Literary (and 'creative') language: a brief history of definitions

In terms of written language, creative uses are most markedly associated with literary texts. Even though definitions of what counts as literary are variable and contestable, the nature of the phenomenon has been widely discussed and analysed in recent years. Defining what counts as literary in writing is an important element in understanding creativity and provides frameworks within which creativity in speech can begin to be described. This next section reviews some of these main frameworks.

Two main models for definition of literary language can be discerned, and these can be grouped, rather loosely and at the risk of oversimplification, into *inherency* and *sociocultural* models. We shall begin with the more formalist inherency definitions because they are both historically antecedent and can be more easily described.

Inherency models: deviation theory and self-referentiality

Inherency definitions are predicated on a division between 'poetic' and 'practical' language. According to deviation theory, literariness or features of creativity inhere in the degrees to which language use departs or deviates from expected patterns of language and thus defamiliarises the reader. Literary language use is therefore different because it makes strange, disturbs, upsets our routinised 'normal' view of things, and thus generates new or renewed perceptions. In a much quoted example, the title of Dylan Thomas's poem 'A grief ago' would be 'literary' by virtue of its departure from semantic selection restrictions which state that only temporal nouns such as 'week' or 'month' can occur in such a sequence. As a result, however, grief comes to be perceived as a temporal process.

Another influential 'inherency' definition is particularly associated with Roman Jakobson. In a famous paper (Jakobson, 1960) he articulated a theory of poetic language which stressed the *self-referentiality* of poetic language. Thus, in the examples *I hate horrible Harry* or *I like Ike* the verbs *hate* and *like* are selected rather than, for example, 'loath' or 'support' because they establish a reinforcing phonoaesthetic patterning. The examples cited (the former is Jakobson's own, the latter a campaign slogan of the former American president Dwight Eisenhower – whose nickname was Ike) demonstrate that creative patterning can *inhere* in such everyday language as political advertising slogans. Jakobson's definition is, like definitions of deviation theory, founded on an assumed distinction between 'poetic' and 'ordinary' language. According to Jakobson, in non-literary discourse the word is a mere vehicle for what it refers to. In literary discourse the word or phrase is brought into a much more active and reinforcing relationship, serving, as it were, to echo, mime or in some way represent what is signified as well as to refer to it. Thus the similarity and repetition of vowel and consonant pattern in *I like Ike* are themselves mutually supportive and thus serve to encode support for the president. In this way such a use of language is also self-referential.

This emphasis on the representational nature of literary discourse is valuable. But it should be pointed out that Jakobson's criteria work rather better in respect of poetry than of prose and that he supplies no clear criteria for determining the *clines* or degrees of poeticality or 'literariness' in his examples or for what might make some messages more strikingly creative examples than others. For example, is *I like Ike* more or less effective than a slogan by a politician who announces 'Education, Education, Education' to support a central plank of policy? Like several deviation theorists, Jakobson stresses too much the *production* of effects, neglecting in the process the recognition and reception of such effects. The reader or receiver (or listener) of the message and his or her sociocultural position tend to get left out of the account.

Schema and refreshment

Most descriptions of linguistic deviation and of self-referential uses of language are exemplified by individual words and phrases. Cook (1995, 2000) attempts to explain the effects of such uses of language in terms of larger units of discourse. For example, he accounts for the pleasure derived by readers from creative patterning in language in terms of mental mechanisms which fulfil basic human-species-specific needs; and among the more basic of mental mechanisms are those which are renewed and refreshed as a result of the destabilising and 'defamiliarising' effects of such literary patterning.

In his book *Discourse and Literature* (1994), Cook underlines different types of discoursal deviance which can act as a specific trigger to what he terms *schema refreshment*. The notion of schema refreshment is based on work in AI (artificial intelligence) and has what might be termed a textual-cognitive orientation, reflecting the subtitle to Cook's study: 'The Interplay of Form and Mind'. Cook analyses a wide range of schema-disrupting properties, arguing that what is generally understood to be aesthetically valued literature, at least within certain cultural (usually Western) conceptions of the term, are the texts which introduce schematic or cognitive refreshment. That is, an advertisement or a joke may disrupt at a textual or linguistic level of deviance but often does not offer any real challenge to cognitive renewal in terms of how the world is perceived. For example, the use of the formal conventions of a children's fable to describe the outcomes of social change and revolution in George Orwell's *Animal Farm* is challenging. The novel departs from formal conventions (it is not the usual subject-matter for a fable) but as a result it also works to renew perceptions and understandings of the political process. Schema refreshment in literary texts results in new ways of seeing and thinking about the world.

Speech acts

Initial accounts of literary language which attempt more boldly to underscore the role of the reader or receiver interacting in a sociocultural context with the sender of a verbal message have been generally termed 'speech act theories' of literary discourse. In the 1960s, work on speech acts by J. W. Austin and John Searle in the context of the philosophy of language drew distinctions between constative and performative language. Constative language is language used to describe things or to make a statement such as *London is the capital of England* and is either true or false. Performative utterances do not describe but perform the actions they refer to. For example, saying *I do* in a marriage ceremony is a performative utterance. It is neither true nor false but is simply either appropriate or not. That is, the phrase will not perform anything in the absence of the right contextual conditions (it has to spoken before someone authorised to marry people and by an intending bride or groom, not by the best man or the person who has just cleaned the building for the ceremony).

In applications of these theories to literary text study, one of the main proponents has been Richard Ohmann. Ohmann's basic proposition is that the kinds of conditions which normally attach to speech acts such as insulting, questioning and promising do not obtain in literary contexts. Instead we have quasi- or mimetic speech acts. As Ohmann (1971: 2) puts it:

> A literary work is a discourse whose sentences lack the illocutionary forces
> that would normally attach to them . . . specifically, a literary work pur-
> portedly imitates (or reports) a series of speech acts, which in fact have no
> other existence . . . Since the quasi-speech acts of literature are not carry-
> ing on the world's business – describing, urging, contracting, etc., the
> reader may well attend to them in a non-pragmatic way and thus allow
> them to realize their emotive potential.

Thus, the literary speech act is typically a different kind of speech act – one
which involves (on the part of the reader) a suspension of the normal pragmatic
functions words may have in order for the reader to regard them as in some
way representing or displaying the actions they would normally perform. In this
sense a literary speech act brings a world into being for its readers or listeners,
but beyond that it does not do or perform anything. It is not like the language
which refers to a prior state of affairs. The constative literary speech act is a
displaced speech act.

Ohmann's theory, like inherency models, again suffers from an essentialist
opposition between literary and non-literary which careful consideration does
not really bear out. Pratt (1977), for example, has convincingly demonstrated
that fictional, non-pragmatic, mimetic, displaced, disinterested, playful speech
acts routinely occur outside what is called literature. Hypothesising, telling
white lies, pretending, playing devil's advocate, imagining, fantasising, relating
jokes or anecdotes, even using illustrations to underscore a point in scholarly
argument, are then, by Ohmann's definition, literary. And we should note, too,
how 'literary' biographies contain true constative speech acts.

There are limitations to the theory of speech acts. Most examples of speech
acts are based on single sentences, and traditional analyses do not really explore
stretches of discourse of the kind seen in the examples cited in the introduction
to this book in which speakers negotiate what is meant and in which several
speech acts are being performed simultaneously. But what work on speech act
theory has done is to pose the question of whether the literary speech act is different or whether all language can be used for literary purposes. It is a tradition
which has led to the insertion of quotation marks around the word 'literary'.
(For related studies see Fish, 1973; Searle, 1975; Herrnstein-Smith, 1978; Van
Peer, 1991.)

Presentationality, pleasure and performance

Anders Petterson's *A Theory of Literary Discourse* (1990) relates to work on
speech acts and literary discourse but develops a further sociocultural definition of literature by locating linguistic analysis within domains of literary and
cultural theory, and raising, in the process, questions of aesthetic pleasure.
Petterson reminds us that what constitutes literary language and literariness
is historically and culturally variable and that many of the issues to do with the
deviancy and self-reflexivity of literary language belong within the twentieth

century and within Modernist accounts of literature. Petterson's main conclusion is that literature in most Western cultural settings is seen as a verbal composition which is especially marked by its *presentationality*. For Petterson, literature differs from other categories he explores such as functionally informative discourse (a standard recipe or a set of instructions for a washing machine) because: 'to verbally understand serious literature is . . . to understand that it is presentational and to apprehend it in the intended manner is to seek to obtain emotional, cognitive or formal aesthetic satisfaction from it'(1990: 256). Petterson's position finds general support in studies devoted to more universalist and *cognitive* preoccupations with aesthetic functions. Bauman (1977, 1986), for example, stresses the 'designed for performance' aspect of literary presentation, drawing many examples from more oral-based cultures and arguing that 'aesthetic' satisfaction may simply result from a display and appropriate evaluation of verbal skill, the evaluation being based on a judgement of the extent to which clear public rules for the performance have been adhered to.[1] (See also work on ethnopoetics below pp. 78 ff. and on the sociolinguistic analysis of ritual insults reported by Labov, 1972.)

The notions of pleasure and of verbal 'presentation' designed to confer satisfaction do, however, suggest an interaction between reader and text. Though Cook's and Petterson's work is concerned with similar effects, their main concern is with the discoursal effects which particular types of text have on readers or listeners (though mainly the assumption is of a reader), while at the same time, however, reminding that cognitive features play a part too. In the process both formal and inherency accounts are linked with more functional and sociocultural frameworks.

Is all language literary language or can readers choose?

In a more extreme version of these arguments, Eagleton (1983: 10) argues that 'anything can be literature' and that it is all a matter of how we choose (or are chosen) to read a text. Because texts are varied and the social and cultural positions from which readers read texts are even more varied, a definition of literature can only be relative to specific contexts. In certain institutionalised contexts such as a department of literature in a school or university, definitions of literature will be made by the selection of texts for study which will in turn do no more than reflect the 'interests', predispositions and theories of those teachers, publishing houses or examination boards which make the prescription. In this sense literature is in the reader rather than to be defined by any formal or textual criteria. A good illustration of this position is that cited in Herrnstein-Smith (1978: 67) of the extended readings made possible if the first line of a newspaper report on the social and economic prospects for the social group of Hell's Angels were laid out in a particular form and lineation:

Only one in ten Angels has regular
Employment.

Herrnstein-Smith points out that, though the language is not literary, it can be read as if it were. For her readers (students of literature) in their social context the language comes to represent a world in which religious values (as symbolised by angels with a capital letter) are in terminal decline. It is a view of literary language as a predominantly social and cultural phenomenon. By extension the same assumptions apply to what is or what is not judged to be creative.

Such a position is echoed in the writings of many twentieth-century literary theorists and philosophers, beginning with pre-Modernist thinkers such as Nietzsche. In *What is Literary Language?* (1988), Tambling points out that for Nietzsche all language is literary language because even supposedly referential language has no original reference point and because even a referential statement is a rhetorical device, one which is designed to persuade the listener or reader to act or to think in a particular way. The position is close to that of Derrida's discussions of textuality (1978) in which for him, as Tambling argues:

> 'Literary language' is a pleonasm . . . all language is literary, because it is all mere writing (the earlier meaning of 'literary'), and it can all be read for the guileful, ambiguous and indeterminate uses of language that literature employs . . . 'what is literary language?' is not a question to be asked merely by those who study 'literature': it affects those who write history, philosophy, political science or science itself.
>
> (Tambling, 1988: 74)

Lecercle (1990) adopts a not dissimilar line, arguing that many models of language have been impoverished by a failure properly to examine the more creative 'remainder' of language. The 'remainder', as he terms it, is necessarily ignored by more formalist inspired models which idealise language systems and which, following the lead of Saussure in particular, focus on *langue* to the exclusion of *parole*. The 'remainder' only comes to our notice when we examine real uses of conversational language, or look at particular forms such as poetry, or explore everyday metaphors, puns, riddles and verbal games. Lecercle questions whether such uses of language can ever be fully formalised, but he argues that linguistic systems would be all the richer for recognising their existence, pointing out in the process that the preoccupation of much modern linguistics with the arbitrariness of the sign, invented data, sentence-level grammar and a narrowly truth-condition-determined semantics does not allow any direct engagement with such language or its associated theories.

Literary-linguistic approaches: literariness and creativity

So, does anything go, and is everything creative, or is it possible to undertake analyses which make such comments more specific? This section will review and explore briefly issues connected with the existence or otherwise of a literary lexicon and, among other related questions, explore the role of tropes such as metaphor which are generally considered to belong to markedly 'literary' or creative domains. In particular, it is argued that it is more accurate to speak of *literariness* in language use (see Carter, 1987b, 1990, 1997: ch. 6) and that there are close connections between literariness and creativity in language. One main aim of identifying literariness in language is to argue that literary language is not an exclusive, once and for all phenomenon, to be located only in certain types of text. But another main aim is to argue that it is important to attempt to identify what is judged to be literary or creative within particular contexts. Literary and creative uses of language are ubiquitous but are also a matter of degree.

Literariness and language

The examples here are taken from passages from two different contrasting contexts of use which are connected by the theme of the motor car. The first text is drawn from an instructional handbook for motor car repair and concerns the replacement of brakes. The second text is taken from a well-known novel published in Britain in the 1950s. The discussion here is reproduced from Carter and Nash (1990: 43ff):

Passage A

> Commence by replacing the hub-bearing outer race (33), Fig. 88, which is a press fit and then drop the larger bearing (32) into its outer member followed by oil seal (31), also a press fit, with lip towards bearing. Pack lightly with grease.
>
> If the hub is to be fitted to a vehicle equipped with disc brakes, a concentric ring of Prestic 5686 must be applied between the shield and axle face. On hubs with drum brakes, apply sealing compounds between shield and back-plate.
>
> Fit hub (28) to sub axle (I) and fit the inner member of the outer race, also greased. Replace the inner nut (34) and tighten to remove all end-float. If discs are fitted check run-out. Slacken inner nut two holes and check end-float (0.0~.006 in.) using a dial gauge.

The most prominent feature of this passage is that the lexical items are only effective in conjunction with another medium, that is, the technical drawing referred to as Fig. 88. It is generally apparent that the text has to do with the fitting of a hub assembly to the axle of a car; but its details cannot be properly understood without the accompanying diagram. Such 'medium dependence' is not a characteristic of what is conventionally understood to be literary language, though there are certainly special cases (e.g. the dramatic text and the film commentary) in which a verbal process is linked with another channel of communication. One of the ways in which such cases differ from the present example is that in them words function descriptively and inferentially rather than directively. This text implies the relationship of the instructor and the instructed. It specifies performances and, in that way, is markedly non-literary.

Literary language is sometimes axiomatic, carrying directives in the form of moral injunctions, but it does not normally direct us to perform particular constative speech acts in current response to the text.

In these two respects, then, Passage A lacks the property of literariness: it depends on a parallel, non-verbal, form of communication, and it treats the reader as an agent responding to a directive process. It is also unliterary in its *monosemy*, that is, its use of precise technical terms which are valid only in special application by a special type of audience. Thus in Passage A the language forms are for the most part register-specific, that is, they are restricted to the domain of car-maintenance and are not used beyond without the traces of that domain being marked accordingly. Some of these terms, like *end-float* and *run-out*, must be obscure to all but the motor mechanic; others (for example, *hub-bearing outer race*, *oil seal* and *stub axle*) are difficult in the absence of the diagram with which they have an ostensive ('What's this called?') relationship.

This brings us back to the question of 'medium dependence'. The uninformed reader of a workshop manual can struggle to come to grips with it by studying the text in relation to the diagram and the diagram in relation to the text. In literary discourse, by contrast, there are vital and increasingly complex relationships between words, for example between these semantic networks created in the reader's own mind and the experiential pattern they imply. This is a difficulty of a different order from that of discovering the meaning of a set of technical terms, a process which contrasts with the uses of language in Passage B, an extract from one of the first 'campus' novels, Kingsley Amis's *Lucky Jim*, first published in 1954:

Passage B

> A minute later Dixon was sitting listening to a sound like the ringing of a cracked door-bell as Welch pulled at the starter. That died away into a treble humming that seemed to involve every component of the car. Welch tried again; this time the effect was of beer-bottles jerkily belaboured. Before Dixon could do more than close his eyes he was pressed firmly back against the seat, and his cigarette, still burning, was cuffed out of his hand into some interstice of the floor. With a tearing of gravel under the wheels the car burst from a standstill towards the grass verge, which Welch ran over briefly before turning down the drive. They moved towards the road at walking pace, the engine maintaining a loud lowing sound which caused a late group of students, most of them wearing the yellow and green College scarf, to stare after them from the small covered-in space beside the lodge where sports' notices were posted.

The basic point to underline is that attention to the fine detail of linguistic organisation here guarantees a place for this text further along the *cline of literariness*. It involves recognition that the lexical items deployed are more *polysemic* in that they are selected as much for the resonance they create, the associations they produce and the interaction they generate semantically (together with syntactic and phonetic contouring) within, across and beyond the text itself. Examples might be 'beer bottles jerkily belaboured' which depends crucially and self-referentially on complementary phonetic syntactic patterning and in the case of 'belaboured' produces an ironic set of transitions between what are colloquial items (*jerkily*, *cuff*, *lowing*) and more formal (appropriate in an academic context) vocabulary such as *involve*, *component*, *belaboured* and *maintaining*. The resulting density of meanings allows much more to be conveyed than a description of a car being started and driven from a college courtyard. There is little restrictive monosemy, the text acquires a degree of sovereignty (or 'medium <u>in</u>depen-dence') and words are not being held, however creatively and skilfully, within any one domain or register nor within any direct author–reader channel. The communication is displaced and indirect.

Some aspects of the analysis here need to be qualified. First, it is clear that density of meaning is not attributable merely to operations at the level of language, however significant or creative such features may be. Meanings are made by more than just the language itself. Secondly, interpretations of literariness are, as we have already seen in the previous section, to an extent dependent on being willing to see things that way. Readers are often competent to read in this way as a result of a course in 'literary' reading, a training which they may or may not choose to apply, depending on the context and purpose of their reading. For example, the novel may be read, as an extract has been here, in a kind of slow motion, or in another context, for example on a train on the way to work, it may be read quickly with an emphasis more on the shaping of plot and character. This means that many of the definitions offered in the above paragraphs are inevitably circular. Thirdly, the exercise raises questions of value and judgement. Some readers in some reading communities may prefer the language of a popular novel or the language of an advertisement or the wordplay of graffiti to the dense patterning to be found in Amis's fiction. It is therefore important to isolate different degrees of literariness, but even more important to understand that literariness and, by extension, literary language is socially and culturally relative. Because literary language is seen as creative, the same applies by extension to creativity.

Clines, values and creativity

The above discussion underlines that literary competence involves strategies of reading which are taught in educational institutions and which may not nor-mally be extended beyond such contexts and, certainly only rarely, to language uses not institutionally authorised as literary. The main point to stress here is that it may be more instructive to see literary and creative uses of language as existing along a cline or continuum rather than as discrete sets of features or as a language-intrinsic or unique 'poetical' register.

This is again an issue of value and values. It is clear that different reading communities within society assign different values to different examples of cre-ativity with language or recognise the existence of literariness in language for different purposes. In this connection Boden (1994) draws a distinction between

H-creativity and P-creativity. H-creativity stands for historical creativity, that is, creative productions which have come to acquire a particular historical value, standing the test of time, in other words, and being regarded as important to the culture of a society; P-creativity stands for personal creativity and refers to the kinds of daily creative productions which have local, personal or inter-personal value but which are not likely to prove of recognised 'monumental' value beyond this particular context.

Carter and Nash (1990) similarly make a distinction between creativity and composition, the latter referring to the capacity possessed by everybody to do things with language and texts. They recognise the greater prestige afforded to creative writing, especially writing in certain culturally valued genres, and allow that some texts may come, over time, to be regarded as enduring arte-facts; such a process of value ascription should not, however, they argue further, blind us to the significance of a *common* capacity for creative composition. It is a position not too far removed from Czikszentmihalyi's systems view of cre-ativity (Czikszentmihalyi, 1999 and pp. 38–9 above).

> Copywriting, report-writing, scholarly exposition, journalism, all fall on the wrong side of a stereotypical fence, the side marked composition. The other side, called creative writing is where we place poetry and fiction and drama . . . The argument for a cline, or gradation, of literariness challenges the stereotype but in practice does little to shake popular conviction. Even the practitioner feels that writing an article for a journal is 'composing'; whereas writing a short story is 'creating' . . . It is, however, a faulty per-ception if it leads us to conclude that so-called creative writing can dispense with the routines and disciplines of composition, or that composition is a mechanical process.
>
> (Carter and Nash, 1990: 175)

Bakhtin, creativity and voicing

> Our speech is filled with others' words, varying degrees of otherness or varying degrees of our-own-ness, varying degrees of awareness and detach-ment. These words of others carry with them their own expression, their own evaluative tone, which we assimilate, rework and re-accentuate.
>
> (Bakhtin, 1986: 89)

The ways of seeing creativity and literariness thus far entail not only a static view of the nature of creative language but also a somewhat monologic account of linguistic processes. The Russian linguist and sociocultural theorist Mikhail Bakhtin takes a different view, and argues that all language is fundamentally dia-logic in so far as every utterance responds to a previous utterance and anticipates what will be said next. This dialogic process is normally a consen-sual and collaborative one, extending in the case of some texts to considerable faith on the part of the consumer of a text that it will eventually prove worth it to have read it or listened to it for a long time, before the point of the text emerges or its 'tellability' (its value as something to be told to others) becomes clear.

Furthermore, conversational interaction can go beyond the individual speaker and his or her discourse. The very idea of a dialogue includes a dual voice. For example, Bakhtin develops the notion of *addressivity* to underline the importance of an addressee, a listener who can also have a creative role to play in a dialogue, even if sometimes only a silent, non-verbal one. Speakers have to take into account a kind of conversational duet, a dynamic of interchange with the listener or the different listeners who are 'addressed'. Of course, there are occasions when speakers simply enact routine exchanges without having to worry too much about voicing; for example when they conform to the needs of a context such as a straightforward service encounter in a post office. But in other contexts, the addressee(s) can influence what they say and how they say it.

This addressivity can also sometimes lead to the projection of different voices for different people and to an improvised, creative interplay between the voices – it is, for example, something which has been studied in the language and play development of young children.[2] Thus, we may talk in a particular way when we know that we are being overheard, when we are addressing a baby who cannot reply but when we want to impress the parents with our 'baby-talk', or when we have a conversation with a friend's cat and we ask the cat's age knowing that the friend will answer. Or when we are addressing a group of people and we suddenly single out and talk directly to one in the group who we know will respond. We can also move between voices as the context changes, developing in the process a kind of 'multivoicing'.

Bakhtin also points out that we can reproduce the voice of others and that when we do this it is nearly always for purposes of evaluation or judgement. This kind of 'speech reporting' can range from direct quotation of the voice of others; or, by more indirect means, it can involve imitation, stylisation or parody of others' voices. In the case of more indirect voicings there can be a tension or even a kind of internal argument or polemic between the different voices.

A dialogue is not always one of agreement and consonance, however. One voice can challenge or contradict or subvert another and dialogic exchanges can result in creativity which is more critical. Furthermore, in medieval society, according to Bakhtin, such dialogue was institutionally supported through festivals and carnival days in which spoof prayers and parodies of serious aspects of public life were an integral part of the occasion, serving, temporarily at least, to undermine traditional authorities and power structures. Bakhtin uses his perception of the dialogic nature of language to underline how in all language use other voices keep appearing which creatively undermine or challenge existing norms, functioning almost as a subversive element of 'carnivalesque' which keeps erupting through the surface discussions of all transactional tasks and targets (Emerson, 1983; Bakhtin, 1986). (We should incidentally note that, although Bakhtin wrote in the 1920s, the references are to subsequent translations of his work.)

It is important to recognise that creative, dialogic play with language is not wholly unidirectional. Creativity is a two-way process and can have a range of social purposes which include entertainment, drawing attention to the language itself (for pleasure and entertainment) as well as highlighting more disruptive purposes in which existing orders can be inverted. In one way or another, and even if consensus is not achieved, creation is always a matter of co-creation.

Bakhtin's ideas developed as a result of literary critical analysis in which he was trying to define issues of narrative style in the novels of Dostoevsky. Bakhtin's positions on these matters are important to note at this stage in our discussion, not least because they have an especial relevance for an understanding of creativity in speech. Many of the ideas are taken further in subsequent chapters, most particularly chapter 6 (see pp. 196–8 and 204 ff.).

Preliminary conclusions

> *Before you check in, check out CNN Hotels*
>
> (CNN advertisement, December 1997)

Although the most immediate focus in this section has been on linguistic features, it should not be forgotten that whether the reader (or listener) *chooses* to 'read' or respond to a text (spoken or written) in a literary way – as a poetic text as it were – is one crucial determinant of its literariness. It is worth underlining the paradox too that some uses of language are designedly less creative than others, while at the same time realising that the production and reception of all language involves creative processes. The argument continues to integrate formal and functional views of creativity, seeing it as an issue of language organisation and use and as a social and cultural practice.

The opposition of literary to non-literary language is thus an unhelpful one, and the notion of literary language as a yes/no category should be replaced by one which sees literary language as a continuum, a cline of literariness in language use with some uses of language being marked as more literary than others in certain domains and for certain judges within that domain. There is no simple definition of what is or is not 'literary' language. In some definitions it is measured against the norms of 'ordinary' discourse; but other definitions illustrate that ordinary discourse has literary properties.

In the next section these definitions are explored further with reference to a growing and ever more influential body of work within the explanatory models and paradigms of cognitive linguistics and of work in the field of cognitive poetics. Such models start from studies of the endemically figurative character of language and from whether such language be judged to be literal or non-literal, literary or non-literary, or otherwise.

Are figures of speech special or normal? The view from cognitive poetics

A continuing inspiration for study of figurative language is seminal work by Lakoff and Johnson which issued in their study *Metaphors We Live By*, published in 1980, and continued in further studies by Lakoff and Turner (1989) and

Turner (1991). The starting point and continuing emphasis of this research are that human language and the human mind are not *inherently* literal. In writings by cognitive linguists figurative language is seen not so much as deviant or ornamental but rather as ubiquitous in everyday language, especially spoken language. Discussions of figurative language proceed on the assumption that the fundamental roots of language are figurative. In previous sections comparisons between literary and non-literary have been made. Within cognitive poetics research a main distinction is between the *literal* and the *non-literal* with, once again, words such as *ordinary*, *everyday*, *creative* and *literary* never very far away.

Such an assumption and the research paradigms which follow from it present a set of beliefs radically different from the beliefs about human thought and language which have traditionally dominated the disciplines of the humanities and social sciences in the Western intellectual tradition. Gibbs, in *The Poetics of Mind: Figurative Thought, Language, Understanding* (1994), has argued for a 'cognitive wager' which contrasts with the more standard 'generative wager'. The *generative wager*, associated with the generative and structuralist linguistics of Saussure and Chomsky, hypothesises that explanations of language and of language universals in particular are structure dependent and that linguistic constructs are autonomous of general conceptual knowledge. The *cognitive wager* of Gibbs and other cognitive linguists aims to show that there is no autonomous language faculty and to illustrate that language is not independent of the mind. Gibbs argues that *figurative* schemes of thought structure many fundamental aspects of our ordinary, conceptual understanding of experience.

An example of this position is provided by Gibbs with reference to the polysemous word *stand* which has a range of everyday meanings: for example, 'He could not *stand* the pressure'; 'The law still *stands*'; 'The barometer *stands* at 29.56'; 'The house *stands* in a field.' Gibbs points out that the basic meaning of *stand* is one of a physical movement or physical act. Other meanings of *stand* extend this basic sense, often metaphorically, to convey meanings of verticality, resistance to attacks (as a result of 'standing firm', remaining vertical in the face of attempts to unbalance or knock you down) and endurance (to remain upright): for example, 'He *stands* over six feet tall'; 'He *stood* up to all the attacks against his theory'; 'The law still *stands*'.

One interesting conclusion from these examples is that there is a link by metaphoric extension between physical action and mental representation. The figurative often has an origin in physical, bodily experience and the figurative framework of everyday thought motivates a surprising number of meanings in this and other examples: so that phrases such as 'to take a stand on something', 'to uphold' (principles/the law), to remain an 'upright' person, derive from the same underlying, conceptually coherent domain. Cognitive linguists also put 'the body back into the mind', arguing that 'metaphor, and to a lesser extent metonymy, is the main mechanism through which we comprehend abstract concepts and perform abstract reasoning . . . [and that] metaphorical understanding is grounded in non-metaphorical preconceptual structures that arise from everyday bodily experience' (Gibbs, 1994: 11).

While traditional lexical semantic studies search for literal meaning on the grounds that literal meaning best reflects the truth of an objectively determined external world, cognitive linguists such as Gibbs recognise that so-called literal language is itself constituted by fundamental processes of figuration. As further evidence, Gibbs regularly cites examples of a figurative predisposition on the part of young children who are shown to be readily and normally capable of interpreting non-literal language as normal (see in particular, Winner, 1988). For Gibbs all language is fundamentally figurative.

Studies by Gibbs and others (Johnson, 1987; Lakoff and Turner, 1989; Sweetser, 1990; Lakoff and Johnson, 1999; Stockwell, 2001; Gavins and Steen, 2003) raise fundamental questions for our understanding of the nature of literary language. For example, metaphor has always been seen as a fundamentally literary property as a result of the apparent propensity of its users to create new insights into human experience and values; and metaphorisation has been conventionally regarded as a liberating process in which novel and de-automatising ways of thinking are made possible. Gibbs offers an alternative mapping of creative metaphoric processes by illustrating the extent to which poetry can depend on basic underlying metaphors which structure our most fundamental, common everyday experiences. In other words, language is metaphorical anyway and creative invention in language often builds from this metaphoric base.

In the case of love poetry, for example, one of the prototypical ways in which ordinary language use construes love is in terms of a basic metaphor of love as a nutrient. That is, love is conventionally described in terms of the energy and sustenance it provides. For example: 'They were *kept going* by their love for each other'; 'She's been *starved* of affection for too long'; '*hungry* for love'; 'I was *given new strength* by her love.' Other everyday metaphorical construals are of love as a force which can cause a loss of control: for example, 'She's *crazy* about him'; 'They are quite *besotted* with each other'; 'He was *burning* with passion'; '*addicted* to love'; 'sexual *obsession*'; 'she *pursued* him relentlessly.' Sometimes these two basic metaphoric frameworks converge, so that the nutrient itself can be intoxicating. Gibbs (1994:) cites a poem 'I taste a liquor never brewed' by the American poet Emily Dickinson in which he illustrates how the poet's description of the experience of love is founded upon such familiar, everyday metaphoric concepts but fuses them into a semantically denser pattern which supports the main themes of the poem.

Gibbs's work on metaphor implicitly accepts the notion of a *cline* between creative and everyday metaphors in ways parallel to that outlined above. But he has less to say on processes of the contextual interpretation of metaphor and on what the communicative 'risks' are when metaphors are creatively extended, especially in literary contexts. For example, Stockwell (1999) argues that attempts to make too invariant a fit between word and meaning in much cognitive linguistic research works against the multiple meanings of words found in many literary contexts.

Furthermore, the data used by Gibbs for exemplification are often not drawn from naturally occurring texts, and there is little or no reference to spoken data (though an important recent exception is Gibbs, 2002). This leads us to question the precise nature of what Gibbs means by 'basic' meanings, not least because the interest in generating universalist applications and insights militates against reference to social and cultural contexts. It also means that issues of the effects and degrees of creativity in particular contexts are underplayed (though see further consideration of Gibbs's work in chapter 4). None the less, the cognitive poetic approach adopted by researchers such as Gibbs raises key questions and makes a major contribution to our understanding of core principles in the use of figurative language.[3]

Homo ludens: creativity and language play

> Civilisation arises and unfolds in play.
>
> (Huizinga, 1949)

> Speech play is instrumental to the acquisition of adult verbal art.
>
> (Sanches in Kirschenblatt-Gimblett, 1976)

Recent work on language play has refocused attention on issues of language, literature and creativity and has begun to offer valuable ways forward, particularly from a social and cultural standpoint. Like creativity, language play or 'ludic' language has been a neglected topic in linguistic studies. Crystal (1998: ch. 1), for example, argues that, although the main purpose of language is normally seen to be that of communicating information, it is language play which is truly central to human lives: 'we need to alter our definition of language to give proper recognition to the importance of language play. For only in this way can we reach a satisfactory understanding of what is involved in linguistic creativity' (p. 8).

Crystal's basic definition of language play is rooted in a human enjoyment of the texture of language, an enjoyment which is built on deviating from rules and structures:

> We play with language when we manipulate it as a source of enjoyment, either for ourselves or for the benefit of others. I mean 'manipulate' literally: we take some linguistic feature – such as a word, a phrase, a sentence, a part of a word, a group of sounds, a series of letters – and make it do things it does not normally do. We are, in effect, bending and breaking the rules of the language. And if someone were to ask why we do it, the answer is simply: for fun.
>
> (p. 1)

Crystal makes interesting chapter divisions to his study. He distinguishes between amateur and 'professional' users and uses of playful language, counting among the former the everyday language in riddles, jokes, limericks, playful uses of accents and dialects, nonce words in popular songs and sayings, and counting among the 'professional' examples of language play in the work of headline and advertising copy-writers, professional collectors of ludic language, comedians and writers of humorous texts. The division between amateur and professional is one between those whose work, paradoxically, involves language play and those who encounter language play for recreation or who do not normally perform ludically in quite so overt a fashion. Other chapters consider the importance of language play in the metalinguistic development of children and the uses of ludic language in a range of written texts. In Crystal's final chapter the argument is advanced that, although conformity in reading materials is important to children functioning in the adult world, greater attention to language play and linguistic creativity in reading books in schools would support the development of the kinds of creativity described in naturalistic child language development.

Cook's *Language Play, Language Learning* (2000) extends many of these themes and issues. Like Crystal, Cook demonstrates the existence of language play at different linguistic levels from the phonological to the discoursal and the textual. He also pulls in examples from child to adult discourse extending from childrens' playground rhymes and chants to tabloid puns, riddles, magical incantations, religious liturgy, verbal duelling, fiction, poetry and songs.

Play is seen as an aid to educational and social development in children and language play in particular is seen as a necessary component in language acquisition. In adult lives, for example, gossip is seen by Dunbar (1996) as closely related to language play and as having a related purpose of learning how to deal with and in some cases compete with strangers within an ever more complex social environment. Gossip, according to Dunbar, helps us to refine the skills necessary for survival by learning how to learn through the truths and distortions of 'fictions' about the people around us, their motives and their behaviours. In a parallel way, play is therefore seen as having an important social function. Learning through play is a common feature of animal and human behaviour, as roles are played out which will be important in core interactions but which, in the context of 'play', do not have serious outcomes or consequences. (For example, the notion of 'role play' has acquired particular significance in a number of fields, from management training to language teaching and learning.)

The preparatory role of play is common to both the animal and human worlds to the point where there may be both a biological imperative and a social need for it. Cook does, however, seek to distinguish between the two worlds, suggesting that human language play may provide a basis for creative responses and adaptation to the social world. Animals may play fight, playfully leap and pounce, attack with withdrawn claws; children may create pretend worlds, play mummies and daddies and so on. But there is

> a possible qualitative difference between animal and human play. It may be that human play, in addition to the function of specific training which it shares with animal play, also performs an educational role by increasing general flexibility, thereby allowing humans to develop, both as individuals and societies, a greater understanding of their environment, and more creative responses to it.

> (Cook, 2000: 107)

Although there may be universal applications to such distinctions between play for training and play for education, Cook also investigates the different status ludic forms have in different cultures and societies, and points out how in some cultures and communities some forms will be more highly valued or salient than others, while others will be an important component of folk memory and be regularly and in some instances ritualistically repeated in discourse. The sociocultural stance taken by Cook in relation to language play parallels the investigations of culturally variable creativity described above (pp. 42 ff.).

While Cook's study is important for its detailed attention to sociocultural contexts and to social and educational functions of language play, it is also valuable for its consideration of the biological aspects of play, drawing on studies of the possible evolutionary origins of language play (Turner, 1982) to argue that humans are simply defined as a species by their play. Furthermore, the more intelligent the species, the more that species is likely to play and the more intricate and complex its games are likely to be. It is a characteristic of human beings too, as *homo ludens*, that their play persists long after infancy and childhood. Playing with language parallels this innate characteristic.

It might also be noted that language play can occur at moments of high seriousness such as the circulation of an ever extending sequence of apocryphal jokes concerning the American President, George Bush, at the time of the war with Iraq in 2003, which pun and play with the supposed limits of his intelligence and cultural knowledge and which possibly act as a kind of defence against or deflection from people's fears about the legality or consequences of such a war. Statements such as the following have been posted on the Internet with attributions, allegedly, to the President:

> *The trouble with the French is that they don't understand the word entrepreneur.*
> *Whatever happens. Don't mis-underestimate me.*
> *This is a real crisis which cannot be over exaggerated*
> *We have the full support of Spain and other South American countries.*

Huizinga, play and universalist explanations

Biological accounts of human play seek explanations of play in terms of its functions and purposes, and Cook illustrates the extent to which biological and sociocultural explanations converge. The theories of play advanced by Johan Huizinga (1949) are primarily concerned with universalist explanations; in fact, Huizinga is distrustful of biological explanations of play which seek some extrinsic function or purpose, preferring to regard play as something which cannot be reduced to motivated categories. For Huizinga the primary purpose of play is play.

> The numerous attempts to define the biological function of play show a striking variation. By some the origin and fundamentals of play have been described as the discharge of superabundant vital energy, by others as the

satisfaction of some 'imitative instinct', or again as simply a 'need' for relaxation. According to one theory play constitutes a training of the young creature for the serious work that life will demand later on. According to another theory it serves as an exercise in restraint needful to the individual . . . All these hypotheses have one thing in common: they all start from the assumption that play must serve something which is not play, that it must have some kind of biological purpose.

(1949: 2)

This position does not, however, prevent him from accounting for numerous social and cultural activities in terms of the development of the predisposition to play on the part of young children and young animals. In advanced human civilisations the most serious of human activities, including warfare, the law, courtship, education, philosophy, the law, have play elements embedded within them and in some cases have their cultural origins in play. This is borne out by the etymology of keywords such as *school* (which in Greek means 'leisure') and the way in which the wordplay exists in relation to core human cultural activity such as drama ('plays', 'playwright'), music ('playing the piano'), sex and courtship ('foreplay', 'playing with yourself'), fighting ('swordplay') and hunting for 'game'. Huizinga's study challenges preconceptions that creative play is confined to the world of children which adults grow out of, and abolishes easy distinctions between the serious and the playful.

Huizinga's study is more markedly cultural and philosophical. Studies of the biology of play stress that play often has agonistic elements, that is, it is concerned with contests (see the accounts of verbal duelling above, pp. 45–6), even though the confrontation may be realised symbolically through ritual or incantation or some kind of formal display. The pleasure which play affords may well be linked to entertainment in many cases, but it is also linked to a human desire for challenge and competition; hence the many links between the world of language play, games, sport and the language of sport. Etymologically, again, the links between sporting contest and 'playing' the game are obvious.

Playing the game

Cook (2000: 128) is also especially interested in exploring the links between games and language play, recognising in the process a number of parallels:[4]

- They are uniquely of the human and animal worlds.
- They contain core components of contest and competition, sometimes with trophies and prizes awarded for victories.
- They can be individual or involve a team or collective grouping.
- They provide an opportunity for individual display and for mutual or, in the case of an audience, communal pleasure and identification.
- Knowing the rules of games, skill within those rules and competence in producing particular effects within the rules, is the mark of a creative 'player'.

- The ability to break out of the boundaries imposed by rules and norms of expectation is an especial mark of competence.
- Improvements can be produced by practice and rehearsals.
- There is no unambiguously defined productive outcome.
- There are elaborate rules for turn-taking and for fixed sequences, but with possibilities for variation and an element of relationship-building.
- There is an element of risk involved in dealing with the unanticipated, even within the context of rule-governed activity.

Literal and non-literal worlds: fictions, facts and creativity

> Hardly has the child comprehended with certainty which objects go together and which do not, when he begins to listen happily to verses of absurdity. For some mysterious reason the child is attracted to the topsy-turvy world where legless men run, water burns, horses gallop astride their riders and cows rubble on peas on top of birch trees.
>
> (Chukovsky, [1928] 1963)

We have seen in the previous section that the relationship between the real world and representations of the real world is a complex one. Children act certain key roles such as playing mummies and daddies; animals play fight; games are seen by spectators in term of real-life contests; soap operas offer imitations of reality. Although the creation of fictional worlds and imaginative entry to those worlds is regarded as essentially the domain of the growing and developing child, the role of fiction in the lives of adults cannot be underestimated.

There is speculation too that as a social species humans need fiction for the smooth running of interpersonal relationships. We need to distort the world as much as we need to see it as it is. Lies, white lies, hyperbole, understatement, degrees of deceit and deliberate misinformation may be as much a part of dealing with others as straightforward factual and cooperative communication. There is speculation too that, having satisfied what is needed for survival as a biological species, we will use fiction of any kind from performed poetry, song and drama to the culturally more recent and 'novel' fictions and films and television programmes as a means to satisfy underlying urges for recreation, re-creation and wish-fulfilment. There is even speculation among some cultural theorists that the creation of fictions, through interrelated forms of play, including language play, is the fundamental defining characteristic of the human mind, from which the basic urges for survival through food and shelter and mating are mere temporary deflections (Winnicott, 1971; Winner, 1988, Meares, 1992). The viewing figures for television programmes in Britain which regularly place soap operas as the most popular programmes, by a considerable margin, offer some evidence for this hypothesis.

Although the primary functions of language are often conceived to be social organization and the accumulation and transmission of factual knowledge, with fiction and formal patterning arising as minor if entertaining by-products, this order of origin and dependency can easily be reversed. It might be that, both ontogenetically and phylogenetically, the first function of language is the creation of alternative worlds: whether lies, games, fictions or fantasies. From this use could have emerged the capacity for intricate social organisation and complex knowledge. But in this case it is these which would have been the by-products rather than the prime movers.

(Cook, 2000: 47)

Summary

Discussions of language play illustrate the importance of considering both linguistic forms and the sociocultural functions of these forms. Research in this field also underlines the importance in thinking about the creation of fictions and alternative worlds. And in this connection language play is seen to be both a species-specific capacity and a creative social practice which pervades many aspects of everyday life.

Chomsky and creativity

At the beginning of this chapter the influence of twentieth-century linguistic theorists such as Chomsky was cited, and his view of the importance of understanding language by means of a primary analysis of the structures underlying use rather than by analysing actual instances of language in use. Perhaps paradoxically, Chomsky's work in the 1960s also shows commitment to the notion of creativity. For him it is defined as the 'infinite' competence of ordinary language users to produce and understand language forms which they could not possibly have heard before.

> The central fact to which any significant linguistic theory must address itself is this: a mature speaker can produce a new sentence of his language on the appropriate occasion, and other speakers can understand it immediately, though it is equally new to them. Most of our linguistic experience, both as speakers and hearers, is with new sentences; once we have mastered a language, the class of sentences with which we can operate fluently and without difficulty or hesitation is so vast that for all practical purposes . . . we may regard it as infinite.
>
> (Chomsky, 1964: 7)

Chomsky sees creativity as a fundamental species-specific capacity for generating an infinite number of rule-governed language choices which are for the most part new to both speaker and listener and yet are readily understood by both. In Chomsky's biological definition (1964: 7–9) the creative capacity also extends to the ability creatively to construct a context in which an interpretation of the language can be made, even if the language is not well formed according to the rules governing that language. Chomsky's stress on the creative capacity of the individual receiver of a message is important, but his view is limited by restricting language use to well formed, usually invented sentences rather than to stretches of text or naturally occurring, contextually variable sequences of speaking turns in which creative patterns can form and re-form dynamically and organically over stretches of discourse, and emerge co-creatively between speakers. Chomsky's notion of creativity here is not a statement about the capacity of the individual to produce strikingly innovative language or to co-create meanings in everyday conversational exchanges involving more than one speaker, but rather a statement about a genetically endowed capacity to exploit an underlying system. It is an essentially biological view, in which language is separate from external social or cultural influences. Its main parameters are the universal properties of language and the underlying competence of language users, not particular creative instances of its use, whether spoken or written. Chomsky's position illustrates a tension in linguistic studies between explanations of universals and explanations of sociocultural and contextualist locations for language use.

Conversation analysis at work: ethnopoetics, cultures and voices

> In the most ordinary of encounters . . . social actors exhibit a particular attention to and skills in the delivery of a message. In speaking there is always an aesthetic dimension, understood as an attention to the form of what is being said. We are constantly being evaluated by our listeners and by ourselves as our own listeners.
>
> (Duranti, 1997: 16)

Work in the fields of the sociology of language, ethnomethodology and conversation analysis (also referred to as CA) contrasts markedly with the concerns of Chomsky and his followers. The main concern of research in these fields is with everyday, common talk, with social and cultural variations of language in context and with working out the underlying rules for conversational exchanges, including the relationships between talk and the transmission of cultures. Such research underlines above all how much effort speakers invest in everyday conversational exchanges and in ensuring their own ordinariness in such encounters (see especially key papers by Sacks, 1984 and Schegloff, 1986). Speakers transmit, reproduce, modify, transgress and continually remake the cultures they inhabit by means of their ordinary speech. In this sense 'culture' is a verb (Street, 1993). Speakers are social actors and agents of culture, and are transitive in their encounters, shaping and reshaping their language in ways which encode that how they mean is a significant component in what cultures mean and what people mean as speakers within their cultures.

Culture is thus not a fixed inheritance of shared meanings, abstracted from ordinary daily experience. It is closely connected with identities which are formed between and among the people and the social institutions with which they engage in their own words. Work in these fields has underlined the significance of speakers who attend to their performances and to those of others through language, however insignificant those encounters may appear to an outside observer. In this sense ordinary everyday language is pervasively creative, and this perspective, echoed in the quotation from Duranti (1997: 16) at the head of this section and in the following quotation from Scherzer (1987: 295), will be one which is constantly acknowledged in this book.

> It is especially in verbally artistic and playful discourse, such as poetry, magic, verbal duelling and political rhetoric, that the resources provided by grammar, as well as cultural meanings and symbols, are activated to their fullest potential and the essence of language–culture relationships becomes salient.

Everyday conversation reveals uses of language that are strongly associated with criteria for 'literariness', that is, with the uses of language that characterise texts held by members of given speech communities to be 'literary'. Traditions of research in ethnopoetics and in anthropological and cross-cultural studies of verbal art have also embraced culturally specific, contextually sensitive accounts of verbal exchanges and encounters.[5] Most studies within this tradition have focused on the relatively restricted genre of stories and of narrative and dramatic performance as manifested in more monologic discourse styles. Studies which have explored the artistry of everyday exchanges and interactions (e.g. Tannen, 1989; Norrick, 1993, 2000, 2001) have been largely confined to the genre of narrative or to restricted social contexts such as dinner-party or family conversations. None the less, detailed attention is given in these studies to spoken creativity and to its contextual conditions and such studies also eschew definitions of creativity which are too formalist, preferring more functional and contextualised accounts.

Recent studies also recognise that casual conversation intrinsically creates a space within which speakers can fulfil what would appear to be a fundamental need to insert a more personal or personally evaluative position into the ongoing discourse. It is as if the relationships which are so important a part of casual conversation cannot be fully realised without an element of verbal play and inventiveness; and it is as if verbal play and creativity in talk are in essence interactive and interpersonal in character. It is a fundamental casual conversational strategy to engage and involve others and there is an underlying recognition that, although, as Cook (1996) suggests, casual conversation is often a space-filling discourse, it comprehends so much more than the transfer into the space of information. These are all issues subsequently explored in this book in subsequent chapters.

Tannen (1989) has commented extensively on this feature of conversational discourse and with particular reference to repetition. 'Repetition is a resource by which conversationalists together create a discourse, a relationship, and a world. It is the central linguistic meaning-making strategy, a limitless resource for individual creativity and interpersonal involvement' (Tannen, 1989: ch. 3). Crystal (1995: 413) has summarised and himself glossed this position in a clear

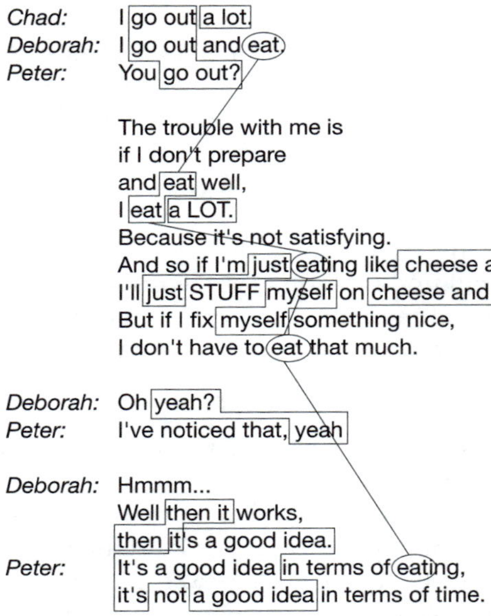

Chad: I go out a lot.
Deborah: I go out and eat.
Peter: You go out?

          The trouble with me is
          if I don't prepare
          and eat well,
          I eat a LOT.
          Because it's not satisfying.
          And so if I'm just eating like cheese and crackers,
          I'll just STUFF myself on cheese and crackers.
          But if I fix myself something nice,
          I don't have to eat that much.

Deborah: Oh yeah?
Peter: I've noticed that, yeah

Deborah: Hmmm...
          Well then it works,
          then it's a good idea.
Peter: It's a good idea in terms of eating,
          it's not a good idea in terms of time.

Figure 2.1 Talking voices and creative patterns.

and helpful way, in the process drawing on data examined by Tannen herself in her book *Talking Voices* (see Figure 2.1).

Crystal comments:

> Not only does it readily admit linguistic deviance, it displays many of the formal features which are traditionally thought to be 'literary', such as metrical rhythm, syntactic parallelism, figurative language, alliteration and verbal repetition.
>   . . . The literariness of a conversation is not immediately obvious . . . Transcribed in a conventional manner, it is difficult to see anything of interest taking place. Laid out differently, several patterns begin to emerge and a more informed comparison can be made with the crafted conversation of drama. Only the lexical patterns are shown . . . several other links can be found between certain grammatical words (*I, if*) and there are signs of phonological repetition too (*in terms of time, lot/not, just/stuff/much*).

But this is not **Paradise Lost:** *another note of caution*

There is a tendency in discussions of demotic creativity – which I acknowledge to be the case in the discussion in this chapter – to suggest that literariness is wholly a matter of patterning at the linguistic level. The literary texts which are valued within many communities certainly have these qualities and hence it is possible to draw points of comparison between a conversation, an advertisement and a lyric poem. It should be recognised that in some literary texts, for example a long novel such as *Middlemarch* or an epic poem such as *Paradise Lost*, such patterns are indeed present but that the patterns operate on a much larger and more extended scale, sometimes spanning several hundred pages, and that they often contribute to the explication and representation of the universal human condition. For some readers this marks them out as more valuable than a newspaper headline, however rich its associations, or everyday casual talk, however subtle its creative patterning across the boundaries between conversational turns. Such works are designated literary by educational institutions and publishers and are therefore subject, as Eagleton (1983) points out, to a certain social exclusivity in the assignment of value. But to point out that creative language in such texts functions in ways similar to those in conversations does not explain why these texts have importance in individual lives. Examining this would be the topic of another book, but the perspective cannot be dismissed as of no relevance to this study. It is a perspective which cautions against excessive claims for comparison between conversation and literature.[6] My position in this book respects this perspective but continues to operate on the grounds argued for in the introduction and prologue above and in the discussion of values and relativity in the final paragraphs of chapter 1 and throughout this chapter.

Conclusion: towards the art of common talk

This chapter has examined a range of linguistic approaches to the study of creativity in the twentieth century.

- It has been argued that issues of creativity are not easily separated from questions of what makes a literary text literary and of the nature of literariness in language. Truth and lies, play and non-play, fiction and reality, ordinary and literary language are not easily distinguished.
- Research in cognitive poetics has shown that the boundaries between the literal and the non-literal are not as clear as is often assumed in linguistic research.
- Creativity is ubiquitous across a range of text-types and is especially salient in spoken discourse too. It depends for its effects on particular patterns of language form and is interactive in that both senders and receivers are involved, dialogically, in the co-creation.
- Creativity is both special and normal and is both ordinary and extraordinary. It is extraordinary in its ordinariness. Ordinary language, in so far as it exists, is the exception rather than the rule. It is problematic to make ordinariness a default condition.
- An emphasis on clines of creative language use should none the less not obsure the fact that some communications are routine and are cases at the limit of the non-creative part of the cline. Examples would be a car-maintenance manual, a sales order, most service encounters and most letters to a bank manager.
- Creativity is connected with language play and draws on figures of speech which have been described as a fundamental characteristic of all language.

- Creativity functions to give pleasure, to establish both harmony and convergence as well as disruption and critique, to express identities and to evoke alternative fictional worlds which are recreational and which recreate the familiar world in new ways.
- Linguistic descriptions have the potential to show how creative language works, but can do so only relatively, that is, relative to the values, beliefs and judgements formed within and according to the needs of different social groups, communities and cultural systems.
- To identify features of literariness in language is a necessary but not sufficient condition for the definition of literature.
- The variable and plural nature of creativity is best discussed in terms of clines and continua.
- It is both necessary and valuable to see creative language in relation to social and cultural contexts.

The next chapter begins by looking more closely at 'the poetry of talk' and starts to unravel the kinds of frameworks and research questions which may help us to investigate everyday creations involving common spoken language. The argument will be strongly advanced that creativity is not simply a property of special individuals but a special, shared property of all individuals, a property which is especially apparent when spoken creativity, as language operating 'at full stretch', is explored and, in particular, when it is explored as a social and cultural phenomenon and with reference to real data involving people actually using the language in daily encounters. It is therefore not simply a matter of a genetically endowed cognitive competence but a matter of socially and culturally mediated expertise with language. As I argued in the previous chapter, creativity is an individual matter but, more fundamentally, it is a matter of individuals in dialogue with other individuals.

Notes

1   In a related way, Bever (1986) points out that aesthetic satisfaction is produced not simply by straightforward arousal but rather by the *pleasure* which ensues when difficulty is followed by resolution, a good example being when a complex narrative is resolved by an ingenious plot outcome or in which a specific moral problem is addressed and solutions proposed. Parallelism is another example in which the first part is resolved by the reinstatement of a related pattern in the second part, a process which serves as a kind of psychological closure or completion. In earlier studies Berlyne (1971) had gone even further, and with an apparent recognition of the demands of many Modernist texts, arguing that a presentation of aesthetic arousal can be autonomous and that, indeed, complexity need not be resolved and may even be all the more pleasurable for remaining so. Cognitive anthropologists in this tradition are, however, less concerned with specific textual functions or with sociocultural reception than with the universal, non-culture-specific character of verbal art.

2   See, in particular, studies by Sawyer (1996, 1997) in which he provides data

from pre-school classrooms and shows very young children learning to extend, distribute and play between the different voices associated with different social positions.

3   Gibbs does, however, provide evidence to support the speculation that there is a delimitable set of core, productive and culturally salient vocabulary items that predominate in both conventional and creative metaphors. See also chapter 4, pp. 115 ff.

4   Games can also be games of chance, involving high levels of risk, some calculated and some involving a more or less complete submission to random forces. Many games and playful uses of language introduce a chance element almost for its own sake, compelling participants to enter into a random 'flow' of events and an associated intensely concentrated and focused state of mind which Czikszentmihalyi (1996) and others see as a core component in creative thinking or in a preparation for creative activity. The influential French play theorist Caillois ([1955] 1969), while sharing a number of Huizinga's understandings of play, lays particular emphasis on what he calls *alea*, which he defines as the kind of play in which, as in a game of roulette for example, the player relies wholly on external forces of chance for any success in the game.

While there may not appear to be overt links between *alea* and language play, Cook pursues the connection in illuminating ways. In language play, Cook suggests, the introduction of patterns of linguistic form (e.g. rhyme, rhythm, parallelism) beyond those demanded by meaning and purpose destabilises the relation of meaning and form, allowing change in the range of possibilities open to both. Exploiting such destabilisation of language may be important to creative thought and in the creative adaptation of language in providing solutions to problems.

5   See, for example, Tedlock (1975, 1977); Friedrich (1979, 1986); Hill (1985); Mannheim (1986); Rubin (1995); Hanks (1996); Hymes (1996).

6   Guy Cook (personal communication) points out that the kinds of intimacy achieved in common talk, and by creativity in talk in particular, are an important feature of literariness. It may, Cook argues, be a feature in language interaction which the greatest creative writers always exploit to some degree, thus allowing readers to feel that writers, even writers from a distant past, are interacting with them in the here and now. Cook also points out that arguments for the universality of literature cannot be ignored in investigations of literariness.

Exploring further

On differences between spoken and written English see Halliday (1989), Cornbleet and Carter (2001) and, with particular references to narrative and narrative ordering, Chafe (1994). Further work by Deborah Tannen on spoken and written literacy events, with particular reference to cross-cultural narrative differences can be found in Tannen (1982). On coherence in spoken and written discourse, see the collection of papers in Tannen (1984a). The understanding of written and spoken encounters with particular reference to frames of understanding is explored in Tannen (1994). Linell (1982) is a fascinating study of a bias towards written discourse in linguistics.

Harris's work (e.g. 1998) has implications too for the initial point of departure for this chapter, as well as for fuller understanding of the underlying theories of spoken–written continua in relation to IRC communication in chapter 6. The past emphasis on creativity in written texts and certain kinds of performed spoken texts (e.g. folk narratives) at the expense of banal, everyday conversation has been underlined, but Harris's notion of 'integrational' linguistics sees both spoken and written texts as co-existing as 'species of situated communicative action' (Fleming, 1995: 94). See also Toolan (1996) for a study in this tradition.

Toolan (2000b) contributes a further valuable study of the representation of speech in modern literary fiction in terms of trends towards spokenness in all discourses. Freeman (1993) has a cognitive poetic analysis of Shakespeare's *King Lear*. Papers in Verdonk and Weber (1995) contain analyses with a cognitive poetic orientation.

Speech acts in literary and non-literary discourse have been explored in classic publications such as Pratt's *Towards a Speech Act Theory of Literary Discourse* (1977) and in seminal papers by Searle (1975). Fish's (1973) paper 'How ordinary is ordinary language?' is a key contribution. Both these studies work from the kinds of distinctions proposed by Ohmann (p. 61 above) and by Carter and Nash (1990: ch. 1). For a critique of speech act theory in the context of studies of intentionality, see Gibbs (1999a). Gibbs underlines the creativity invested by listeners and receivers of messages in recovering the meanings *intended* by a speaker.

For further discussion of the nature of literary language, see Short and Candlin (1986), Carter and Nash (1990: ch. 2), Carter (1997: ch. 6), and Tambling (1988). Definitions of literary language in terms of foregrounding as a result of deviation from linguistic norms owe much to literary analysis by early Russian Formalists. Further discussion in this tradition can be found in Havranek (1932), Mukarovsky (1932) and Attridge (1988). Several of these studies attempt to reverse existing paradigms, in particular that literary language has to be motivated against a background of non-literary language and that non-literary language is therefore by default of less value to us in reading the language of the world. Bennett (1990) studies the 'literary' in relation to institutional and non-institutional discourse. Palmer and Jankiowak (1996) link similar 'spectacular' and 'mundane' domains from an anthropological perspective. Kuiper and Hago (1984), Shepherd (1990) and Kuiper (1996) focus on the relationship between everyday language and poetic art. Turner (1996) argues that basic questions about the organisation of language and thought can be found by exploring the 'literary mind'. Widdowson (2002) debates a range of issues surrounding verbal art, arguing for the centrality of personal rather than social meanings in literary communication.

Derrida (1978) asks fundamental questions about the primacy of speech. Conventionally, spoken language is seen as open to scrutiny by the speaker whose presence in the speech event guarantees its authenticity. Derrida challenges such a privileging of speech and a subsequent downgrading of 'writing'. For Derrida, writing is primary because it represents a truer version of the system of language whose meanings are always undecidable. Writing is therefore a primary system because we delude ourselves into believing that meaning in spoken language can be determined by the speaker. According to Derrida, speaking derives from and is secondary to writing.

McRae (1991) and Holliday (1999) look at 'small' cultures and literatures, while

Hall (2001) gives a very useful survey of the 'poetics of the everyday'. Herrnstein-Smith (1988) explores the assignment of different values to different cultural products.

The conversational studies of Norrick (e.g. 2000, 2001), in particular, provide a lucid and convincing account of the extent to which ordinary language is far from ordinary and of how what is conventionally seen as literary language pervades many everyday conversations. His work in this tradition is orientated largely to research in conversation analysis and is especially impressive with reference to the centrality of prosody to a poetics of conversation. Norrick covers a wide range of creative patterns in his analysis of conversational data. He is especially alert to uses of humour (see Norrick, 1993 for a much fuller study) and bases most of his examples on naturally occurring narrative events, recorded mainly within family and generally within domestic settings within which joke-telling is a key creative source for self-display, entertainment and communality. It is crucial to Norrick's method that he is able to utilise his own knowledge of the participants and of the context of the recordings, as in so doing he overcomes one of the main difficulties in analysing such data: the danger of ascribing intentions and uses of language to speakers who may have not intended such effects, as well as the danger of inter-preting listeners' or co-conversationalists' responses in ways which may distort the data. In fact, Norrick is especially convincing when writing about methodology, and his sensitivity to the need for constant alertness to contextual factors is eloquently displayed.

There is controversy surrounding some of the works of Bakhtin, with certain pieces being attributed to a contemporary of Bakhtin, V. N. Voloshinov. Relevant further reading on voicing may therefore be found in Voloshinov, *Marxism and the Philosophy of Language* (1986). A valuable study of voicing in relation to educational discourse and the institutionalisation of the school is made by Maybin (2003).

Several of the above commentators on 'literary', creative and non-literal dis-courses have pointed to the pleasure conferred by and derived from verbal play. The notion that ordinary language users regularly and typically communicate in ways from which pleasure may be derived has gained considerable ground in recent years and correspondingly the assumption that pleasure is the sole preserve of the highest forms of artistic encounter may need to be reinspected.

Discussions of the role of schema (and what are termed scripts and scenarios) in language interpretation are extensive, though applications to literary and creative uses of language are more limited. Brown and Yule (1983) provide a thorough survey of the foundational literature on these topics, while recent work which engages with the studies of Cook and others, for example by Jeffries (2001) and Semino (2001), provides critique and counter-critique of the fact that such 'schema-based' models appear to assume universalist paradigms and are often therefore narrowly ethnocentric in their potential application.

For further discussion of vocabulary and prototypes, see Stubbs (1986, 1998). Zelinsky-Wibbelt (1993) and O'Dowd (1998) contribute studies of core vocabu-lary and discourse processing with particular reference to prepositions.

There is a long tradition of investigation of creativity in spoken discourse within anthropological linguistics, a tradition which has been influential in traditions of conversation analysis. Typical examples would be Mannheim's (1986) study of the 'poetic' language of popular song, Friedrich's anthropological reformulation of poetics (1976) and the studies collected by Friedrich (1986). Rubin (1995) is a more psycholinguistically orientated study of popular literature in different cultural settings. See Hymes (1996) for a classic study, drawing on many years' fieldwork experience of narrative analysis in different cultural settings and synthesising a number of different ethnopoetic and conversational research traditions. Hanks (1996) also provides a powerful and influential synthesis of work in the field, with a continuing stress on the 'contextually saturated' nature of language and on the importance of an evaluation of context for full understanding of different communicative effects (see especially, ch. 7). By contrast Levelt (1989) provides a classic and influential study of speech processing from a psycholinguistic perspective.

Chukovsky [1928] (1963), Nelson (1996) and Bruner *et al.* (1976) have rich sources of observations and insights into the creative language behaviour of young children. Winnicott (1971), Winner (1988) and Sawyer (1997) all write convincingly on play and creativity in child language use as both a basic instinct and a basic constituent of the developing human mind. See also Meares (1992).

There is a wide range of further discussion and analysis of the role of language play in its own right and in relation to theories and practices of creativity, for example Victor Turner's foundational study of performance and play, *From Ritual to Theatre: The Human Seriousness of Play* (1982). The term 'liminality' used extensively by Turner is crucial. It derives in particular from Turner's anthropological studies in agrarian and tribal societies of adulthood initiation rites. Turner points out that liminal practices can involve a kind of limbo for those passing through these stages but basically such practices underline and support a smoothly functioning social system. But Turner also draws attention to more creative 'liminoid' practices of specific individuals and groups where the ritualised play is intended more as critique of wrongs in social systems. See also chapter 6 for discussions of liminal and liminoid linguistic practices.

Contemporary researchers are continuing to exploit insights of seminal researchers such as Gregory Bateson (e.g. his paper 'A theory of play and fantasy' in his book *Steps to an Ecology of Mind* (1972)) and Lev Vygotsky in his book *The Psychology of Art* (1971). Both offer illuminating insights into the nature of, for example, play fighting and play as display, drawing in the process on analogies with artistic production.

Part II

Forms and functions

3 Creativity and patterns of talk

Owen slips slightly, he's up, he's back on his feet but Owen is through, he's on his own, he slips it past the goalkeeper. 3–0. Now Liverpool are back up there, they're on cloud nine.
(Radio 5 Live football commentary, December 2002)

It is a question of how many birds we can kill with this particular stone.
(CANCODE data)

See you later alligator.
In a while crocodile.

Introduction

This chapter looks at spoken discourse in the light of the theoretical issues and descriptive approaches examined in the preceding chapters. The main part explores the extent to which examples of everyday spoken discourse display creative properties. Among the questions posed in this chapter are:

- Are there differences between creativity in written and spoken texts?
- Can particular creative patterns of spoken language be identified?
- Can a corpus of spoken language reveal features of creativity which other sources of data cannot?
- Is it reasonable to talk of the 'art' of speech and, if so, what kinds of frameworks, both theoretical and descriptive, are best suited to its analysis?

Corpus and data

The data for discussion in this chapter are drawn almost exclusively from a unique corpus of spoken English. Interest in spoken discourse has been re-awoken recently by the large multimillion-word collections of naturally occurring spoken data which have become increasingly available (for example, the BNC (British National Corpus) and the spoken sections of the Bank of English, held at the University of Birmingham, UK). The data on which this chapter is based are all taken from the CANCODE corpus assembled in the School of English Studies at the University of Nottingham, UK. CANCODE stands for Cambridge and Nottingham Corpus of Discourse in English and is a multimillion-word computationally accessible corpus of spoken English. The working corpus from which examples in this book are drawn totals 5 million words and the data were collected between the years 1993 and 2001. Although data from the CANCODE project form the main material for discussion in this and the following two chapters, no corpus study can reasonably rely wholly on one particular set of data: accordingly, other data are used as appropriate and in chapter 6 there is a distinct move beyond CANCODE data to embrace samples of language use from a wider range of contexts.

In the construction and design of the CANCODE corpus the main aim has not been simply to construct a corpus for purposes of quantitative measurement, important though that is; it has been to construct a corpus which also allows more qualitative investigation. In particular, data have been carefully collected with reference to a range of different speech genres, with an emphasis on 'common' informal discourse collected mainly in non-institutional settings. Plans are already laid to extend the corpus to include a wider variety of international Englishes produced in different discourse communities and to compare British and non-British spoken Englishes. Although the emphasis in work on the corpus is on lexico-grammatical description with the aim of producing a new pedagogical grammar of English, what cannot be ignored (indeed, it leaps out at researchers from almost every transcript of the data) is the inherent creativity of significant proportions of common language use.[1]

A subsequent chapter (chapter 5) discusses in greater detail the CANCODE corpus and its organisation into differerent speech genres and social contexts of use. The Note on Transcription (see Appendix 1) discusses the processes involved in transcription and how these can affect what we see and 'read' of the spoken data represented on the page. This Note also discusses some of the limitations which apply to studying spoken language data collected as part of a corpus. Readers who remain properly sceptical about the claims for using large quantities of data, however impressive the numbers may sound, may want to read this Note before engaging with the remainder of this chapter.

The aims of this chapter are, however, principally question-raising, providing initial frameworks for further exploration of key terms for the book and laying a basis for fuller investigation in subsequent chapters. In the first part of the chapter there is a review of some key figures of speech and forms of language used for what can be considered to be creative purposes. Appropriately, figures of 'speech', which are normally examined (paradoxically) in written texts, are examined here almost exclusively in spoken examples.

Punning and playing and patterning

<S 01>: Aston Villa are playing with er a Christmas tree formation with an angel at the top . . . Juan Pablo Angel – ANKHEL I believe it's pronounced – who joined them from the Argentinean club River Plate and erm that's I suppose the last time we'll be able to use that pun.

<S 02>: I hope so Jeff.

(Sky television football commentary, Sky Sports, December 2000)

Peace is not just on the back-burner; it's not on the stove at all.

(CNN TV report, March 2001)

Speakers in the CANCODE corpus regularly pun and play on and with words. In the introduction to this book we saw a group of friends engaged in minor DIY (do-it-yourself) tasks whose discourse, for a time at least, was taken over by a bout of remorseless punning, mainly by means of sexual analogies with particular details of the activity of putting up shelves. Puns are simultaneously reputable and disreputable. In written texts puns are regularly seen as a lower form of wit or are associated with less highly regarded genres such as tabloid newspaper headlines, graffiti or advertising copy. However, puns are ubiquitous, occur in a range of different types of texts, and are multilayered in so far as some puns involve simple ambiguities of sound, sight–sound relations (homonymy) or grammatical pattern, while other puns can have semantically dense resonances. In terms of canonical literature, too, the range of texts which incorporate punning is also wide and incorporates everything from Elizabethan drama to the modernist texts of Joyce and Beckett. Puns are a particular feature of demotic creativity:

> In studying the ludic element in culture, literary and everyday, I should logically also posit a similar element in those who receive and respond to wordplay: that is, all of us. Punning is a free-for-all available to everyone, common property; it is a democratic trope. It is the stock-in-trade of the low comedian and the most sophisticated wordsmith: James Joyce and Max Miller . . . It is and always has been.
>
> (Redfern, 1984: 175)

The fact that puns are a common rather than special property may explain uncertainties in attitude. In any event there is a certain reflexiveness prompted by puns in both speakers and listeners. Speakers and writers often use the phrase 'no pun intended', recognising that to produce punning is also often to elicit embarrassed laughter, groans and apologies. It is as if there is always a recognition that puns do not belong within the serious realms of adult discourse but are rather associated with joke books (especially those for children) or Christmas cracker trivia. As Cook (2000: 81) has commented, 'all puns, even good puns, are bad puns'.

Puns are common in the CANCODE corpus. In the following example the participants are engaged in a game. A joke is told which depends on an intertextual reference to a well-known television and film series (*StarTrek*). A common reference in that series is to progressing to the final frontier in outer space. The pun in this case is on the words *frontier* and *front ear* (a reference also to the unusual ears of one of the main characters in the programme). The self-conscious reference to the pun in the joke, the disparaging comments and the (possibly) mock laughter all conspire to underline prevalent social attitudes to the use of puns in discourse.

Example 3.1

[Holiday cottage in north Yorkshire, England, occupied by one family. There are eight people present but only four talk in this extract. The group consists of a father and children, and the children's friends and partners. <S 01> is the father (58). All the children and their friends/partners are in their twenties and thirties.]

<S 01>: Hey. Who's telling this joke? Who's telling this joke?

<S 02>: [laughs]

<S 01>: He's got a left ear he's got a right ear and he's got a final frontier.

<S 02>: Frontier. Yeah.

<S 01>: [laughs]

<S 02>: Oh.

<S 01>: Oh.

<S 01>: [laughs]

<S 02>: You're supposed to point though.

<S 01>: Are you?

<S 02>: Mm.

<S 01>: [laughs]

<S 02>: You're supposed to point though.

<S 01>: Are you?

<S 02>: Mm.

<S 01>: [laughs]

<S 03>: Run it by us again.

<S 02>: [laughs]

<S 01>: Right. Why? What's, what do I need to point at you?
[laughter]

<S 02>: I thought it was funny anyway.

<S 03>: [laughs]

<S 01>: Have you got it?

<S 04>: [claps]

<S 03>: [laughs]

<S 01>: It's a pun. It's an English pun.

<S 02>: I've got it.

The following two examples offer some further representative samples from the CANCODE corpus.

Example 3.2

[Members of a family in Cardiff are preparing food for a party. <S 01> is female (45), <S 02> is male (19), <S 04> is male (49), <S 03> is male (46). <S 03> is <S 04>'s brother and is visiting. <S 02> is the son of <S 01> and <S 04>.]

<S 01>: Now I think you'd better start the rice.

<S 02>: Yeah. What have you got there?

[pause]

<S 01>: Will it all fit in the one?

<S 02>: No. We'll have to do two separate ones.

[pause]

<S 03>: What next?

[pause]

<S 03>: Foreign body in here. What is it?

<S 02>: It's raisins and [inaudible]

<S 03>: Er oh it's rice with raisins is it?

<S 04>: No. No. No. It's not supposed to be.

[laughter] Erm

<S 03>: There must be a raisin for it being in there.

Example 3.3

[<S 01> female (42) (Glam.); <S 02> female (13) (Kent); <S 03> male (46) (Glam.); <S 04> male (12) (Kent). <S 01> is <S 02>'s and <S 04>'s mother; <S 03> is an old childhood friend. At <S 01>'s house, Birchington, Kent, November 1993. This story refers back to an earlier ghost story involving a man having a premonition of his own death on the ship Hood. *<S 01> begins by describing how the members of the crew were all lined up prior to being selected for the* Hood. *The data belong to Michael McCarthy ©.]*

<S 01>: Oh yes. I mean they were all eager to get (<S 02>: Yeah) to get on it you know. They were really looking (<S 02>: Mm) forward to being the chosen ones. And er he was one of the ones who was called up (<S 02>: Yeah) and he getting ready to go and the Chief Petty Officer came back and said Oh no. It's a mistake. Erm Dixon+

<S 03>: We've got one extra.

<S 01>: +Dixon er you're not needed. (<S 02>: Mm. Yeah) And er he was a bit disappointed and he went back carried on with what he was doing and the boat sailed out and was torpedoed and all hands lost.

<S 03>: By a German ship.

<S 02>: Oh yes. Yes.

<S 04>: Every= everyone died.

<S 03>: Anyway all hands lost but legs saved.

[laughter]

<S 01>: Do you remember?

<S 03>: Well sailors were always getting legless weren't they anyway.

[laughter]

<S 01>: Finding their sea legs.

<S 03>: Mm. Yeah.

The creativity of speakers and listeners in examples 3.2 and 3.3 here produces a widespread form of punning and verbal play – a kind of verbal schizophrenia with words pointing in two directions at once. In example 3.2 the comic identification of the phrase 'foreign body' with a *raisin* results in puns on the word 'raisin/reason'. In example 3.3 the puns operate as a result of double meanings in the word *leg*. For example, the fixed expression 'find your sea legs' (meaning to learn how to be a sailor) combines with the word 'legless' (meaning to be unable to stand up or 'find your legs' as a result of being drunk). We should also notice in example 3.3 a creative play with the metonymy ('hands'). The word *hands* is used metonymically to refer to people (for example, workers in a factory or, as here, sailors on a ship) and is also in a semantic pattern with *legs*. The hinges of punning and ambiguity on which the discourses turn in these examples clearly work to establish a common viewpoint of the topic on the part of the group of speakers, and the commonality and convergence are reinforced by the not infrequent laughter in the groups. Speakers play on these forms spontaneously by exploiting the real, immediate context for humorous effects, in contrast with ready-made or rehearsed jokes which normally exploit more remote fictitious contexts.

In the following extract, a group of young female students are taking tea together, and two verbal ambiguities are exploited within a very short stretch of text.

Example 3.4

[An extract from a multiparty conversation involving three art college students. The students are all female, are the same age (between 20 and 21) and share a house in Carmarthen, Wales. Two of the students (<S 01> and <S 03>) are from the south-west of England and one (<S 02>) is from South Wales They are having tea at home on a Sunday, sitting in a relaxed and informal manner around a tea-table.]

<S 01>: Yeah. Did you ever do erm erm, what was it called. [inaudible] Cilla.
<S 02>: Did I ever do Cilla?
<S 01>: [laughs] No. [inaudible]
<S 02>: [laughs] [inaudible]
<S 01>: [inaudible]
<S 02>: Did you?
[laughter]
<S 01>: You know Cilla last year on Three D.
<S 02>: Oh this is wonderful.
<S 01>: [sighs] [inaudible]
<S 03>: Bakewell time.
<S 02>: Tea and tarts.
[laughter]
<S 03>: Tea and tart.
<S 02>: Tea with some
<S 01>: Tea with tarts.

<S 03>: They're not tarts.
[inaudible] [laughter]
<S 01>: Tarts for tea.

'Do' is exploited for its sexual ambiguity (the word also has a vulgar meaning of having intercourse with) and 'tarts' for its meanings of (a) a sweet pastry item and (b) a slang term for a prostitute.

Wordplay involves more than puns, of course. Creative play can be illustrated by the examples 3.5–3.7 which follow. (Example 3.7 is also discussed briefly in the introduction to this book.) In these contexts the verbal play is with larger units or 'chunks' of language. The chunks consist of patterns – which are familiar as a result of common use or because the 'chunk' is a proverb or formulaic utterance – and the strategy is to play with these larger patterns by deviating from what is expected, creatively disfiguring them to produce and play with perspectives and ways of seeing.

Example 3.5

[Two friends in London are discussing a third friend's stormy marriage and the fact that, as a result of continuing infidelity, relations between the couple are 'frozen' and they are barely talking. <S 01> female (32), <S 02> male (36).]

<S 01>: He's at it again but he really wants you know just to sit down.
<S 02>: Like they just talk about how they both feel.
<S 01>: Out of the frying pan into the deep freeze this time.
[laughter]

Example 3.6

[Two colleagues in Leicester, who are social workers, are discussing a third colleague who has a tendency to become too involved in individual cases. <S 01> female (45), <S 02> female (47).]

<S 01>: I don't know but she seems to have picked up all kinds of lame ducks and traumas along the way.
<S 02>: That that's her vocation.
<S 01>: Perhaps it is. She should have been a counsellor.
<S 02>: Yeah but the trouble with her is she puts all her socialist carts before the horses.
[laughter]

Example 3.7

[Three students in Bristol are talking about the landlord of a mutual friend. The students are all male, aged 19–22.]

<S 01>: Yes, he must have a bob or two.
<S 02>: Whatever he does he makes money out of it, just like that.
<S 03>: Bob's your uncle.
<S 02>: He's quite a lot of money erm tied up in property and things. He's got a finger in all kinds of pies and houses and stuff. A couple in Bristol, one in Clevedon I think.

Example 3.5 shows speakers playfully and creatively extending metaphors involving the words 'hot' and 'cold' which are both words used as metaphoric figurations in the expression and evaluation of human feeling. Both words are also used alongside a creative extension of a formulaic saying ('out of the frying pan into the fire') (meaning to go from one bad situation to a worse one), so that the comment that the situation has got even 'colder' between the couple is inflected in the reference to a deep freeze. In a similar way examples 3.6 and 3.7 also show standard idiomatic chunks being creatively displaced into new patterns. For example: *She puts all her socialist carts before the horses* (Don't put the cart before the horse); *He's got a finger in all kinds of pies and houses and stuff;* (He's got a finger in every pie).

As has already been discussed in the introduction to this book, example 3.7 also contains the intriguing possibility of subliminal phonaesthetic echoing across speaking turns. The word *bob* here operates in the fixed expression 'bob or two' (where 'bob' is a shilling, a pre-decimal unit of currency worth about five pence) and in the idiom 'Bob's your uncle' meaning 'that's the way it's done'). There is also a further semantic 'repeat' in that the phrase 'Bob's your uncle' has the same meaning as 'Just like that' in the previous turn. It is clear that this 'fixedness' of idioms is something which can be bent and remoulded for particular expressive purposes. In fact, all the examples (3.5–3.7) illustrate how speakers can create new or extended meanings through a playful reformulation of fixed patterns of language. Such expressions also function for evaluative purposes and we should note that the speakers here use the structures to comment adversely on the behaviour of a third party. This commonly creative feature is highlighted here as an aspect of playing imaginatively with words along the lines described in the sections on language play in chapter 2. The topic is also given fuller treatment in chapter 4.

In spite of the shared laughter it should not, however, be supposed that punning and playing with words and phrase structures function solely as a kind of socially cohesive glue or to allow individual speakers collaboratively to display verbal skills which entertain or cause laughter. Puns, in particular, can operate for competition as well as convergence. They can arise from aggression, a revenge for being mocked or condescended to. In the extensive literature on the ritualised insults used in Black English Vernacular and known as *sounding* or *playing the dozens*, the winner of the contest is often the one with the largest range of effective insults, usually based on metaphors and similes structured around complex puns. The ability to use these insults both reflects and enhances the social status of the contestant, and the most effective performer wins the contest (see Abrahams, 1962; Labov, 1972). In any case, it is not simply the identification of puns or forms of wordplay that we are interested in but also a fuller understanding of the effects they create and the functions they perform in stretches of discourse.

In all these examples it is noticeable how puns are self-referential, as described on pp. 59 and 91 above. They draw attention to themselves and draw the attention of speakers and listeners. There is an overt, more openly presentational element in punning which involves speakers in degrees of verbal display. The ways in which they occasion laughter and elicit comment indicate the extent of metalingual awareness on the part of many speakers. They are an example of speakers' common awareness of their own creativity, underlining that concepts and ideas are being combined and re-formed in striking and noticeable ways.

New words for old: morphological inventiveness

The parsley has to be kind of finelyish chopped.

(*The Naked Chef*, BBC TV, 6 May 1999)

His dancers . . . are so undancerly they look as if they'd never say no to a McDonald's.

(*Independent on Sunday*, 29 May 1995)

Also prevalent in CANCODE data are several instances where speakers invent new words from existing words, a feature termed 'morphological creativity' (Carter and McCarthy, 1995b).[2] Here are two examples, in the 'invented' words *heart drawers* and *crawly*:

Example 3.8

[Four student friends discussing a craft stall at <S 04>'s house.]

<S 01>: I mean stuff like this is what we need because it's quite an quite easy thing to design and (<S 02>: Yeah) it that looks really pretty. So what's that?
<S 02>: It's got a lovely heart as well.
<S 03>: Heart drawer.
<S 01>: Heart drawers.
[laughter]
<S 03>: Heart drawers.
<S 01>: Somebody's knickers. And how much was that? Seventy-five?
<S 03>: Seventy-five pence.

Example 3.9

[Three female teachers, all mid-twenties, are in a school staff room discussing the composition of a letter that <S 01> has written seeking information from her local tax office.]

<S 01>: Oh I've done the letter.
<S 02>: Right.
<S 03>: But it's a bit bloody abrupt. It's quite sort of [inaudible]
<S 02>: Ah.
<S 03>: You can sort of [inaudible]
<S 02>: No that's fine.
<S 01>: That's fine?
<S 03>: That's fine.
<S 02>: Are you sure?
<S 03>: Yeah. You don't want to feel crawly do you?
<S 01>: No it's not crawly is it. It's all right if I want this information
         isn't it.
<S 03>: Yeah.

In example 3.8 the invented phrase 'heart drawers' makes a punning analogy between the word *knickers* and the word *drawers* (a word which can also be used to mean underwear such as 'knickers'). But in terms of morphological creativity the word in example 3.9 *crawly* is a neologism derived from the verb *crawl* which also has a meaning of to be unnecessarily flattering or sycophantic. Speakers regularly create new words in this way by deriving new words from established forms. Sometimes these words are created as what might be termed 'survival' words; that is, the word needed does not immediately come to mind so the speaker is forced to invent a word as a kind of survival mechanism to ensure that the conversation continues to flow. Such words are often emergent in the discourse and do not precede it in any deliberative way. It may be that such inventions only occur in particular types of exchange (for example, as here, informal conversations between friends). In the above examples speakers clearly find the interaction sufficiently supportive and co-productive to allow the invention not only to be accepted but also to be seen to be necessary and motivated. Indeed, the invented item is picked up and recycled by the following speaker. If this process happens sufficiently widely, with enough speakers working on the same word(s) in the same way, then the word becomes more established and may even enter the written language and become an established rather than invented item.

Morphological creativity, whereby the derivational potential of words and morphemes is creatively exploited, is surprisingly common in everyday talk. Vizmuller-Zocco (1985) sees lexical derivation as belonging to 'that linguistic competence which is based on creativity', while Howden (1984) sees the native speaker's knowledge both of existing derived words and of the potential for choice as centrally important; she also stresses the interrelationships of meaning set up by new combinations of stems and affixes, many of which, as the following examples illustrate, can be used not simply playfully but also to intensify meanings or to add an evaluative tone to what is said (see Bolinger, 1950 for a classical study and Becker, 1994, for more recent further examples). In these examples the *-y* suffix is highly productive and is becoming an established process by which 'new' words can be produced (see also Appendix 2 for further study).

In the examples that follow, the focus is often on no more than an individual word and the examples given may be no more than a single line or conversational turn. This runs counter to the many other examples in this book which illustrate extensive stretches of discourse. However, the following sections of this chapter return to more extended examples and to the ways in which forms and meanings unfold across several speaking turns.

Example 3.10

[<S 02> who is preparing food, has asked <S 01> to get her a bowl.]

    <S 01>: You said you wanted the little ones as well. Want the little ones?
    <S 02>: Not really . . . sort of *salady* . . . that fruit bowl would be ideal.

Example 3.11

[The speaker is describing what she believes to be some 'newfangled' shoelaces she has bought.]

    <S 01>: They're well sort of like lycra, *elasticky* sort of stuff.

On another occasion, using the *-ing* inflection, a speaker 'derives' a verb from a noun while telling a story of a dangerous game he and his friends played as children, rolling down industrial spoil heaps inside old lorry tyres. As a result the nightmarish rolling movement is intensified.

Example 3.12

    <S 01>: And you'd just roll, like *circusing* right the way down and get
        right up the top.

In another extract from the CANCODE corpus, two women are assembling a portable baby-cot which involves twisting the metal parts until they become rigid. Note in this example how speaker <S 02> uses morphological creativity, this time with a prefix (instead of using the more conventional 'loose' or 'slack'), to satirise her own mistake in the twisting movement.

Example 3.13

    <S 01>: There, that's solid now.
    <S 02>: I think I've made it *unsolid* . . . sorry . . . I've done it the wrong
        way round, have I?

Morphological creativity can be combined with satirical cultural reference too, as in this extract where a hostess (<S 01>) is apologising to her dinner guests (one of whom is <S 02>) that they are a little short of home-grown vegetables.

Example 3.14

> <S 01>: And so I'm afraid we're a bit sort of erm challenged *greenwise*.
> <S 02>: *Greenly* challenged.
> <S 01>: We're *greenly* challenged so erm sorry about that.

Here we have the morphological creativity of *greenwise* and *greenly* combined with an oblique cultural reference to phrases such as *visually challenged*, *physically challenged*, etc., as current 'politically correct' euphemisms for 'blind' and 'disabled', just as being 'green' (growing one's own vegetables organically, etc.) is a politically correct stance. The creative play with words works on several levels, and it is significant that the joke is jointly created or 'co-produced' by the two speakers, emphasising the high degree of shared cultural knowledge as well as alignment and convergence between the speakers.

Repetition and converging

The above features are characterised by their overt attention-getting characteristics and by an inherent capacity to be used for purposes of play. It is, however, also noticeable in the above examples how often speakers repeat each other's words, and work to co-construct and then reinforce each other's invented words. Speakers regularly pattern each other's sayings, producing parallel structures in the form of lexical and syntactic echoes. For example, the repetition of words, invented and otherwise, is especially marked in example 3.9 above, where all the words here are repeated at least once: *That's fine*; *sort of*; *crawly*; *yeah*.

A continuation of the discussion of the family preparing food in the kitchen in example 3.2 also illustrates patterns similar to those noted in example 3.9:

Example 3. 15

> <S 01> How long does it take?
> <S 02>: Erm+
> <S 03>: Oh that'll make a noise.
> <S 02>: +takes about thirty-five minutes. Yeah. That'll be that'll, that'll destroy your tape.
> <S 01>: Thirty-five minutes?
> <S 02>: Yeah.
> <S 03>: Yeah.
> <S 01>: I thought the microwave did everything in about two minutes.
> <S 03>: You may as well turn it off now then.
> <S 01>: Yeah. You can do it on the cooker for thir= in thirty-five minutes couldn't you.
> <S 02>: Then if you have to watch it. You just ignore it.
> <S 01>: Oh.
> <S 04>: You don't have to wash the saucepan either do you.

<S 02>: You don't have to wash the saucepan after [laughs]
<S 01>: Mm.
<S 02>: And you don't have to erm, you don't have to drain the water off either.
<S 01>: I didn't know that microwaves ran that long.
<S 02>: Yeah. You don't have to erm drain the water off either cos [inaudible] Yeah.
<S 01>: I'll switch it off when you turn that on.

This multiparty sequence of exchanges contains several examples of the seemingly random topic switching and overlapping, interruptions, unanswered questions, hesitations and false starts which characterise informal conversations. On the surface and to the outsider (though not to the participants) there is much divergence, disconnection and incoherence. Beneath the surface there is, however, much convergence and coherence marked in a distinctive range of pattern-reinforcing linguistic features, especially repetition. For example, the speakers use each other's words, employ parallel syntactic forms and generally pattern question and answer replies in such a way as to suggest high degrees of affective connection and convergence. Note, for example, the regular recycling and echoing of the following words and structures: *take*; *thirty-five minutes*; *do/did*; *yeah*; *drain the water off*; *you don't have to wash/drain*; *off/on*.

This feature of echoing and repetition has been remarked upon in the previous chapter where the work of Tannen and others was referred to (see introduction and p. 80). It is worth requoting Tannen at this point for an insight into one of the functions of repetition. 'Repetition is a resource by which conversationalists together create a discourse, a relationship, and a world. It is the central linguistic meaning-making strategy, a limitless resource for individual creativity and interpersonal involvement' (Tannen, 1989: ch. 3). The patterns established through repetition are less obvious, and do not merit the same attention and reflexive comment that puns or other more overt forms of wordplay command from speakers, but they are no less significant as creative instances of language interaction. However, can the two main types of pattern we have identified, the more overt and the less overt, be brought into any kind of synthesis?

Creative patterns: a hypothesis

Don't give up on giving up
(NHS anti-smoking advertisement, October 2000)

Patterns are always potentially present in language, and language users always have options whether or not to establish patterns and, if so, what kind of patterns to create. In the data from the CANCODE corpus discussed above patterns of various kinds can be discerned. There are patterns which are based on repetition. Such patterns are not always noticed by speakers when they are speaking although they are easily identified when a transcript is analysed.

There are also patterns that are more likely to be noticed by speakers because the patterns created are more overt. That is, such a pattern draws attention to itself. It is made more transparent because it involves a deliberate play on or with words and it is overt because it can involve a break with an expected pattern. For example, a second meaning of a word is picked up on or a fixed expression is displaced or a newly coined or invented word or phrase is produced.

It might thus be hypothesised that there are two main motivating choices involving words and word patterns: *pattern forming* choices, and *pattern re-forming* choices.

Most of the examples we have examined in this chapter fall into the pattern re-forming category. They draw attention to patterns by re-forming and reshaping them and sometimes by directly and overtly breaking with them. In extreme versions of *re-forming* there is a more radical position created by the 're-form'. Co-conversationalists are prompted to pleasure and laughter, to more evaluative and affective viewpoints and to a more innovative reshaping of our ways of seeing. They involve new words and novel expressions, implying change and normally involving a single producer who brings about 'novel' changes to the language in ways which are innovative, schema-refreshing and in keeping with the post-Romantic views of creativity outlined in chapter 1.

In the case of pattern forming choices such as various forms of repetition, the speakers use the patterns to converge their way of seeing things and to create a greater mutuality between them. The creativity grows from mutual interaction rather than from individual innovation. The patterns may not draw attention to themselves in the same way as pattern re-forming choices; and it is also more likely that rules for linguistic structures will be conformed to rather than departed from, a process more in keeping with pre-Romantic views of creativity. The patterns operate discretely but they can be and often are combined, as is illustrated by the following extended example.

Patterns in action: a sample analysis

Part of the following extract was discussed in the introduction to this book. It is from a conversation involving three art college students. It is returned to here and examined in greater detail, with fuller transcription, together with a longer stretch from the same exchange.

Example 3.16

[The students are all female, are the same age (between 20 and 21) and share a house in Carmarthen, Wales. Two of the students (<S 01> and <S 03>) are from the south-west of England and one (<S 02>) is from South Wales. They are having tea at home on a Sunday, sitting in a relaxed and informal manner around a tea-table.]

> <S 03>: Does anybody want a chocolate bar or anything?
> <S 01>: Oh. Yeah. Please.
> <S 02>: Oh. Yes please.

[laughter]

\<S 03>: All right. You can have, you can have either a Mars Bar Kit Kat or erm Cherry Bakewells.

\<S 02>: [laughs]

\<S 01>: Ooh.

\<S 02>: Oh.

\<S 01>: Er er er erm [inaudible]

\<S 02>: Oh it's a toss up between the Cherry Bakewell+

\<S 01>: [laughs]

\<S 02>: +and the Mars Bar isn't it.

\<S 03>: Well shall I bring them in? And, cos I mean might you want another one. Cos I don't want them all. Cos+

\<S 01>: Yeah.

\<S 03>: +I'm gonna be

[laughter]

\<S 02>: Miss paranoid about weight here.

\<S 03>: [from distance] Yeah. But you know.

\<S 02>: You're not fat Sue.

\<S 03>: [from distance] I will be [inaudible].

[laughter]

\<S 02>: God.

[laughter]

\<S 03>: I ate almost a whole jar of Roses this weekend.

\<S 02>: Did you?

[laughter]

\<S 03>: And my mum [inaudible].

\<S 02>: Look at her neck.

\<S 01>: [laughs]

\<S 03>: She goes Ooh. Do you [inaudible].

\<S 02>: My God.

\<S 01>: What was that about you you said about your, you and your mum don't get on?

[laughter]

\<S 01>: I'd say you got on all right with that+

\<S 03>: Well we can relate to chocolate.

\<S 01>: +wadge of food there.

[laughter]

\<S 03>: I think they're the little ones actually.

[inaudible]

\<S 03>: So you can have one of them and one of them as well.

\<S 02>: Oh those Cherry Bakewells look lovely.

\<S 01>: They do don't they.

\<S 03>: Don't they. Oh they were [lowers voice] [inaudible]

\<S 01>: Gorgeous aren't they.

\<S 03>: Shall we save it for a cup of tea?

\<S 02>: [laughs] Yes.

\<S 01\>: All right then.

\<S 03\>: Sound like a right mother don't I.

\<S 02\>: [laughs]

\<S 01\>: You do.

\<S 02\>: Well they would go smashing with a cup of tea wouldn't they.

\<S 01\>: Oh they would.

\<S 02\>: Yeah.

\<S 03\>: Cup of tea and a fag.

\<S 01\>: [laughs]

\<S 02\>: Cup of tea and a fag missus. We're gonna have to move the table I think.

\<S 01\>: Yeah. Do you like this ta= this table she's constructed of erm boots and and a book?

\<S 02\>: [laughs]

\<S 03\>: Ah. That's brilliant.

\<S 01\>: Hey. That's really good there look.

[laughter]

\<S 02\>: And it's got the Milky Way wrapper.

[rustling noises]

\<S 01\>: That's right.

\<S 02\>: As that little extra support.

\<S 03\>: I like Sunday nights for some reason. [laughs]

\<S 03\>: I don't know why.

\<S 02\>: [laughs] Cos you come home.

\<S 03\>: I come home+

\<S 02\>: You come home to us.

\<S 03\>: +and pig out.

\<S 02\>: Yeah. Yeah.

\<S 03\>: Sunday is a really nice day I think.

\<S 02\>: It certainly is.

\<S 01\>: It's a really nice relaxing day.

\<S 02\>: It's me earring.

\<S 03\>: [inaudible]

\<S 02\>: 's me earring.

\<S 03\>: Oh. Lovely. Oh. Lovely.

\<S 02\>: It's fallen apart a bit. But

\<S 03\>: It looks quite nice like that actually. I like that. I bet, is that supposed to be straight?

\<S 02\>: Yeah.

\<S 03\>: I reckon it looks better like that.

\<S 02\>: And it was another bit as well, was another dangly bit.

\<S 03\>: What+

\<S 02\>: Separate.

\<S 03\>: attached to+

\<S 02\>: The top bit.

<S 03>:   +that one.
<S 02>:   Yeah. So it was even.
<S 01>:   Mobile earrings.
<S 03>:   Oh.
<S 02>:   [laughs]
<S 03>:   I like it like that. It looks better like that.
<S 02>:   Oh what did I see. What did I see. Stained glass. There w= I
         went to a craft fair.
<S 01>:   Mm.
<S 02>:   C= erm Bristol. And erm I know. [laughs] I went to a craft fair
         in Bristol and they had erm this stained glass stall and it was all
         mobiles made out of stained glass.
<S 01>:   Oh wow . . .
<S 02>:   And they were superb.

As we have seen, the analysis of conversational snippets allows an appropriate focus on particular creativity-prone features of language but it can also be an atomistic practice. The following commentary analyses specific features in local contexts but also examines more global creativity-enabling conditions, how these conditions are constituted and what we can learn from the existence of different densities of creative language use. Such conditions cannot normally be easily examined if only single conversational turns or shorter snippets of dialogue are investigated.

Commentary

This conversational extract is typical of casual talk. The topics drift from one to another, sometimes provoked by what the speakers are doing (e.g. eating and illustrating – by physically pointing out – weight problems), or by simple reference to objects in the immediate situation (the discussion about the earring). Sometimes, however, the topic is dictated by something which springs to mind by association (the remarks about the craft fair), or by the overall present situation itself (talking about the day Sunday itself). No one person is in control of the topics, and almost anything may be talked about.

The casual nature of the talk and the constant topic-switching create a sense of surface incoherence. However, closer inspection reveals that there is coherence but that it is largely interpersonal rather than topical. Indeed, how what is said is as significant, if not more so, than what is talked about. In other words, the symmetry of the relationships between the girls is reflected in the nature of the talk in which re-establishing and/or reinforcing the interpersonal relationship is as important, if not more important, to the participants than the conversational themes or topics they may pursue.

In the course of their seemingly random exchanges these three students draw on a number of patterns of language which are generally characteristic of spoken interaction. The patterns involve both *pattern forming* and *pattern re-forming* tendencies. For example, speakers invent particular words. Either these are neologisms or they are created by means of morphological extensions from existing items in the lexicon. *Wadge* (of food) is an invention (though based on the word 'wodge') and *dangly* is for some an instance of creative morphology (derived from 'dangling'). (The word 'wodge' is normally associated with material such as paper but is here particularly creative in its association with food.) More marked instances of pattern re-forming wordplay occur, most noticeably in the word *mobile*, which is metaphorically linked with dangling earrings and which puns on the meaning of mobile (with its semantics of movement) and the fixture of a 'mobile' – a brightly coloured dangling object which is normally placed over a child's bed or cot to provide distraction or entertainment, or which, as here possibly, is a piece of moving art.

Further verbal play is an example of a more directly interpersonal 'voicing' (see pp. 67 ff.) and involves a playful projection or 'throwing' of the voice. Within the first twenty lines one of the girls engages humorously in a play with the concerns of her friend by inventing names for her (*Miss paranoid about weight here*). And two of the girls then deliberately take on parodic voices by mimicking low-prestige accents. The chorus-like repetition by speaker <S 02> of speaker <S 03>'s parody and her addition of *missus* underlines the collaborative nature of the humour. The girls membership themselves temporarily as 'working-class cockney women', such a self-categorisation being among the key elements in the movement in and out of identities in talk emphasised by Antaki and Widdicombe (1998).

<S 02>:   Well they would go smashing with a cup of tea wouldn't they?
<S 01>:   Oh they would.
<S 02>:   Yeah.
<S 03>:   Cup of tea and a fag.
<S 01>:   [laughs]
<S 02>:   Cup of tea and a fag missus. We're gonna have to move the table I think.

Thus, some uses of language are creative by following standard rules (pattern forming); others, such as word-class conversion or playing with the voice, are more conventionally creative and involve individuals being more markedly inventive, either on their own or with the help of others (pattern re-forming).

Here pattern forming and re-forming coalesce. Identical patterns are formed across speaking turns but the parodic voices depart from the normal expected speaking voice to draw more overt attention to what is being said. In the process the revoicings generate a self-consciously ironic tone, reflecting on the speakers' own needs while at the same displaying a playful, metalingual awareness of the creative possibilities of the voice. Less overt pattern re-forming forms include similes expressly inviting comparison; in this case, a perceived likeness between stained glass mobiles seen at a craft fair and a colour wheel, features of language use embedded in a narrative recount which is discussed below in greater detail. There is also a case for seeing some of the formality switches (for example, *pig out*) as constituting ironic-comic reversals of the kind often linked with pattern re-forming creative effects.

Other features have a more pattern forming effect and create conditions in which speakers feel they occupy shared worlds and viewpoints, in which the risks attendant on creativity are reduced and in which intimacy and convergence are actively co-produced. Such features are predominantly interpersonal, relationship-creating and relationship-reinforcing. These essentially convergent, shared worlds and viewpoints are created in a number of ways: for example, by means of supportive backchannelling – *Oh lovely, oh, lovely*; *yeah, yeah*; by means of specifically interpersonal grammatical forms such as tails – *They were superb, they were*, and tags – *sound like a right mother don't I?* . . . *They do don't they?* and by means of affectionate vocatives (e.g. *Mand*). In a related way too, these convergences are created by intertextual references to familiar worlds and objects, in this case mainly to popular chocolate and cake varieties (*Milky Way wrapper/Mars Bar, Kit Kat, Cherry Bakewell*). The exchanges are also impregnated with vague language forms (Channell, 1994) (for example, *or anything*), affective exclamations such as *wow* and a range of evaluative and attitudinal expressions (often juxtaposed with much laughter) which further support the inclusive solidarity and membershipping established within the triangle.

The most marked form of convergence and mutuality is created by means of a wide range of repetitions, functioning above all as pattern forming elements. The extent of the underlining adopted here illustrates the density and pervasiveness of the pattern forming which is created at this point in the exchange. For example:

<S 02>: [laughs] Cos you <u>come home</u>.
<S 03>: I <u>come home</u>.
<S 02>: You <u>come home</u> to us.

<S 03>: Sunday is <u>a really nice day</u> I think.
<S 02>: It certainly is.
<S 03>: It's a <u>really nice</u> relaxing day.

<S 03>: Oh I think it <u>looks better like that</u>.
<S 02>: And there was <u>another</u> <u>bit</u> as well, <u>another</u> dangly <u>bit</u>.
<S 03>: What, attached to.
<S 02>: The top <u>bit</u>.
<S 03>: <u>That</u> one.
<S 02>: Yeah. So <u>it</u> was even.
<S 01>: Mobile earrings.
<S 03>: <u>I like it like that. It looks better like that</u>.

There is a clear sense here that the term the *art* of talk is not exaggerated. Indeed, it is almost a poetry of talk. There are repetitions and echoes which are verbatim almost in the manner of full rhymes (e.g. *come home/come home*;

that/that; better/better; what/what), there are half-rhymes in which the vowels are not identical but are assonantly related and in which there are consonantal repetitions (e.g. *it/bit/better* and *really/relaxing; what/that*); and there are rhythmic correspondences in which there is pattern forming involving syllables of identical or near identical length:

> *<S 03>:* What . . . attached to+
> *<S 02>:* The top bit
> *<S 03>:* +That one
> *<S 02>:* Yeah. So it was even
> *<S 01>:* Mobile earrings

One marked effect here is that the repetitions and other convergence-creating patterns do not simply support the symmetry dynamic of the group of students. More significantly, and as mentioned above, the speakers work with them to co-produce creativity-enabling conditions. In general, pattern re-forming structures and forms involve greater risks to the speaker. Here, however, pattern forming creates a basis for pattern re-forming. There are, as it were, peaks and troughs of creativity, with different patterns forming reliefs against which different effects are keyed by the speakers.

Thus, as the conversational exchanges develop, an impetus to further verbal creativity is produced. And as these conditions are continuously reproduced, creative forms are generated which in their overall function are denser than some of the other more local turn-by-turn effects. Thus the verbal inventions of *dangly*, *mobile* earrings are complemented by the narrative recount at the end of this sequence of the visit to the craft fair in Bristol in which creative analogies are drawn between the earrings, mobiles and stained glass mobiles, all of which are imaginatively connected, visually and kinetically.

Research involving the CANCODE corpus reveals a number of characteristic features of such spoken discourse: first, that ordinary, everyday language is far from being either everyday or ordinary (on the contrary, it is pervasively 'artful'); second, that verbal play with language is often undertaken for humorous purposes, serving in part to bring people closer together and membershipping them inclusively; third, that this kind of linguistic creativity and inventiveness is almost always contextually embedded in so far as it depends on the social relations which obtain between participants (relations between people in the above data are informal, and participants are on a mainly equal social and psychological footing); fourth, creativity involves not only more overt attention-drawing *pattern re-forming* forms but also more covert *pattern forming* forms, the latter especially across speaking turns; fifth, that it is a *frequent*, not exceptional feature of ordinary, everyday language use and that it is not an uncommon but a *common* practice to share pleasure, align viewpoints and create convergence in and through language and to do so often by means of creative play with language.[3]

The above observations emerge from a recognition of the social and cultural nature of creative language as discourse and situate speakers and listeners (as well as writers and readers) as essential constituents of the definition. The definitions and frameworks discussed so far do, however, raise a number of questions about the nature of such discourse, especially when they are examined, as here, dynamically, in stretches of text rather than, as is more usual, in isolated single words, in single sentences or in instances of single conversational turns.

Demotic creativity: conclusions and further theoretical questions

In relation to spoken-language uses in the CANCODE corpus examined to date the most frequent forms of linguistic creativity include:

- speaker displacement of fixedness, particularly of idioms and formulaic phrases;
- metaphor extension;
- morphological inventiveness;
- verbal play, punning and parody through overlapping forms and meanings;
- 'echoing' by repetition, including echoing by means of allusion and phonological echoes.

There are clearly two levels of 'creative' interactions: first, more overt, presentational uses of language, open displays of metaphoric invention, punning, uses of idioms and departures from expected idiomatic formulations (*pattern re-forming*); second, less overt, maybe even subconscious and subliminal parallelisms, echoes and related matchings which regularly result in expressions of affective convergence, in signals of intimacy and in implicit symmetries of feeling (*pattern forming*). The categories of *pattern forming* and *pattern re-forming* in speech are not purposeless non-pragmatic embellishments. They fulfil, as we have seen, fundamental communicative purposes.

Creative, non-literal, playful language is purposeful and not merely ornamental. One main purpose is, as we have seen, to play with such language in order to confer pleasure. Another purpose is in order to display identity (see Boxer and Cortes-Conde, 1997). Speakers may signal that they like to be thought of as individuals who are 'fun to be with' or who can offer a new perspective on things. They may want to signal a sense of belonging, to indicate their membership of a group or to establish that they are on the same affective plane as others. It is a use of language not far removed from gentle hugging, touching and other forms of physical bonding. Purposes and functions vary and can change in the course of a conversational encounter.

There is always an element of risk-taking in creative verbal procedures. The risks mainly involve potential failures of uptake, the embarrassment of unsuccessful performance or ineffective 'presentationality'. Puns and extended or newly minted metaphors, in particular, involve acts of language use which are relatively self-conscious. Punning may not work and attempts at morphological inventiveness may fail. But, when performed successfully, there are corresponding rewards because speakers establish greater intersubjective accord, intimacy and involvement through a discourse with a clear affective overlay.[4] The effects can also be 'schema-refreshing'.

Creativity should not be decontextualised. In CANCODE data, speakers appear to use verbal play where social relations between participants are broadly symmetrical. Thus features of the kind listed above are less apparent in the data in relatively more formal and asymmetrical settings such as interviews, legal cross-examinations, business meetings, conversations between strangers or being stopped by the police for speeding on the motorway. In this connection the topic of conversation may also be significant, as deliberating on string quartets or the bombing of a hostile nation, exchanges in a funeral parlour or discussions of our voting preferences, may not normally allow of language play.

Informal settings are the contexts of use which are most frequently encountered by most speakers. In such settings the main purposes of verbal play can be interpreted to be involving, affective and 'convergence-creating'. Speakers and listeners jointly co-construct playful discourse with the aim of aligning, harmonising and sharing ways of seeing, so re-forming and reinforcing the informality of the relationship.

However, even though such functions have not been manifested in the data examined so far, it is important not to neglect the possibility that the close relationship between creativity and affect can also result in verbal play which is the basis for disagreement and opposition and which is highlighted in the work of Bakhtin and others (see p. 45 above). Creative dialogue can also be constructed not simply to create interpersonal convergence but also in order to oppose an existing convention or to critique an established institutional order.

Quite properly, questions continue to be asked. For example, do listeners creatively co-construct discourse solely in order to achieve greater mutuality? Is the interaction more or less successful if precise interpretation is not achieved? How far can we account for the *pattern forming* and *pattern re-forming* tendencies of the (largely) socially symmetrical spoken CANCODE discourse in terms of providing pleasure? Can we say that the pleasure results mainly from the registering of new morphologies, extended idiomatic constructions and convergent parallelisms or are there other processes at work?

Not all these questions can be answered here, but to answer one question raised at the beginning of this chapter, it can fairly be said that it is not out of place to speak of the 'art' of common everyday speech. Although the study here does not include analysis of rhythms and sound patterns, it may not be out of place either to refer to such patterns as having properties of literariness. Patterns of creative language, especially the use of wordplay and the use of repetitions, are part of this common art.

Language, creativity and models of language

At the beginning of this chapter it was asked if there are differences between creativity in written and spoken texts? Another question was to ask about frameworks for description and analysis.

Table 3.1 Creativity and dimensions of discourse.

Written	Spoken
sentence	stretches of discourse
invented data	naturally occurring data
ideal individual speaker	real speaker
rule-governed creativity	co-creative talk
referential	representational and expressive
ideational	interpersonal
transactional	interactional and affective
literal	non-literal
truth-conditional meaning	contextual meanings
serious	playful
monologue	dialogue

Spoken creativity is contrasted with creativity in writing on a number of axes. First, spoken creativity is unplanned and unrehearsed. Although there are public performed occasions such as wedding or retirement speeches and sometimes even formal lectures and parliamentary debates where humour, wordplay and creative interventions can be inserted, such contexts are closer to contexts of writing than to speech. Although speakers do rehearse jokes and anecdotes and do improve by prior telling, in the case of writing there is a more in-built polishing process of revision and recasting. Second, spoken creativity grows from interpersonal interaction in which a shared context allows the marking of attitude in a more overt manner than in written contexts. In spoken contexts indications of intimacy, evaluation and intensity are much more closely bound up with creative expression, though the generally more expressive and emotive character of spoken creativity does not of course preclude the expression of ideas. Third, as we have seen in chapter 2, it cannot be claimed that reading is not an interactive process between reader and writer; but it is a more one-way process. Spoken creativity is co-produced, growing organically from those contexts which best support such dialogue and in which meanings are made interpersonally as well as conveyed transactionally.

In terms of descriptive frameworks it may be useful at this stage and by way of summary to diagrammatise the particular focus on language which is now beginning to be adopted. Table 3.1 attempts such a representation. It has to be stressed, however, that within the discipline of linguistics world-wide many of the models of description and many of the theories of language have followed the orientations listed in the left-hand column. The kind of investigation undertaken in this book presumes a number of points of theoretical and analytical orientation and, although both ends of the clines and lines intersect in all kinds of ways, the principal points of exploration and focus are towards the right-hand column. It is a focus which is markedly in keeping with the nature of the data.

As we have seen so far, the nature of the CANCODE corpus means:

- that creativity can and should be explored in stretches of naturally occurring text, involving authentic data and real speakers;
- that the language investigated involves interpersonal exchanges in social and cultural contexts with speakers affectively involved in the co-creation of meanings;
- that figures of speech such as metaphor and idiom can be shown to be common to spoken discourse, such language being commonly used to represent and express things as well as to refer;
- that the transfer of information is important but the creation of relationships is as significant;
- that play with language form and function leads to a range of social and cultural purposes, including pleasure and entertainment and the creation of fictional speech acts;
- that, compared with written text, creative spoken language use may be more closely connected with expressions of feeling and identity.

Once again I underline here that creativity is not simply individual or best measured as an individual product. Examining CANCODE spoken data reveals creativity at work as a process, with several individuals in dialogue, working at full-stretch, in real time, improvising, duetting, creating individual riffs, harmonies and local indirections, making things up for the nonce, for the occasion, *en passant*, and always remaining attentive to the social and cultural context they are in themselves as well as to others within it.

Conclusion

This chapter has set a number of questions running, some of the more elusive of which may not, of course, be captured in subsequent chapters. However, questions about the nature of corpus data and their sociocultural and psychosocial provenance need to be explored further. This is undertaken in chapter 5 where the questions raised in this chapter about the nature of verbal play, from the literary to the demotic, are also examined further in relation to other examples of CANCODE data and explored in a much wider generic and sociocultural range of contexts. The question raised about the possibility that creativity, in both pattern forming and pattern re-forming manifestations, has a probabilistic relation with certain types of social context and certain types of social interaction is explored further. Subsequent chapters refine the definitions and theoretical underpinning of both creativity and common talk by examining data which go beyond that of the single CANCODE corpus of spoken English.

The next chapter, chapter 4, considers further data from the CANCODE corpus, in respect of a wider range of figures of speech in action, and raises further questions of both theory and analytical practice. The basic aim of the next chapter is to explore the corpus further and to amass more data and examples as additional evidence for the provenance of the art of common talk.

Notes

1   The spoken section of the British National Corpus amounts to 10 million words, and nearly 20 million words of spoken data are available through the Bank of English. All CANCODE data collected are the property of Cambridge University Press © which has funded the project. For further discussion of the design of this corpus see chapter 5, as well as Carter and McCarthy (1997a) and, especially, McCarthy (1998a: ch. 2). The CANCODE bibliography in Appendix 3 also contains a number of discussions in which a range of ideological and other issues connected with corpus design are aired. The Note on Transcription (Appendix 1) also raises key issues. Appendix 2 takes a number of points raised in this chapter and explores them further with particular reference to the creative extension of the morphemes *–y* and *–ish*.

2   More extended examples are given in Carter and McCarthy (1995b) and Carter (1997: ch. 8) with particular reference to a pervasive creativity with the *–y* suffix and with further analogies suggested with parallel patterns in modern poetry.

3   Chris Candlin (personal communication) asks here if membershipping means that individuals cannot be creative to themselves and in their own eyes, as their creativity only exists in the context of the cultural group.

4   Both Bhaya *et al.* (1988) and Carter (1997: ch. 7) explore the extent to which the existence of creative and inventive language involves risks for the creator.

Exploring further

For discussions of corpus linguistics see Biber *et al.* (1998), Kennedy (1991), Stubbs (1996), Barnbrook (1996), Sinclair (1991). See also McCarthy (2001a), Aston and Burnard (1998) on the significance of corpus design and on the construction principles of the British National Corpus. Knowles *et al.* (1996) provide a prosodically transcribed account of a highly formal spoken corpus.

Culler's study of *Puns* (1988) adopts a more literary stance on the question. By contrast, Anderson and Trudgill (1992) explore the role of demotic speech, including slang, swearing, etc., in part as a creative sociolinguistic phenomenon. Susan Phillips's paper (1975) on puns and 'putting people on' is still regarded as a classic sociolinguistic account. Bolinger (1950), Mertz (1989) and Becker (1994) offer further illuminating accounts of processes of lexical innovation and invention. Bublitz (1988) contains numerous insights on the uses of repetition in naturally occurring discourse.

On formulae and routines in conversation see Coulmas (1981), Cheepen (1988), Cowie (1988), Dörnyei and Thurrell (1992), Burke (1993) and Aijmer (1996). For a critique of the restrictively formulaic and routinised talk in call centres and service industries in general see *Good to Talk?* (Cameron 2000: ch. 3).

For studies of conversation in traditions related to those explored in this chapter see Cheepen and Monaghan (1990), Stenstrom (1994), Tsui (1994), Blum-Kulka (1997, 2000) and Eggins and Slade (1997). Coates (1989, 2000) offers illuminating discussions of all-female talk. Goodwin's (1988) work combines gender study and play activities. Tannen (1991) gives a well-known popular account of male–female talk.

On questions of identity in relation to language use, works by Norton (2001) and Le Page and Tabouret-Keller (1985) are significant, the former with particular reference to contexts of teaching and learning. Schiffrin (1996) makes a valuable study of identity and 'self-portrait' in relation to story-telling practices.

For fascinating studies of musical (jazz) improvisation and 'jamming' with clear analogues to patterning, duetting and ensemble creation in talk, see Berliner (1994), Monson (1996) and Sawyer (1999 and 2001).

4   Figures of speech

How every fool can play upon the word.
(William Shakespeare, *The Merchant of Venice*, III, v)

Introduction

The previous three chapters have laid the ground for an exploration of spoken creativity by examining theoretical issues, procedures for data collection and classification, and the kinds of frameworks considered appropriate for the analysis of spoken discourse. This chapter takes the discussion further by adopting a sharper linguistic focus. The main aim is to consider some further resources for spoken creativity which speakers and listeners have at their disposal, with an emphasis on figures of 'speech', a topic, as we have noted, which is often analysed only with reference to written examples. The previous chapter considered figures of speech such as puns and wordplay, repetition and neologisms. This chapter considers further resources open to speakers, including figures such as metaphors, idioms and hyperbole. There is a particular emphasis on the need to describe creative uses of language with reference to clines and continua of meaning and function, especially with reference to the expression of feelings and identities. Throughout there is an emphasis not simply on particular linguistic forms but also on the speakers and listeners who use and negotiate the use of such creative language.

Core and non-core vocabulary: a baseline for creative lexis

The term 'core vocabulary' is used to describe those elements in the lexical network of a language which are unmarked. That is, core vocabulary usually constitutes the most normal, basic and simple words available to a language user. There are many ways in which such words might be isolated. Psycholinguists would probably argue that core words are those which are most perceptually salient; that is, they mark dominant areas of prototypical sensory perception such as size (*large/small*), weight (*heavy/light*), colour (*red/green*) (but not *mauve* or *fawn*) (see Rosch *et al.*, 1976; Dirven, 1985, 1993). Sociolinguistically, they might be isolated as the items most likely to be used in talking to foreigners or to small children. The following criteria for core vocabulary (developed more extensively in Carter, 1987a and 1998: ch. 2; Stubbs, 1986, 1998) are linguistic tests, designed to isolate the main structural and functional features of core vocabulary.

- Core words often have clear antonyms. Thus, the antonym of *hot* is *cold*, the antonym of *laugh* is *cry*, the antonym of *fat* is *thin*. It is more difficult to locate antonyms for non-core words such as *corpulent* or *skinny* or *emaciated*.
- Core vocabulary is generally characterised by weak collocational patterns. A core word such as *fat* has a wide collocational span which includes *fat man*, *fat* salary, *fat* cheque. Words from the same lexical set such as 'corpulent' or 'chubby' have a more restricted range and are, by contrast, strong collocations; for example, one does not say 'corpulent cheque', 'chubby salary'.
- In any lexical set there will be an unmarked word which can be pressed into service to define the meanings of the related words. For example, in the set *snigger, grin, smirk, beam, smile*, all the words except *smile* can be defined by *smile* (the core item) plus an adverb. For example, *beam* = smile happily; *smirk* = smile knowingly. And so on. *Smile* itself, on the other hand, has to be defined by reference to basic semantic components and cannot be defined using any of the other words in the set.
- Core vocabulary items are those which do not carry especially marked connotations or associations. Thus in the set of words surrounding a core item such as *thin*, lexical items such as *skinny* or *slim* carry marked negative and positive associations respectively. Similarly, items such as *emaciated* or *scraggy* carry marked associations of, respectively, formal and informal contexts of use. By contrast, thin is a relatively unmarked or core word.
- Core words do not normally allow us to identify from which field of discourse they have been taken. Thus, the words *galley, port, starboard, fore* and *aft* and *knots per hour* immediately recall nautical or aeronautical fields. Corresponding items such as *kitchen, left* and *right, miles per hour*, etc., are unmarked, more neutral in subject matter and thus more core.
- Core words are often superordinates. Thus, in the set of words *rose, tulip, peony, dahlia, carnation*, the superordinate item *flower* can regularly do service and stand in for the other items in a number of contexts. Core words are also positioned in the middle of a lexical hierarchy. For example, *dog* would be so positioned in a 'radial' set which stretches from *toy-poodle* to *poodle* to *dog* to *animal* to *mammal* (see Lakoff (1987) on radial structures and categories).

These tests are not intended to be in any way either final or absolute. It is clear that it is preferable to refer to degrees or clines of coreness in lexical items, since there can be no clear yes/no divisions among words into core and non-core categories. But recognition of coreness in vocabulary can, at least, enable us to begin to identify degrees of expressivity in vocabulary, and to begin to isolate the kinds of non-neutral expressive vocabulary which, it is argued here, are commonly marked for creative language use.

The notion of core vocabulary is basic to the argument in this chapter as there are clines from core to non-core vocabulary. While categories of definition such as the tests proposed are useful for purposes of overall definition, it is clear that respective degrees of coreness vary according to the particular socio-cultural contexts and registers, according to individual speakers' preferences and according to the uses to which the vocabulary is put. It is clear that coreness in vocabulary use is especially sensitive to interpersonal exchanges.

It is also clear that the clines which run from core to non-core vocabulary represent a continuum of expressive possibilities for making utterances more intimate, as well as for intensifying and evaluating utterances. At such points in the discourse, speakers are doing more than convey information or transmit ideas; they are allowing their own attitudes to emerge, they are interacting with others, they are signalling affective and expressive responses and accordingly they are making vocabulary choices which often creatively encode their own feelings. It is important therefore to construct clear, retrievable hypotheses which enable such explorations to be undertaken.

Clines of intimacy, intensity and evaluation

When speakers interact, they do more than transmit information. (Almost all Internet communication, for example, is highly interactive.) Speakers also often wish to give a more affective contour to what they or others are saying. It is hypothesised here that there are three essential expressive options open to them: the expression of intimacy, the expression of intensity and the expression of evaluation. Such expression is clinal and involves continua from one pole to another:

- *Intimacy cline* involves an expression of formality; an indication of the degree of social distance between interlocutors. Thus, when a group of care assistants, discussing in a weekly meeting recent work that one of them has done in a residential home, uses the word *pop off* when referring to the death of one of the occupants, one outcome is to create a more intimate and interpersonal contour to the talk, reinforcing the familiarity of the group.
- *Intensity cline* involves an expression of the strength or weakness of feeling and attitude invested in the utterance. Thus, when a speaker says, in the context of discussing a recent victory of the team supported by his conversational partner: *You didn't just win. You* annihilated *us*, he is expressing intensity and strengthening the statement by choosing the word 'annihilate' in preference, say, to more 'core' items such as *beat* or *defeat*. Intensity in vocabulary can also mark such things as relative degrees of urgency.
- *Evaluation cline* involves an expression of a positive or negative stance towards what is said. Thus, when a speaker describing a flat she has been living in moves in a sequence from a more core word 'small' to a more non-core word *poky*, she is expressing a negative evaluative stance to the accommodation: *I wouldn't say it was* small, *it's* poky *actually. But what choice have I got at the moment?*

The extent to which such clines operate and the extent to which they overlap in the course of a few utterances is illustrated in the following sequence in which two close friends are discussing the behaviour of <S 01>'s sister. Both speakers are forty years old, female, and are talking on the phone.

Example 4.1

> <*S 01*>:　She is Naomi. But I think that both of them are strong.
> <*S 02*>:　Mm.
> <*S 01*>:　They're very much alike the two of them.
> <*S 02*>:　Yes.
> <*S 01*>:　You know. So. Oh I don't know. I mean she's she's whittling on to me about Christmas. That er she's been invited over to Mel's moved into big place down this [inaudible] priory and it's it's sort of, I think she's t= trying to think she's got airs and graces and she hasn't type of thing you know.

Here one particular lexical choice *whittling on* can be seen to operate on several clines simultaneously. The phrasal verb 'whittle on' (which may be derived from the more standard 'witter on') could be replaced by the more core or neutral choice 'talk'. However, *whittling on* is more informal (it is a lexical item more closely associated with spoken than with written contexts); it intensifies the core lexical choice (it is a stronger, more intense item than 'talk') and it adds a more evaluative contour (it carries negative connotations, suggesting that the talk is unnecessary and continues at length).

It should also be noted that a core word *strong* is also used here expressively for evaluative purposes (the speakers are complaining that Kath and her mother are both strong personalities and probably mean the word to have negative associations). Core words, though usually used for neutral purposes, can be negotiated into less neutral more affective meanings. It should also be noted that the attitudinal and affective contours to the exchange here involve more than lexical items. The first speaker uses hedges and discourse markers to converge with her interlocutor and to prevent her statements sounding too authoritative and assertive: for example, *I think . . . she's got airs and graces and she hasn't type of thing you know*, where *type of thing*, in particular, functions deliberately to convey vagueness. Similarly, her uses of *sort of*, *I mean*, *I don't know* serve to soften her statement in terms of intimacy clines while still ensuring that the evaluative comments are conveyed.

Of course, it would be a mistake to suggest that only core and non-core vocabulary clines are involved in expressivity, as the following extract from an earlier segment of the exchange between these two friends illustrates. The topic of discussion is still the sister Kath and her behaviour *vis-à-vis* the rest of the family.

Example 4.2

> <S 02>: So it couldn't be jealousy.
> <S 01>: No. She had a real go at Laura. And then you know like at Laura's had, she's got two little ones and you know at the christening she+
> <S 02>: Yeah.
> <S 01>: +caused such a that her and Laura had a real barney and+
> <S 02>: Oh no.
> <S 01>: +Laura ended up in floods of tears and walking the streets of+
> <S 02>: Oh no.
> <S 01>: + [inaudible]. Oh. It's terrible.
> <S 02>: So she ruins every event.
> <S 01>: She ruins. She has to be star attraction.
> <S 02>: [tuts]
> <S 01>: She cannot play second fiddle.
> <S 02>: What about her wedding? What was she like at that then?

Here non-core vocabulary choices (*barney* in preference to the more neutral *row* or *argument*) express greater intensity and intimacy. Additionally, though, other items such as metaphors, idiomatic expressions and hyperbole also play a part in providing an overlay of evaluation, intensity and intimacy to the discourse. *Floods of tears* hyperbolically intensifies 'crying' while the idiom *to be the star attraction* negatively evaluate Kath's behaviour; likewise, the idiom *to play second fiddle* intensifies attitudes while at the same time negatively appraising her and imparting, in particular, a more highly charged emotional quality. The evaluative character of the discourse is in part possible because the person referred to is not present but the lexical choices serve to create even greater solidarity between the speakers.

Thus the notion of core vocabulary is important in providing a framework for a creative expressivity in vocabulary. But it is not a static category; there are overlaps and intersections between different clines, and the expression of attitude and affect goes beyond individual words into multiword units as well as the more conventionally creative realm of metaphor and other figures of speech. We have seen from work in cognitive poetics how central metaphor is to the unpacking of supposed divisions between literal and non-literal language (see chapter 2, pp. 69 ff.). And it is to these topics that we now return.

Metaphor, metonymy and literal language

> Metaphor is a device for seeing something in terms of something else.
> (Burke, 1945: 503)

Metaphor is one of the most extensively discussed figures of speech and is often bracketed with metonymy for purposes of classification and for comparison of functions and effects. Metaphors work by drawing analogies, usually between domains of meaning which are not normally linked. (In classical Greek the word *metaphora* means to 'transfer' or to 'carry over' and meaning is carried over when one layer of meaning is compared with another.) For example, to say *This book is a gem* is to say that the properties associated with the meaning of *book* can be extended so that, by analogy, the book is seen as having a value or uniqueness or age (or perhaps all these properties simultaneously) of an expensive jewel and is therefore something to treasure. Metaphors treat something as something else, making semantic links between things mainly by means of similarity between a literal meaning (book) and a non-literal meaning (jewel), since a book cannot literally be a jewel. Conventionally, the process of analogy-drawing is from *vehicle* or literal meaning (the book) to *tenor* (non-literal meaning) by means of the *grounds*, the linking relation between the literal and the non-literal. The link between vehicle and tenor is not always transparent, however, and some metaphors display greater incongruity than others between vehicle and tenor. For example, to say 'This book is a sardine' would require a reader or listener to work harder to infer meanings.

Metonymy, on the other hand, links things by means of contiguity rather than by means of similarity. Thus to say *The Crown has lost popularity in recent years* is to say that the royal family has lost popularity. The crown is something worn ceremonially by the king or queen and the word *Crown* is therefore made to stand, by a process of contiguous association, for royalty. Metonymy does not seek to draw analogies; instead, it works by an altogether more overt process of similarity, linking things in a spatial or temporal sequence within a given semantic domain.

The discussion of metaphor, especially in literary criticism, normally revolves around its uniqueness and imaginative range. Within linguistics, and cognitive linguistics in particular, the main stress within recent studies has been on metaphor, not as an exception or distortion but rather on metaphor as a fundamental and ubiquitous structure of language. In particular, and as we have seen in chapter 2, work by Gibbs (1994), Lakoff (1987) and others[1] underlines how metaphor represents a fundamental cast of mind in so far as particular core words within the lexicon structure perception of the world and ways of thinking about the world. Once again, some uses of such metaphors require greater processing effort than others. In poetry, for example, the metaphor may be more densely packed and/or elaborated. In academic discourse, theories themselves are regularly explained in metaphorical terms; but the root analogy that *theories are buildings* is commonly used and therefore generally more easily decoded.

For example, certain analogies are root analogies; that is, they organise in a very basic way how things are seen. Among these prototypical categories are such core analogies as *Life is a journey* which generates a range of related metaphors such as: *They've lost their way*; *We're always going round in circles and never seem to get anywhere*; *She really knows where she's going*; *They've reached a bit of a dead end with their son*; *We're at a crossroads*.

In the following example from the CANCODE corpus a root analogy is drawn on. Two students are talking about career choices and organise their discussion in terms of an extended association of career paths with 'getting through' life. 'Getting through/to', 'going on/into' and 'being/making it through' involves a journey to be undertaken with obstacles or 'hurdles' to be overcome. The prepositions 'in' and 'into' work in particular to metaphorise change of status and profession while at the same time making the process sound as straightforward as walking into a room, a process which leads to a question of whether certain metaphors are conducive to certain ideas and topics and vice versa.

The speakers themselves also have metalingual awareness. They recognise the metaphorical nature of their exchange and at one point comment explicitly on the metaphor. Notice, furthermore, how the two speakers here run with the metaphors, bouncing them back and forth, co-creatively recycling, extending, fine tuning and retuning each other's metaphors as yet another instance of creativity as a dialogic process.

Example 4.3

[<S 01> is 24, male, and a PhD student in American Studies, <S 02> is 22, male, and an MA student in American Studies. They have known each other for about a year and are good friends. The speakers are sitting on the grass in <S 01>'s garden.]

<S 02>: Yeah. I wonder now about people who go into the army these days like m= I had a friend erm who went who was a good friend of mine when I was at school you know+

<S 01>: Mm.

<S 02>: +up till sixteen. After that we lost touch a bit but he only lives round the corner from me now. But he went erm on a army course recently and he did really well and he got to the last thing at Sandhurst where you would go+

<S 01>: Yeah. [laughs]

<S 02>: +in as an officer+

<S 01>: Yeah.

<S 02>: +and he did the thing there and he fa= he fell at the last hurdle. And

<S 01>: What he he, you're talking metaphorically here?

<S 02>: and and er fitness trainings and did really well and now he's gotta go in as a, as a yu= you know as a regular.

<S 01>: [tuts] Oh no.

<S 02>: He was so close. But but you know

<S 01>: What was the last hurdle?

<S 02>: I dunno. It's just that it was at Sandhurst and it was that last sort of test of the people who'd made it through that far and he didn't get through that part you know entailing various things and that.

<S 01>: Oh how annoying.

<S 02>: Yeah. So he'd been through all this and he'd been waiting for six

months. But you know going into the army now it seems like such a career.

Some researchers (for example, Birdsong, 1995) have explained such metaphoricity in terms of both universal modes of perception and prototypical human actions. In other words, we naturally look up before we look down, upwards movement always involves rewarding human effort, is nearly always challenging and so on. Language thus represents the reality of the speaker and the speaker's position, and there is thus a fundamental iconicity between language form and metaphorical mapping. For Birdsong this iconicity is carried not only in the equation between individual prepositions and semantics or between phrasal structures and basic human action sequences (*they got up and out of it*) but also extends into the most easily processable phonetic structures involved in some of the most frequent fixed phrasings, such as *bed and breakfast*, *short and sweet*, *safe and sound*, and into expressions such as '*hot and cold* running water' where the perceptual sequence of the taps in English language-based cultures is standardly left to right. Metaphorical thinking may thus be directly derivable from basic bodily experiences (see Deignan, 1995; Stockwell, 2001: ch. 8 for a range of examples and discussion).

Of course, some metaphors are more obviously metaphors than others and one factor central to the discussion of metaphor, especially in everyday spoken discourse, is the fact that many metaphors are not consciously recognised as such. Some metaphors and idioms which have a metaphorical basis are described, employing further metaphors in the process, as *dead* or *fossilised* metaphors. Even the expression *This book is a gem* may function in most contexts as a conventional expression for the ascription of praise or value rather than be marked out and valued as overtly metaphorical. Such metaphors are sometimes devalued in that they are perceived to be so automatic and entrenched that they lack originality, a parabola of discussion which takes us back to historically situated estimations of creativity, where in modern 'Western' industrialised cultures it is largely what is new and original and striking that is most valued (see above chapter 1, pp. 26–9). Discussion so far should, however, caution against oversimplistic reference to what is 'ordinary' or 'core' or 'non-literary' or a 'dead' metaphor.

Metaphors and processing

What should be recognised in such discussions is, however, the fact that some metaphors require greater processing effort than others, particularly if concept combining is involved. For example, in the following three deliberately decontextualised metaphors: *elephant bottom*; *butter mountain*; *genetic roulette*, different degrees of inferential and interpretative work are needed for understanding, even though different degrees of effort may be required in different contexts. Thus, the link between elephant and size and the common cultural practice of describing anatomy (often hyperbolically) in terms of size is sufficient to generate a relatively smooth decoding process. In the case of *butter mountain* the processing effort required is greater in order to link large stores of unused butter with the kind of stock piles which might resemble a mountain. The association with the tenor is, of course, in both these cases non-literal and requires some degree of imagination on the part of the reader or hearer. In the third example of *genetic roulette*, fuller contextual background (in this case a newspaper article on the dangers of genetically modified foods) may be needed in order to allow associative links to be generated. In this last example, however, a fuller degree of operationalising of what Turner and Fauconnier (1999) have termed 'conceptual blending' is demanded. Here the projection from *genetics* to *roulette* is more complex and less entrenched than the projection from *elephant* to *bottom*, involving connections between producing crops for human consumption and a casino game of chance in which the player has to submit to random processes. (This is especially so in the case of Russian roulette, a non-game-based challenge, in which the protagonist has a gun loaded with just one bullet and a normally only one-in-six chance of dying when the gun is fired.)

These metaphors do not, of course, appear in discourse contexts and a decontextualised sentence-based exemplar form should not be seen as wholly typical.[2] But it can be said, for example, that the use of a sports or game metaphor such as *You've been a backstop for far too long* is likely to be more easily processed in a context in which both participants share common frames of reference or in which both speakers are at a sports game or the role of the backstop has been previously identified and explained. See, in particular, chapter 5, pp. 159–61 below for further discussion.

And metonymy and synecdoche

Waitress 1: The ham-sandwich at table 11 wants the bill.
Waitress 2: OK. I'll get it.

Waiter: Are you the fish?
Customer: No, my husband's the fish.

Metaphor is a very basic figure of speech in so far as it is sometimes difficult to distinguish between metaphor and other tropes, and other common formations such as idioms and proverbs. Metonymy is, as we have seen, formed by a process of contiguity rather than by one of similarity or analogy-making. Metaphor involves a blending of two conceptual domains; metonymy involves only one conceptual domain. Thus the utterance cited at the heading of this section and spoken by a waitress to a colleague:

Waitress 1: The ham-sandwich at table 11 wants the bill.
Waitress 2: OK. I'll get it.

involves a metonymic process in which ham-sandwich is taken to refer to the person at table 11 who has been eating a ham-sandwich.

The trope of synecdoche is related to metonymy and is used similarly, referring to ships as *sails* or to manual workers as *hands* and standing contiguously for the whole as part of a similarity process in which no indirect interpretation is normally required. The close interrelation of these tropes also explains the presence of blends between the categories. For example, the phrase *He's always shooting his mouth off* involves both metaphoric and metonymic processes. And well-established sayings such as *Religion is the opiate of the masses* or *The Child is the father of Man* can involve underlying metaphorical analogy-drawing formulations which simultaneously stimulate a number of inferential maps and projections (see Turner and Fauconnier, 1999).

In this connection it should not be forgotten either that most discussion of metaphor is undertaken with reference to decontextualised examples, usually in written sentence form, and that metaphor also needs to be examined in relation to naturally occurring written and spoken uses, especially across speaking turns. The reinsertion into naturally occurring discourse of one of the metaphors from the above discussion (the reference to *elephant bottom*) underlines how metaphors operate within a frame which includes real participants in real contexts. Here our processing of the metaphoric usage is determined in part by its use for playful insult and ironic self-disparagement, its creative stimulus to laughter, its hyperbolic function and its extension into further hyperbole (*my bottom is so enormous*). The metaphoric constellation of 'elephant' with 'bottom' also illustrates a creative layering of *intensity* (hyperbolic extension with reference to size), *intimacy* (the reference generates laughter and clear convergence between the speakers) and *evaluation* (the reference to size and the accompanying self-criticism places a value on the speaker's estimate). The clines intersect in productive ways to show the complex communicative dynamic functioning of metaphor in context.

Example 4.4

[A group of four middle aged friends are planning a holiday. <S 02> (male) and <S 03> (female) are husband and wife.]

<S 04>: Where's the *Rough Guide* then?
<S 03>: It's in that bag.
<S 02>: Erm.
<S 01>: You're s= You're sitting on it.
<S 02>: I'm not am I?
[briefly inaudible]
<S 03>: [inaudible] elephant bottom.
[laughter]
<S 01>: I told you.
<S 02>: I couldn't feel it cos my bottom is so enormous.
[laughter]

And simile

Simile is also very closely related to metaphor; in fact, one definition of metaphor is that it is an elliptical simile and that for specific communicative reasons simile involves the explicit signalling of comparison between one thing and another. The explicit markers of comparison take several forms ranging from copular and verbal similes involving *like* and *as*, specific phrases such as *the equivalent of, tantamount to, close to, nothing less than* and clausal similes such as *as if* and *as though*.

> *I think of illustrating books rather like being in a play.*
> *It was as though they were passing before us in a dream.*
> (Sandra Cornbleet's data)

There is evidence that simile is more frequent than metaphor in everyday speech, most markedly in contexts in which speakers are recording reactions to events which usually impact on the speaker personally and have a powerful affective dimension. In the following example, an eye witness gives an account of the sight of the roof of a train buffet car which had been ripped off in an accident:

> *the top peeled back as if it was a sardine can*
> (Sandra Cornbleet's data)

In the next example two women, who are being interviewed by a news reporter, give their account of the effect of a car crash on the house where they live:

> <S 01>: It just went into a massive bang and at that point all the windows came in glass everywhere and we were . . . like
> <S 02>: all the stones being hit against the window like gunshot the only way I can seem to describe it is like someone was shooting at the house.
> <S 01>: like gunshot.
> <S 02>: because all the stones kept banging and you could hear all the glass all slowly breaking.
> (Sandra Cornbleet's data)

The examples illustrate (i) that simile cannot be explored wholly in isolation and is best seen in relation to the specific discourse contexts in which it is patterned and (ii) that simile co-occurs with other figures of speech (here most markedly hyperbolic expressions) and specific forms of language play. Simile is more designed for the recipient than metaphor, which often requires more interpretation. In contexts such as the above it would be unusual if the contours of the experience were mediated without reference to analogy or some kind of creative representation of the experience. Using metaphor may make things less immediate and make the listener work harder.

Figures of speech, metalingual awareness and discourse context

> The human and discourse context of language use is inherent in the joint construction of discourse goals and in the use of metaphor to achieve those goals. Processing metaphorical language takes place in context and draws on the discourse expectations of participants. It follows that the theoretical frameworks used to operationalise metaphor must do so too.
>
> (Cameron, 1999: 25)

As has been acknowledged already, different figures of speech in use require different degrees of conscious processing effort by speakers and listeners. In spoken discourse, in particular, some metaphors can, for example, be disambiguated by reference to the immediate context. But sometimes the producer of a metaphor is conscious of the interpersonal functions of a choice of metaphor, and generally speakers may become quite conscious of the varying degrees of approximation to the literal truth which the metaphors convey and may even comment quite explicitly. Speakers are also in varying degrees conscious of when they draw comparisons to underline meanings. They are often aware of the degrees of exaggeration implicit in utterances and adopt a number of different communicative strategies which signal that awareness. Such strategies regularly take the form of intensifiers, downtoners/hedges and approximations or vague language. For a fuller account see Goatly (1997: ch. 10).

The following example illustrates a speaker who is conscious of new words being invented and who embeds the new words within a discourse co-text which does not draw too much attention to the new words and in which vague language and approximations signal the speaker's own consciousness of how the discourse might be received and interpreted by the listener.

> *My parents were very kind of* booky *and literary I know it sounds quite sort of I don't know really.*

Such discoursal triggers also apply in the case of comparisons, including metaphorical use. For example, particular intensifying structures are employed to strengthen the truth claims of statements. The word *literally* serves both to intensify statements, especially hyperbolic statements (see below, p. 136) and to show recognition of the incongruity inherent in some comparisons. It is sometimes collocated in the phrase *both literally and metaphorically* in the use of which speakers show a degree of metalingual awareness. Other words which similarly work on an *intensity cline* include *actually*, *in fact*, *indeed*, *really*, and *simply*.

> *The journey here was a nightmare actually.*
> *She's simply a bit of a mouse, in fact and I can't see them ever promoting her, can you?*

Women have to look up to men, literally as well as metaphorically in fact, if you see what I mean.

Sometimes speakers signal, metalingually, their awareness that the metaphoric force of the statement is deliberately approximate and should not be seen as a typical analogy or comparison. Such discoursal uses are interpersonally sensitive and tend to operate along an *intimacy cline*. In particular, vague language and hedges are employed as signals to the listener; they include lexical items and phrases such as *a bit, a touch, somewhat, in a way, nearly, almost, I'm afraid, in a sense, more or less, quite, not exactly* and so on.

I'm afraid that Jack is a bit of a dickhead.
She's more or less burrowed herself away in her room and won't let anyone near her.
Noirin's been something of a crutch to him during his mother's illness.
They've dug themselves in a hole somewhat, in a sense, Alan's team have, like.

And in almost all the above examples there is an evaluative dimension, with the statements and comments simultaneously operating along an *evaluation cline*. The close connection between metaphor and its use for evaluation and appraisal should be recognised.

And sometimes there is a recognition of multiple meanings which result either in one meaning being explicitly privileged or in all the available meanings being accepted as relevant. Again such recognition results in the speaker showing concern for how the utterance might be or might need to be interpreted, with words such as *regular*, *right* and *real* signalling the preferred interpretation.

He's a regular pisshead.
That's a real burden off her shoulders, isn't it?

The corpus evidence seems to suggest that speakers are more reflective than might be assumed and that there is an underlying *metalingual* awareness of language which is a common property and which is especially manifest in respect of creative uses of language. Metaphoric salience is recognised and the metaphoric character of the utterance is intensified, evaluated and made more or less intimate according both to varying communicative demands on participants and according to the contextual dynamics which operate. Listeners (and readers) also engage in varying degrees of processing and reflectiveness on what they hear or are guided to hear. This can range from straightforward online processing in which there is unconscious and more or less immediate recognition of meaning to awareness that there is metaphoric usage and then further to, in certain contexts, fuller and explicit appreciation of the skill with which words have been deployed. And although the examples here are drawn from metaphor, further examples of this kind of metalingual awareness can be noted across a range of figures of speech.

Fixed expressions and formulaic language: creativity and constraint

> *The trouble with the Germans, Sir, is that they don't like it up 'em, they don't like it up 'em.*
>
>   (Spoken by a character in the UK television comedy, *Dad's Army*)

> *I guess now you are over the moon, Mars, Jupiter and the whole galaxy*
>
>   (Sports report, Sky Sports, 2 July 1999)

In the introduction and in chapter 3 (pp. 95 ff.) it was observed that playing and creatively disfiguring the fixed patterns of pre-formulated and formulaic chunks of language constituted a common feature in interaction between speakers in the CANCODE corpus. This observation is carried further in this section.

Fixed expressions are notoriously difficult to define and to classify, especially in idiomatic formations. Such expressions are complex because of the *degrees* of fixedness or frozenness which affect the syntactic and lexical patterns of their component parts. For example, the idiomatic phrase *forty winks* (meaning 'a brief sleep') is a 'frozen' pattern in so far as changes to its form alter the idiomatic meaning to literal meanings. Thus you cannot say 'I'm just going to have a forty wink' or 'She's just having twenty winks'; in this respect, the collocation *forty winks* is immutably fixed. Yet the phrase is not completely frozen as the verbs which pattern with *forty winks* are not so restricted. *Have forty winks*, *get forty winks*, *enjoy forty winks* are all possible, for example, and various adjectives may also be inserted (e.g. 'I'm just going to grab a *quick* forty winks'). Semantically, many expressions are similarly difficult to pin down because they cannot all be interpreted in the same way on the basis of the literal meanings of their component parts. Thus *to spill the beans* or *to have cold feet* are both semantically opaque even if the meaning of each individual word in the phrase is known; whereas *to blow your top* is more likely to be worked out by reference to a core conceptual knowledge linking anger to liquid in a heated container. However, some fixed expressions, for example *to be yellow* (cowardly), can be fixed in form and be opaque semantically.

The fuzziness of definitions in this whole domain has been well described by Kövecses and Szabó (1996: 327):

> The category of idiom is a mixed bag. It involves metaphors (e.g. *spill the beans*), metonymies (*throw up one's hands*), pairs of words (e.g. *cats and dogs*), idioms with *it* (e.g. *live it up*), similes (e.g. *easy as pie*), sayings (e.g. *a bird in the hand is worth two in the bush*), phrasal verbs (e.g. *to come up*) as in 'Christmas is coming up', grammatical idioms (e.g. *let alone*) and others.

It is unlikely that such categories and associated structures could ever be united under any single theory of fixed expressions and, certainly, analysis of formal and semantic properties alone would only get us so far (see McCarthy and Carter, 1994; Carter, 1998: ch. 3; McCarthy, 1998a: ch. 7). However, although there are disadvantages to blurred and overinclusive definitions and to a consequent categorial overlap, there are advantages too. The main advantage is to compel recognition that such patterns are widespread in everyday speech, that some of them are routinely used for conventional and formulaic speech functions but that some of them are also sufficiently flexible in form that they can be made open to freshly reconfigured and creative patternings.[3]

In terms of the main creativity principles proposed in the previous chapter, we might suggest here that fixed expressions are at the heart of what have been argued here to be key components in linguistic creativity in common talk: *pattern forming and pattern re-forming.* One particular aspect of pattern re-forming with fixed expressions in spoken discourse has been noted by McGlone *et al.* (1994) and more specifically by McCarthy (1998a: 117):

> Another noteworthy feature of idioms in everyday talk is the way speakers use them creatively by a process of 'unpacking' them into their literal elements and exploiting these; even in opaque idioms, literal meanings of component words are in some sense activated, or are at least potentially available.

Such comments are underpinned by empirical studies which provide evidence against the idea that idioms can be dismissed as no more than 'dead' metaphors. People are able to work with, process and interpret fixed expressions because of a knowledge of underlying metaphorical concepts, a capacity, when interpreting meanings, to move seamlessly between the literal and the figurative and an as yet imperfectly researched and understood sense of which words are semantically key within each fixed expression and of how fixed or otherwise they are. Such keywords, however they are identified, prompt both creative extension to some lexico-grammatical and semantic patterns and a related creative intuition that some other patterns should be repeated and reinforced. What the cognitive linguistic research reported by Gibbs (1994: ch. 6) does underline is that idioms are not simply comprehended without some kind of metalingual analysis of component parts by speakers and listeners.

A good example of this feature is part of a conversation between two retired male schoolteachers who are reminiscing about former pupils and colleagues.

Example 4.5

<S 01>: The second year I had, I started off with 37 in the class I know that, of what you call dead wood the real dregs had been taken off the bottom and the cream the sour cream in our case up there had been creamed off the top and I just had this dead wood. I mean it really was and he was so impressed with the job that I did with them and the way that I got on with them and he immediately said right how do you feel about taking a special class next year and I took one from then on.

<S 02>: Rather you than me.

The first speaker begins with the metaphor of bottled liquid in which bad elements (*dregs*) fall to the bottom. The liquid metaphor is extended to *cream* which means what is left at the top of the milk but which also signifies what is the best part of something. This phrase is then idiomatised into the phrase *sour cream* (meaning something unpleasant) and then further extended into the phrase *creamed off* (meaning to select the most worthwhile – the metaphor here involves the process of cream floating to the top of milk). The metaphor of liquids is then mixed with the idiom of *dead wood*, a phrase which means that something is of little value. The comments of the first teacher are then responded to by the second teacher with a more routinised fixed phrase *rather you than me*, which evaluates what has just been said. Of course, as the suggested category list above illustrates, there are difficulties of overlap and unclear borderlines between fixed and unfixed and between metaphor and idiom in this extract. For example, to what extent is *dead wood* or for that matter *sour cream* or the reference to *dregs* metaphoric or idiomatic? But this instance does underline how in fixed expressions some component parts remain alive and open to reformulation and innovative extension.

A related feature of idiom reformulation occurs in the following example where two students are discussing their relatives – in this case speaker <S 01>'s grandfather. The context and the speakers are the same as in Example 4.3.

Example 4.6

[<S 01> is 24, male, and a PhD student in American Studies, <S 02> is 22, male, and an MA student in American Studies. They have known each other for about a year and are good friends. The speakers are sitting on the grass in <S 01>'s garden.]

<S 01>: What were your grandparents by profession?
<S 02>: My grandfather who's still alive was erm plumber he had his own business. But that's why he's er so ill now. It's cos
<S 01>: Own plumbing?
<S 02>: No Burrows.
<S 01>: Burrows plumbing.
<S 02>: It's my mum's father. He erm has got bad asbestos poisoning now.
<S 01>: [tuts] Oh dear.
<S 02>: He's been on like you know doomed to die death's door for about three years now.
<S 01>: Oh that's terrible.
<S 02>: So he's, it's really good that he's you know still alive. Touch wood again as this morbid+
<S 01>: I know.
[laughs]
<S 02>: +morbid banter goes on.

The extract shows that idiom form can be creatively distended and played with, even, as here, as a possible way of lightening and/or distancing speakers from an unpleasant topic. The idiom *to be at/on death's door* is here reformed and made more interactive by the vagueness markers of *like* and *you know*, and the self-consciousness of metalingual reference to *morbid banter* seems to reinforce this interpretation. There is even perhaps in 'doomed to die' a verbal allusion with a mock-morbid ring of Victorian melodrama. The formulaic reference to the superstition of touching wood (*touch wood*) in order to prevent ill-luck also shows how the full range of fixed expressions from routinised, pre-formulated chunks to a creative reworking of established idioms is commonly found in stretches of talk and how in fact the two ends of the cline may be much more closely related than it may at first seem.

What has not yet been established in current research is how and why particular items are selected for metaphoric extension or for further literal play with ambiguity or how and why idioms vary in the way in which particular literal meanings are blocked. Giora (1999: 185) has suggested that there is a semantic core to some idioms which invokes a different comprehension process: 'If a word has meanings that can be retrieved directly from the lexicon, the meaning more popular, or prototypical or more frequently used in a certain community is more salient.' Such a suggestion may well lead us back to the notion of core vocabulary (see above, p. 115 ff.) and to the fact that certain lexical items have a greater salience than others. Initial corpus analysis in this area does suggest, for example, that words for parts of the body and basic perceptual processes are active in this kind of way. Searches for words such as *back*, *head*, *arm*, *shoulder*, *head*, *eye*, *teeth*, *foot*, *heart*, together with *see*, *hear*, *talk*, *breathe* show how regularly such prototypical items enter into idiomatic form. For example: *catch someone's eye*; *keep an eye on*; *turn a blind eye to*; *eye up*; *eye to eye*; *to turn one's back on*; *back to back*; *to back up*; *to stab you in the back* are all items which seem to involve both metonymic and metaphoric readings and can thus activate both literal and metaphoric interpretation. Advertisements, in particular, utilise such features. For example, a well-known slogan for the National UK Blood Transfusion agency, *Anyone with a heart can give blood,* plays effectively on just such a network of interrelated meanings from the core words *heart* and *give* and *blood* to the institutionalised cultural metaphor of 'heart' (meaning 'feelings', especially feelings for others).

Thus, while non-core vocabulary is often more expressive and a source for creativity, generalisations can be dangerous. For example, it is worth noting in this connection that the most frequent words in a corpus of English (and in other languages) are grammatical words such as *the* and *a*, though such words do not by definition have any extractable lexical meaning. However, corpus analysis also underlines the significance of lexico-grammatical words such as prepositions. For example, very frequent prepositions such as *down* are commonly associated with core feelings and meanings connected to disadvantage and depression (*he's feeling very down today*, *they're always down on him*) and the preposition *up* is commonly connected with happiness and a positive stance (though paradoxically in several phrasal verb structures it is connected with problems and evaluative attitudes, for example, *muck up*, *screw up*, *it gets up your nose*).

Note, too, how prepositions such as *up/down/in/out* are often core items, especially in sexual innuendos, insults and scatological wordplay. The relation of these words to sexual innuendo is interesting and appears to work as if there were a creative connection between core bodily functions and core words in the language. The connection in part explains the humour in the brief extract from the British TV comedy drama *Dad's Army* cited at the beginning of this section which consists almost entirely of core vocabulary.

Idioms, creativity and evaluation

> *I always wanted to go [retire] while I retained the odd marble.*
> (Sir Michael Levy, *The Daily Telegraph*, 11 August 2000)

> *That sounds like the wag the dog syndrome to me.*
> (Reporter, Channel 4 News, 16 December 1998)

The above exploration of idioms in use clearly shows that idioms are not simply neutral alternatives to less semantically opaque expressions. There is a difference between 'I smell a rat' and 'I am suspicious', or 'She's on cloud nine' and 'She's extremely happy', or 'The garden's a real mish-mash of different herbs' or 'The garden's a real mixture of different herbs.' In all cases the idiomatic expression is used evaluatively and represents a more intense version of the literal statement. For example, McCarthy and Carter (1994: ch. 3), following leads in Strässler (1982), demonstrate that idiom uses do not simply describe but comment in positive and (more usually) negative ways on events, processes and persons. They are also used in face-sensitive ways which is why they are used most commonly about absent third parties or about non-human objects and, less rarely, by or about participants in face-to-face encounters. In spoken interaction there is also a degree of intimacy and informality created by choices of idiomatic rather than 'equivalent' literal expressions. Using CANCODE data McCarthy (1998a: ch. 7) also demonstrates the extent to which idioms occur at topic transitions and, in the context of narratives, at the points at which the main meaning of the narration is being conveyed. In other words, their occurrence at particular junctures in, or in particular contexts of, spoken discourse is not random.[4]

The following example in which the speakers are discussing disk-jockeys (the expression *disk-jockeys* itself is a remarkable metaphor) on a BBC radio programme contains extensive idiomatic choices as evaluations are made of the different personalities.

Example 4.7

[<S 01> 27-year-old male, environmental scientist, <S 02> 31-year-old female, environmental scientist, <S 03> 30-year-old female, receptionist. All very good friends (intimate), chatting at <S 02>'s house.]

    <S 02>: Oh she's not on any more [DJ's name]. She's a pain in the arse.

<S 01>: Has she been thrown off?

<S 02>: Yeah. Ah she's, well she's just not not a DJ there anymore now. I mean [DJ's name] in the morning is a pain in the arse. Simon Mayo is basically there the housewife's choice. Er then there's Jo Wiley on a lunchtime twelve or two. And she's quite good. She's a bit of a muso anyway. She used to do the evening session which was all Indy stuff+

<S 01>: Yeah.

<S 02>: +and new stuff. Erm

<S 01>: There's Nik erm is it Nik Kershaw or John Peel have been stuffed to some really late hour.

<S 02>: Yeah. I mean they're they're still great. Erm and then there's Mark Radcliffe and Lard in the afternoon. They're hilarious. And they're the ones?

<S 03>: I sometimes find them quite irritating.

<S 02>: Ah I think they're really funny. Erm but recently is all these ratings and everything and Radio One have got even more listeners again. And, but I really hate this self-congratulatory kind of atmosphere in Radio One. Some of the DJs knocking other DJs and say er they're just like er er Smashy and Nicey and that kind of thing. But I'm thinking in five years time you'll be exactly like that and being thrown off for being too old and out of touch so you really shouldn't be sort of tempting fate you know.

The fixed expressions ranged here are characterised by a pervasive clustering as the discourse becomes increasingly personalised, affective and critical. Metaphoric expressions such as *stuffed to*, *thrown off*, morphological inventions (*Smashy and Nicey*) and ironic, cultural allusions (*the housewives' choice*) sit alongside more standard idioms such as *a pain in the arse* or *a bit of a muso* or *out of touch* and more transparent idiomatic/proverbial phrases such as *you shouldn't be . . . tempting fate*. The cultural allusion to *Housewives' Choice* is to a cosy BBC radio programme from the 1950s for female listeners.

As with several of the examples cited in this chapter, it is noticeable throughout that the two speakers jointly produce the discourse, creating effects as they go so that the creativity emerges from their interaction and co-production.

Have a nice day! Some language just isn't creative

In selecting idiomatic forms speakers are deliberately making pattern re-forming moves in that they want their words to have a distinct and discernible impact as well as to serve to foreground the ideas, feelings, attitudes and evaluations which are being expressed. However, running in parallel with these creative extensions and reconfigurations is the existence of a range of non-creative, formulaic expressions which, as we have seen, operate primarily to stabilise and routinise the communicative event. Formulaic language has been variously described involving a range of metalanguage; in each case the language is used by speakers in an off-the-peg, ready-made kind of way. The language is prefabricated, normally non-propositional and often deliberately monosemic. It allows messages to be conveyed easily and straightforwardly, often when a transaction of information is the main purpose of an exchange. And that is the main point. There are times when communication or a part of a message needs to be highly routinised and non-creative.

There are clearly many occasions when speakers use clichéd, formulaic language in distinct preference to more freshly minted expressions, rather in the way they might shake hands with someone and accompany the gesture with a conventional greeting or farewell (see Wray, 1999 and Wray and Perkins, 2000). Not for the first time in this book, and in support of the argument that creative language use is relatively ubiquitous, it has to be also pointed out that there are distinctly routine and formulaic encounters in which language is used transmissively and transactionally, and often necessarily so. Unmodified pre-formulated, formulaic chunks of language allow for this by providing scaffolding from which other language structures can be built, though, as we have seen many times, such forms can be made creatively active at any moment.

Proverbs and slang expressions

Proverbial expressions convey familiar folk wisdom through statements and sayings. The well-known truths expressed by proverbs are usually oblique and implicit rather than direct statements, they often have a metaphorical basis and their indirectness prompts interpretation and a 'creative' inferencing of meaning. In specific discourse contexts proverbs usually occur at the end of a discourse sequence, are normally evaluative (similarly to idioms) and often include reference to social and moral matters. Proverbs in use in actual discourse environments often protect face and are used rather than direct statements in order not to give offence. Thus, to say *Don't count your chickens (before they are hatched)* to someone implies a negative evaluative comment but one which is less direct and face-threatening than saying 'don't spend money you haven't got' or some such equivalent. In the case of positive evaluations the proverb serves even more to reinforce solidarity. Thus to say: *Where there's a will there's a way* to someone who has battled against the odds to achieve something is an on-record approbatory statement. In both cases speakers and listeners gain in mutuality by converging in interpretation of meaning and in social alignment and accommodation. It can also be observed in the CANCODE corpus how many times proverbs appear at a discourse boundary, as if functioning to close down a conversation by summarising an attitude or by indicating a particular stance towards what has been said or to allow a smooth transition from one topic to another.

Empirical research, summarised by Gibbs (1994: 309–18), shows that the move from literal to figurative readings of proverbs is a complex one, involving in the process basic conceptual frameworks and mappings, but he points out that proverbs are often interpreted not out of context but in the context of dynamic interaction. Proverbs may appear to be dormant structures which exist as a collection of quaint folk-sayings but they are actually very much alive and are often creatively revived and resurrected in the art of everyday discourse. They function, Gibbs (2001) points out, to unite speakers by appeal to generally accepted or universal truths, performing a binding role within a community of speakers. Their primary function is as part of pattern forming; but pattern re-forming functions do occur when speakers create novel proverbs, making up new formulations or extending existing ones in order to question the validity of a particular way of doing or seeing things. Wallace Stevens and William Blake are among the canonical literary writers who create novel versions of established proverbs as a way of questioning basic assumptions. But in everyday discourse, speakers can create a new way of seeing by taking proverbs such as 'We'll cross that bridge when we come to it' or Don't burn your bridges' and re-forming them. For example, the following: *He's impatient and just fancies burning a few bridges before he has to cross them* was spoken by a contributor to the CANCODE corpus (a thirty-two-year-old business man) turning the two well-known proverbs inside out and into an ironic commentary on the behaviour of a friend who had engaged on an over-risky business venture.

Slang and intimate discourse

Slang expressions can be categorised under the general heading of fixed expressions. We have noted how the use of some idiomatic language, particularly when used about third parties, creates an in-group or personalised lexicon, membershipping participants as belonging socially and culturally. In particular, recent research has shown how small groups, including intimate couples and families, reinforce their intimacy and insulate themselves further against the outside world, by developing highly personalised and sometimes humorous and euphemistic fixed expressions (see Gibbon, 1981; Hopper *et al.*, 1981).

The choice of slang and in-group expressions in preference to more literal equivalents is once again no neutral act. It is almost always affective and attitudinal and often interpersonally and context sensitive. In a fascinating study of hospital slang Gordon (1983) connects the use by hospital staff of an opaque set of slang expressions with helping them to help each other to cope with severely injured patients in contexts where direct literal reference would be too emotionally involving. Gordon also shows how particular varieties of slang are developed to refer to patients who are judged to take up time and attention from patients the staff believe to have greater needs. The slang is often richly inventive and has striking analogical and metaphorical bases; for example, *apple-bobbing* is used to refer to the process of unblocking cases of constipation. In most instances, greater intimacy and strength of group feeling is established by the slang usage. Slang is, however, regularly the subject of social stigma. Slang users are seen as taking easy and ephemeral linguistic options and its use is seen as inhibiting careful thought or original expression. By contrast, Hayakawa (1941: 194–5) refers to slang as the 'poetry of everyday life' and to how it 'vividly expresses people's feelings about life and about things they encounter in life'.

Hyperbole (and *thousands* of examples)

Hyperbole is a further common feature of informal discourse. Speakers often need not simply to convey information but also to insert an attitudinal contour towards what is said. As we have seen, the resources for doing this take many forms and in the case of hyperbole there are formal and discoursal similarities with metaphoric and idiomatic expressions. In CANCODE data (McCarthy and Carter, forthcoming) have pointed out that hyperbole takes the following main forms:

* Vague quantifiers: e.g. numerical quantifiers (e.g. *dozens of, scores of, thousands of, millions of*); measurement expressions (e.g. *yards of, miles of, tons of*); general size quantifiers (e.g. *heaps of, loads of, stacks of*); container quantifiers (e.g. *buckets of, truck/lorryloads of, oceans of*); time quantifiers (*seconds, minutes, hours, centuries, aeons*);
* Modifiers: e.g. *gigantic, enormous, gi-normous, massive, vast, endless, wall-to-wall*;
* Verb phrases: e.g. *to be covered in, to be dying of, to be up to one's eyes in*;
* Counterfactual expressions: (often used in conjunction with *literally, nearly/almost* and related metalingual 'triggers'), e.g. *I ran a mile when I saw her*; *we literally froze to death*; *I almost wet myself when I was waiting to go on*; *I nearly died of thirst waiting for them.*

As is the case with a number of figures of speech, hyperbole functions to evaluate, to introduce humour and informality into proceedings, to mark solidarity and mutuality between speakers as well as to gain attention. In some contexts speakers use hyperbolic expressions as a normal and natural way of conveying or reacting to information, although it should be noted that hyperbole is common in arguments and disputes and in narrative recounts, especially in settings which are more intimate and informal.

Hyperbole is, however, different from other figures of speech in so far as its primary function is to intensify an utterance. Hyperbole involves speakers in saying things which cannot be true or which are recognised as untrue or contrary to perceived facts. An element of deliberately fictional exaggeration or overstatement is almost always introduced, and hyperbole normally works by stressing one particular feature, normally features of size, shape or movement, and by deliberately overplaying its extent. As indicated above, a wide range of hyperbolic structures are available, normally in and around the noun and verb phrase, and they allow a range of expressive choices. Many of these structures are at the same time sufficiently productive to generate creative extensions and creative combinations of items.

Similarly to metaphor and related tropes, hyperbole is usually signalled as such, as speakers show awareness of the extent to which they are playing with normal perceptions or with standard accounts of reality. Hyperbole is especially closely related to metaphor in that some of the overstatements lead to an incongruity of comparison between the real and the created exaggerated or fictionalised account; hyperbole is also closely related to irony in that the exaggeration can also sometimes be interpreted as marking an ironic tone of voice, not least because listeners or readers may be made unsure of how far to take what is said at face value (see Bhaya, 1985; Roberts and Kreuz, 1994). A further related issue is the degree to which many hyperbolic expressions are 'frozen' to the point where the fictionalised alternative worlds are not noticed as creative exaggerations but rather regarded as normal institutionalised expressions and thus at the more non-creative end of the creativity cline.

Just some examples

Corpus examples of hyperbole are not always easy to locate because they cannot be automatically retrieved and have to be presupposed. Searches can be made through metalingual and discoursal triggers such as *literally*, *almost* and *nearly*, and after initial searches further instances can be sought through searches on such items as quantifiers, measurement expressions and specific modifiers.

The following examples are all drawn from the CANCODE corpus and are to be found mainly in contexts involving relationships which are symmetrical rather than asymmetrical. Note too how often the speakers jointly create meanings and effects by repeating or rebuilding each others' words and phrases.

Example 4.8

    <S 01>: Titchy little bag.
    <S 02>: Titchy yeah. It's got *tons* of stuff in it though.

    <S 01>: I am getting *so many millions* of crow's feet round my eyes. I think it's the ozone layer cracking up and it's making my skin get really wrinkled.

    <S 02>: Well all the cars are like that. Oh every vehicle is *twice the size of its equivalent in Britain*. The lorries are *huge*. The cars and trucks are *massive*. You don't realise until very occasionally you see a British type car and it's *minuscule*.
[laughter]
    <S 02>: [inaudible] to have to deal with these great big American things. *Everything out there is just so big*. The mountains are *huge*.

    <S 01>: If you get behind Jim Taylor in the photocopying queue you can wait for *hours and hours and hours, quite literally*, you know.

    <S 02>: I mean it's funny where they, where they live now it's er it's right out in the s= in the sticks in a tiny tiny village. And if you blink you've you've driven through it. And er the only amusement is one pub.

<*S 01*>:   [laughs] Yeah. Mm.
<*S 02*>:   The Post Office opens only three mornings a week and *that's in somebody's front room.*

(The reference here to the post office being in someone's 'front room' is an ironic comment meaning that service is slow and the room is cramped.)

It is noticeable from these extracts how instances of hyperbole co-occur with other tropes such as metaphor and idiomatic expressions, how the hyperbole is not infrequently re-duplicative (e.g. *hours and hours and hours*; *titchy little*) and occurs with other intensifiers such as *absolutely* and *bloody*, how such uses prompt self- and other-directed evaluation and are a constant source of congenial laughter with the speaker. And as we can see from the above data, hyperbole regularly (creatively) stimulates laughter and enables participants to achieve a degree of convergence.

Hyperbole is a common strategy and has an inbuilt creative potential. Some words and phrases are used principally and some almost exclusively with a hyperbolic meaning. Hyperbole operates along clines of intensity, evaluation and intimacy but is most marked in operation along an intensity scale. By marking reference with higher degrees of intensity, speakers can produce different perspectives, stimulating listeners to laughter, to new ways of seeing, or simply to appreciation of affective and interpersonally creative language choices. Hyperbole is closely related to metaphor and irony and contrasts with other rhetorical figures such as understatement or litotes.

Indirectness and creativity

The words 'burning' and 'bridges' come to mind.

(CANCODE data)

Figures of speech often consist of words, phrases and smaller units of language and can be examined in single conversational turns or short extracts from a corpus. Some figures of speech require more extensive treatment. For example, innuendo, understatement, irony and other more indirect modes such as allegory often require a complete stretch of text in order for their functions to be more fully discerned. In this connection further work by Gibbs (1999a: 171–4) illustrates, with an example from the Managalese culture of Papua New Guinea, how indirectness is a primary mode of polite communication. An allegorical story is narrated in order that all parties come to understand for themselves the significance of a particular action (in this case concerning elopement of members of a family). The allegory is used figuratively to resolve a potential dispute with a much greater reliance on listeners to receive, to interpret and to accept responsibility for the underlying message.

Patternings: creativities and clines – a summary

You're not with it, without it.

(Brylcreem hair-gel advertisement, June 2000)

Don't put it off, put it on.

(Barclaycard TV advertisement November 1998)

In this chapter the scalar and clinal nature of creativity has been discussed and its significance underlined, with particular reference to lexis and figures of speech. The following points summarise the main evidence gathered so far in this chapter concerning spoken creativity and the final section concludes with the main arguments concerning spoken creativity.

- Figures of speech constitute a potential resource for creativity. In addition to puns and wordplay in general, other key forms have been shown to include: repetition, metaphor, metonymy, simile, idioms and hyperbole. Such figures are not in themselves creative. They can be used for routine, transactional purposes. But such forms can be and often are made to function for a range of different purposes with a range of different creative effects. The notion of coreness in vocabulary can help in the identification of such effects.
- Spoken creativity is instantial and emergent. It emerges from local, particular instances, often unplanned and unprepared for by participants. It is produced and co-produced, improvised and interpreted in the instance of its manifestation. Speakers are, however, often aware of such uses of language, demonstrating a metalingual awareness of such forms as puns and wordplay in particular. While they are being creative, speakers are sometimes, though by no means always, aware of what they are doing.
- Creativity is a matter of degree. It is pervasive in the daily commerce of language, especially in ordinary everyday exchanges. But it is not so omnipresent as to be everywhere all the time. Creativity varies linguistically: some forms of language are or are made by users to be more open to creative deployment. So non-core vocabulary is more susceptible than core vocabulary; metaphor is more susceptible than synecdoche. Creativity is thus not a yes/no category. We are dealing with tendencies and not with absolutes. Creativity is clinal. As a result, and particularly in respect of spoken language, operating 'at full stretch' in the cut and thrust of dialogue, it is more accurate to say, once again, that we deal with different creativities rather than with one singular or essentialist creativity.
- Spoken creativity can occur in monologues and in the context of a transmission of information but it is more likely to grow out of dialogic interaction in which creative forms and functions are co-produced. In this sense, too, creativity is emergent rather than pre-formulated, though it may crucially contain elements of pre-formulation.
- There is often a sense in which the co-production of creativity, especially, though not exclusively, by pattern re-forming means, results in our not

seeing things subsequently in quite the same way. A sense of re-creation and 're-vision' is almost always involved.

• What is clearly illustrated by the data in this and the previous chapter is that figures of speech are employed and deployed by speakers as communicative resources to negotiate and to position ideas, feelings and attitudes. Such properties and processes are not normally observable when figures of speech are seen detached from real speakers, out of context or as single words and phrases. Different questions are therefore raised by recognising them as dynamic rather than as static entities.

Conclusions from chapters 3 and 4

Creativity is difficult to define. The extent of the presence of creativity in different conversational contexts is difficult to measure in any quantitative way. It is not a wholly linguistic phenomenon but it is often manifested in language. Its manifestations in language also vary in terms of linguistic level. And there are differences between spoken and written creativity. In many spoken contexts creativity does not normally announce itself by formally displaying its properties in the manner of a book of poetry or a piece of fiction assigned to a creative category by the rules of a librarian's index or by its placement on a canonical syllabus for a literature course. In particular, spoken creativity is both emergent and discourse-internal. It is recognised, stimulated, promoted and supported by insider-dealing. There are occasions where it is openly recognised by both speakers and there are other occasions where it may not be consciously recognised. While there may be set-piece scripted occasions for it to be manifest, such as wedding or after-dinner speeches, it is normally co-produced, rather than produced. It requires internal, personal and context-specific, 'insider' recognition and acceptance, a process which makes external, 'outsider' verification difficult. The values ascribed to creative manifestations also, as we have seen, vary over time and across different cultures.

Creativity engages us intellectually. It can prompt thoughts, provide new angles on things, make us laugh at the absurdity of a situation, enable us to express a critical stance. It also engages us emotionally and affectively, enabling speakers and listeners to feel more intimate and at ease with one another, to intensify utterances or to add an expressive contour to statements. It can prompt evaluation and the expression of attitude. Creativity is a mentalistic phenomenon and draws for its effects on basic conceptual categories and prototypical experiences of the world. And it is also a social phenomenon, marked by tendencies, though only suggested at this stage, to be manifest and 'presentational' in some social settings more markedly than in others.

There are, of course, distinct dangers in positing creativity as a predominantly clinal phenomenon marked by intersecting social, psychological and linguistic continua. We may be in danger of saying that creativity is everywhere and nowhere, that it is sufficiently emergent and diffuse as to be indefinable and that it is certainly inaccessible to outsider scrutiny. We may be in danger of retreating behind creativity as a continuum because of a failure to make it

subject to the more stable and fixed categories of replicable linguistic definition. But we may also be in danger of relying on modes of definition belonging
to traditions of linguistic enquiry and description which simply do not in their
present form meet the nature of the phenomenon concerned.

Towards creativity and social context

Chapters 3 and 4 have considered the relation between creative forms and creative functions but the emphasis has been on identifying and categorising
particular linguistic forms. This has been necessary in order to illustrate its
diversity and ubiquity and to construct both hypotheses concerning particular
types of creative language and observations about its distribution.

One important next step forward is to continue to explore the extent of the
connections between creativity and social context. In the next chapter, chapter
5, examples of creative language use are investigated with particular reference
to a range of different sociocultural settings involving different interpersonal
contexts and relationships. In particular, it is important to see whether clines
and continua, and the framing of creativity in terms of continuities and in terms
of patterns such as 'forming' and 're-forming' structures, also apply in respect
of such data and to take forward the more formalistic orientation of chapters 3
and 4 into a fuller consideration of social and cultural functions and contexts of
language use.

Notes

1   See also, for example, Lakoff and Johnson (1980), Lakoff and Turner (1989),
    Turner (1996), Turner and Fauconnier (1999), Fauconnier and Turner (2002).
2   On concept combinations see Ward *et al.* (1997) and, in relation to particular
    contexts of interpretation, Gerrig and Bortfield (1999).
3   In an extensive computational and lexicographical study of collocation Sinclair
    (1987, 1991) has suggested a division into two main opposing categories of
    fixed and less fixed structures which he terms: the *idiom principle* and the *open
    choice principle*. He stresses the particular significance of the *idiom principle* in
    written and spoken text formation, arguing that phraseologically motivated,
    delexicalised formulaic expressions play a major 'building block' role. Sinclair
    recognises that open-choice patterns run counter to but can also emerge from
    idiom principle patterns and argues that the 'open' to 'closed' cline has a scalar
    rather than an either/or constitution. Howarth (1998) proposes a four-point
    scale which stretches from free combination through restricted collocations and
    figurative idioms to 'pure' idioms. Giora (1999) uses a 'graded salience' hypoth-
    esis to describe similar phenomena (see also Moon, 1998 who looks at
    fixedness in terms of scales and gradients). See also Choul (1982) and Fernando
    (1996) on the fuzzy borderlines between metaphor, extended metaphor,
    fossilised idiom and idiom reconfiguration.
4   See also Low (1988), Cameron and Low (1999) and Cameron (2002) on
    the interpersonal and evaluative functions of metaphors, the latter source with

particular reference to educational contexts. Drew and Holt (1995, 1998) offer interesting insights into idioms, figures of speech and topic transitions.

Exploring further

The literature on metaphor is voluminous, but on the topic of metaphor identification see papers in *Language and Literature*, 11, 1 (2002). Goatly (1997) offers a major study. Gibbs (1999b) provides useful updates on his own previous work. Dirven (1985, 1993) contributes pioneering studies of the centrality of metaphor to concept formation. Reddy (1993) gives a much-quoted account of the use of metaphor to convey a whole theory of communication. Goddard (1996) is illuminating on metaphors in talk. Stubbs (1997) looks at the relationship between cognition and linguistic experience. Turner (1996) sees the 'literary mind' as the basis for everyday thought. Blending neuroscience and literary history, he argues that structures such as parable are fundamental to an understanding of the workings of the human brain.

On metaphor in discourse, see Cameron and Low (1999), Cameron (1999, 2002 – the latter with particular reference to educational discourse) and Glucksberg (2001). On the fascinating notion of speaker awareness of metaphor production in spoken discourse and the respective pragmatic 'tunings' to accommodate listener interpretation, see Cameron and Deignan (2003). Deignan (1999) offers research on metaphor using corpus-analytical techniques. Steen (1994) makes an empirical study of metaphor in literary text and Fernandez (1991) an anthropological study of the cultural formation of metaphor. Pulman (1982), in an interesting paper, examines creative metaphor and risk-taking in language use.

On irony in conversation, see Clift (1999). On humour from a linguistic point of view, see also Alexander (1997). On joking and verbal play, see Chiaro (1992) and Crystal (1998). Dienhart (1999) looks at riddles as a form of linguistic play.

On idioms and idiomaticity see Cowie (1988, 2001), Cernak (1994) and Hudson (1998) for work on fixedness and phraseology. Moon (1998) makes a study using the COBUILD corpus. Makkai (1972, 1978) offers classic work in relation to idiomaticity as a language universal. Pawley and Syder (1983) is a much-quoted study with particular reference to language teaching and learning. Gibbon (1981) looks at idiom formation in amateur-radio talk. Sadock (1993) and Rumelhart (1993) gives a classic account of figurativeness in relation to linguistics. Sperber and Wilson (1986) offer insightful analyses of a range of tropes; for example, irony is discussed as a conversational strategy requiring an 'echoic' repetition or mention of a previous utterance understood by a listener to be played against for its truth to a shared context of understanding.

Stockwell (2002) provides illuminating cognitive poetic analysis of a range of texts, including application of insights from metaphor theory. Gavins and Steen (2003) and Culpeper and Semino (2002) make very useful further analyses of cognitive poetic structuring in a wide range of texts. Stockwell (2001) illustrates how cognitive analysis also needs to be complemented by analysis of ideological components which the metaphors reveal and conceal. For example, discussion of war can be distanced by using metaphors, but a 'critical' cognitive poetics points out the ingrained association of certain metaphors with the conduct of war.

Gerrig and Bortfield (1999) explore creative noun/noun combinations (in this case the phrase 'Evian boy') to examine how discourse meaning is created when a phrase is interpreted out of context.

Although the focus in this and previous chapters has been on linguistic forms, it is interesting to ask how creative use of language occurs in non-verbal communication systems such as sign language or gaze, proxemics, etc. which draw on general communication semiosis. For starting points, see Kendon (1994) and Finnegan (2002).

Part III

Contexts and variations

5   Creativity, language and social context

> To be a fluent speaker of a language means to be able to enter any conversation in ways that are seen as appropriate and not disruptive. Such conversational skills, which we usually take for granted (until we find somebody who does not have them or ignores their social implications) are not too different from the way a skilled jazz musician can enter someone else's composition, by embellishing it, playing around with its main motif, emphasising some elements of the melody over others, quoting other renditions of the same piece by other musicians and trying on different harmonic connections – all of this done without losing track of what everyone in the band is doing.
>
> (Duranti, 1997: 17)

Introduction

This chapter continues the steady and unfolding scrutiny of creativity in spoken language and continues to itemise and record features in relation to observations of formal patterns and co-creative functions. However, it takes further one particular but major insight from previous chapters and extends it by means of further analysis of the CANCODE corpus. The insight, drawn particularly from chapter 3, is that spoken creativity may be more prevalent in certain types of social context and within certain types of interpersonal relationship. It is an insight which is difficult to quantify but it will never be subject to analysis if the data taken for illustration are based on only narrowly contextualised snippets of dialogue.

In this chapter, therefore, the full power of the CANCODE corpus, especially its sociolinguistic and interactional design features, will be utilised to offer a preliminary test of these hypotheses concerning the relationship between creative language use and social context. A full range of different social contexts will be explored, but once again the discussion will eschew easy one-for-one correspondences and pay due attention to both the forms and functions and the speaker and listener purposes of creative language use.

Corpus and creativity? Basic frameworks, definitions and research questions

Research so far on the CANCODE corpus has identified both verbal repetition and a wide range of 'figures of speech' in the corpus such as metaphor, simile, metonymy, idiom, slang expressions, proverbs, hyperbole. It is not possible to define creativity in wholly formalist ways by identifying particular forms in the corpus, not least because in spoken interaction what counts as creative use is instantial and varies according to the dynamic established as part of a dialogue or as part of membership of a group.

In a sense, of course, and except for the most routinely formulaic or inattentive turns, almost all conversational exchanges are creatively co-produced, and the main argument so far in this study is that, as Sacks (1984) argues (see p. 78 above), ordinary talk has to be achieved and that it is a human, social and creative accomplishment which is far from being 'ordinary'. In some contexts some figures of speech pass unnoticed as normal, routine, even pre-formulated units; in other cases, the same figures of speech are drawn to the attention of speakers. In other contexts so-called 'dead' metaphors or clichés can be put to effective creative use in the dynamics of spoken encounters. The purposes for creative language in common everyday speech are also highly varied and can, as we have seen, include: offering some new way of seeing the content of the message; making humorous remarks; underlining what is communicated; expressing a particular attitude, including negative and adversarial attitudes; making the speaker's identity more manifest; playing with language form to entertain others; ending one bit of talk and starting another; or simply oiling the wheels of the conversation (as well as several of these functions and purposes simultaneously). In this book creativity is principally defined as instantial and emergent, occurring when particular patterns have come to be perceived by conversational participants as purposeful and motivated uses of language. Creativity almost always depends for its interpretation on the intentions and inferences of the participants.

It was argued in the conclusion to chapters 3 and 4 that it is a mistake exclusively to follow the well-trodden path of formal definitions. Definitions and categories proposed in previous chapters such as *pattern forming* and *re-forming* which recognise forms such as repetition and particular parts of speech as central to creative language are clearly significant. But a focus on forms can result in definitions which are too language-internal. It is important to explore definitions which also take account of functions *in context* and which acknowledge that much depends on how creative language is used by speakers in relation to local, contextual purposes and engagements with language.

One aim in this chapter is to attempt to underline this point by exploring creative functions across a variety of social and generic contexts involving a variety of different speakers in different types and contexts of interaction. It is argued, in particular, that creative language choices compel recognition of the social contexts of their production: principally but not exclusively, the maintenance of interpersonal relations and the construction of social identities. The main aim in this chapter is, thus, to explore the *extent* to which creative language use is evident in different speech genres.

Generic organisation and speech genres in CANCODE[1]

The data collected and transcribed for the CANCODE corpus are classified along two main axes according to *context type* and *interaction type*. Context type reflects the interpersonal relationships that hold between speakers, embracing both dyadic and multiparty conversations, and in all cases it is the relationship between speakers, that is, their wish to communicate at this level, which qualifies data for inclusion in the category, and not simply the particular environment in which the audio-recording is made. Four broad types are identified along a cline from *transactional*, *professional*, *socialising* to *intimate*. The 'transactional' is the most public and often involves contexts in which there is no previous relationship established between the speakers. In the 'professional' category the speakers are not necessarily peers but they do share either a profession or a regular place of work. 'Socialising' typically involves contexts such as sports clubs and pubs, as well as recreational and other group meetings. An 'intimate' context type is normally a private, cohabiting relationship where speakers can be assumed to be linguistically most 'off-guard'. Although there are points of overlap between categories, the relationship categories do represent, albeit roughly, a cline of 'public' to 'private' speech, with the 'transactional' and 'intimate' categories respectively at each end of the cline. The 'professional' category is more public than the 'socialising' category which in turn is more public than the 'intimate' category.

Along the axis of *interaction type*, distinctions are made between data that are predominantly collaborative and those that are non-collaborative and, further, for the collaborative type, those which are task-orientated and those which are not. In non-collaborative texts one speaker dominates significantly, supported by backchannelling from the other speaker(s). Typically, the dominant speaker in these texts relates an event, tells a joke or gives instructions, explanations or professional presentations. On one level, of course, these exchanges are also collaborative; on another level they resemble a unilinear transfer of information. The blanket term adopted for such an interaction type is *information provision*.

The two other interaction types represent more collaborative and dialogic speech encounters. *Collaborative idea* involves the interactive sharing of thoughts, opinions and attitudes, while the category of *collaborative task* is reserved for task-orientated communication. Also included in this category are the exchange of goods or the discussion of an entity that is referred to during the exchange, such as a catalogue or a computer screen. Overall, *interaction type* texts have proved more difficult to categorise owing to the problem of embedding. It is not uncommon to find that what starts out as a collaborative task becomes after a time a collaborative ideas discourse; and sometimes there is impregnation of a cell by more than one other cell. Category membership is thus allocated according to activity that is dominant in each conversation. A more detailed account of the

Table 5.1 CANCODE text types and typical situations in which they might be found.

Context type	Interaction type		
	Information provision	Collaborative task	Collaborative idea
Transactional	commentary by museum guide	choosing and buying a television	chatting with hairdresser
Professional	oral report at group meeting	colleagues window dressing	planning meeting at place of work
Socialising	telling jokes to friends	friends cooking together	reminiscing with friends
Intimate	partner relating the story of a film seen	couple decorating a room	siblings discussing their childhood

CANCODE corpus and its design is given by McCarthy (1998a), where the dangers inherent in reifying the categories are also fully acknowledged.

Combining the two axes provides a matrix of twelve text types as may be seen in Table 5.1, which also suggests some situations in which the text types might be found.

Organising the data: a brief note on 'evidence'

The data for this chapter were collected by random searching of the corpus cells using standard software tools such as Wordsmith (Scott, 1999) and a programme developed by Cambridge University Press. Although ten extracts (varying between 500 and 800 words) were searched in each cell, the overall approach is primarily qualitative rather than quantitative, not least because, in the current stages of automatic retrieval of language, instances of creative language are not easily identifiable by quantitative means. Searches in a corpus will always be limited by the current state of the available software and such a situation should help corpus analysts of all persuasions to guard against excessive claims for any one methodology. In any case it is difficult to imagine a situation in which corpus analysis of creative language use could be undertaken without an appropriate integration of quantitative and qualitative methods.

Thus the corpus is 'read' like a transcribed, living soap opera, in a series of representative extracts. In short, a methodology which combines the fine-tooth comb of conversation analysis with the immediate availability of the large number of contextually controlled samples which the corpus offers seems to be one clear and realistic way forward in the current state of corpus technology. One problem with the method adopted is that much has to be taken on trust, and this is true of many statements in this book concerning the ubiquitous nature of creativity. Examples found in the corpus are analysed and their representative nature argued for, but the analyst cannot provide evidence which goes beyond the extracts cited. And there is, as we must continue to observe, always the danger that what is perceived by the analyst will be of a different order from that perceived by the participants, especially when certain pattern forming structures operate for the speakers with varying degrees of conscious awareness. Claims for 'evidence' always need to be inspected closely.

Lifeguards and journalists

The provenance of different types of creative language can be illustrated by the following extract from the CANCODE corpus, extracts from which have already been discussed above.

Two main examples, lifeguards and journalists, are taken from contrasting contexts within the corpus matrix. The first example involves two lifeguards who have taken a break from their duties at a swimming pool. In such circumstances it is of course difficult to know whether the lifeguards are operating in a professional capacity or are sufficiently disengaged from their professional roles for the genre of talk to correspond more closely to a friendly socialising encounter (see Eggins and Slade, 1997, for many such examples). Such blurrings of category are inevitable, but may in fact provide a more accurate portrayal of a notion such as 'workplace talk' than monolithic categorisations of professional or task-orientated discourse. It is decided to retain the term *professional* for the context, since the location, uniforms and roles occupied by the participants are closer to the professional than to the non-professional socialising axis. Small talk and casual conversation of varying types is endemic in professional settings, as the papers edited by Coupland (2000) demonstrate.

Example 5.1 Lifeguards

[Lifeguards in the office, chatting in-between taking entrance fees from customers. <S 01> lifeguard: male (32); <S 02> lifeguard: male (31). The speakers are discussing possible reading matter for a forthcoming holiday. In this example the speakers are engaged in the genre of 'professional/collaborative idea'.]

<S 01>: The thing about hard-backs is if you take a hard-back on the beach pages don't blow up. Some pages are bound and if you take a paper-back on the beach all the bleeding glue melts.
<S 02>: Oh.
<S 01>: You end up pages all over the place.
<S 02>: That might do there and all cos it's like about ninety to hundred degrees at the moment there.
<S 01>: Yeah.
<S 02>: So.
<S 01>: It's er. I was in, I was in, reading F H M on the sunlounger happy as hell. Not very hot. Pages open. Mm. The next thing

you know this page came in my hand and all glue that holds the pages had melted and there were pages blowing all over the place.

<S 01>: Not a happy hamster.

<S 02>: [laughs] Not a happy one. I've gotta take something and there's like a good book-shop er in Manchester airport. So you get there early enough anyway. So.

<S 01>: Mm.

<S 02>: Straight down to W. H. Smith's and er see what books I can get.

<S 01>: Mm.

<S 02>: I'm not gonna like leave it 'til we get there cos they'd be like you know. Separate tales of Doctor Duck or sommat.

[laughter]

<S 01>: I were taking, I bought Marvin Gaye's biography and taking that and erm what's the other one. Phil Lynott you know him out of Thin Lizzie?

<S 02>: Yeah.

<S 02>: [unintelligible]

<S 01>: +died of drugs and er+

<S 02>: Yeah.

<S 01>: +his erm, he married Leslie Crowther's, Crowther's daughter didn't he?

<S 02>: Yeah.

<S 01>: I'll have a look through them two. Something about like biographies I find them more interesting than than fiction. Fiction's all right innit.

<S 02>: I like some of=yeah.

<S 01>: When you're reading something you know that somebody's done+

<S 02>: Made up.

<S 01>: +or been through that+

<S 02>: Yeah.

<S 01>: +or experienced like it's it makes it a little bit more interesting.

<S 02>: See I like er last time, well not last time but a couple of times before I went to er Tenerife wit t'ex-missus like.

<S 01>: Mhm.

<S 02>: Er I took er a book on on the Holocaust at er, well no like.

<S 01>: A bit of light reading.

<S 02>: Well yeah. A bit of light reading.

The lifeguards' discourse is especially marked by a mutuality within which both participants strive to align knowledge and viewpoint, establishing inter-textual co-reference and reinforcing shared knowledge. For example: . . . *he married Leslie Crowther's daughter, didn't he*; . . . *you know him out of Thin Lizzie* (Leslie Crowther was a well-known British TV personality; Thin Lizzie were a famous pop group of the 1970s). In particular, the mutuality is achieved by: overt agreement by means of simple acknowledgement (*yeah*); supportive backchannelling (*Mm*); acceptance of propositions by repetition (for example: the repetition of the phrase *all over the place* when discussing the dangers of soft-back books in high temperatures or the parallels of *a bit of light reading*). Such mutuality is assumed from the earliest stages of this exchange. From the beginning metaphors are in evidence (*the pages don't blow up, all the bleeding glue melts*) and the lifeguards appear to feel sufficiently at ease with one other. Having further aligned and realigned their mutual knowledge, feelings and attitudes, co-productivity leads organically into more overt creative language choices: deliberate hyperbole (*all the glue had melted; pages blowing all over the place*); extravagant similes (*happy as hell; They'd be like you know Separate tales of Doctor Duck*); ironic understatements (*not a happy hamster; a bit of light reading*).

Nearly all of these formulations result in laughter or further elaboration as the speakers continually take up each other's words and signals. For example, *all the bleeding glue melts* <S 01> is hyperbolically intensified by *to a hundred degrees* <S 02>; *not a happy hamster* <S 01> is reinforced by *not a happy one* <S 02>; and the final sequence shows a highly collaborative piece of co-constructed creative language as the reference to the *Holocaust* is picked up by speaker<S 01> *a bit of light reading* and then further accepted and reaccented by speaker <S 02>. The term *involvement* used by Tannen (see chapter 1, p. 79) does not wholly capture the extent to which conditions are achieved within which creative language choices are made. Here shared feelings and attitudes are mutually constructed as a frame or 'platform' for creative verbal play which is then in its turn further co-produced.

In both extracts so far, there are also 'footing shifts', after Goffman (1979, 1981). Goffman (1981: 128) describes footing as 'alignment, or set, or stance, or posture, or projected self'; changes in the alignment establish new 'frames' in which the talk is interpreted. Turn construction and placement can signal shifts in footing and creatively render a conversational frame or schema more visible. Shifts are often marked by discourse markers, and in the two extracts markers such as *the thing about X is* . . ., *the next thing you know*, . . ., *like, you know*, suggest that new conversational frames are projected in which evaluation or stance of some kind is to be creatively displayed.

Example 5.2 Journalists

In this extract journalists on a local radio station are in a meeting, the main purpose of which is to decide which stories to programme. The context is professional (even though the relationships are clearly sufficiently familiar to suggest that the context could be marked as socialising). And the nature of the interaction (predominantly collaborative task) also shifts in a dynamic way as goals change, so that parts of the talk are clearly more relational than transactional and in some stretches of the discourse the contours are closer to collaborative idea. The dominant speech genre is, however, that of 'professional/collaborative task'.

*[<S 01 radio producer: male (40s); <S 02> journalist: female (20s); <S 03> jour-
nalist, female (20s); <S 04 journalist: male 40s; <S 05> journalist: female (20s).
(These people don't appear on the transcript: <S 06> journalist: male (30s); <S 07>
radio engineer: male (30s); <S 08> news editor: male (40s).)]*

<S 01>: Erm. This isn't really any= anybody's patch but you might want
        to do it tomorrow. Bea= Beatrix Potter's diary is going on sale
        at Phillips in London tomorrow and apparently we talked about
        this last week it tells of her unhappy life in the Lake District.
        Which is a complete, everybody thought.
<S 02>: Oh I thought she was happy as a sandboy.
<S 04>: All the bleeding tourists going round her house she didn't like.
[laughter]
<S 01>: Yeah.
<S 02>: No it's not her unhappy life in the Lake District.
<S 05>: It's all them mice wasn't it. [laughs]
<S 02>: It was her happy life in London cos she lived in Kensington
        didn't she?
<S 01>: Oh is it.
<S 02>: Yeah. She lived in Kensington and that was how she spent her
        childhood. Trapped by the city and+
<S 01>: Oh that's+
<S 02>: +retreated into a+
<S 01>: +that's boring isn't it.
<S 02>: +pet pet
<S 04>: No it's not such a good story+
<S 01>: Yeah.
<S 04>: +now is it.
<S 01>: No. [laughs]
<S 03>: Oh well. I'm not gonna bother with that.
<S 01>: [laughs]
<S 02>: Sorry. I mean I di=
<S 05>: Who did that?
<S 02>: I was reading a piece. Erm
<S 05>: That's good.
<S 02>: Beatrix Potter did that. [laughs]
<S 01>: Right.
[laughter]
<S 04>: Erm.
<S 01>: What's this Mafeking relieved? Erm.
[laughter]
<S 01>: Erm+
<S 03>: [unintelligible]
<S 01>: +Earl of Derby officially opening Liverpool airport's upgraded
        passenger facilities.
<S 03>: Ooh yeah. We'll have that one.

<*S 01*>: Erm tomorrow evening apparently. Half past six. If these prospects are for the right day.

<*S 02*>: Never heard of this guy. The Earl of Derby.

<*S 03*>: Derbyshire versus [unintelligible].

<*S 05*>: Earl of Derby.

<*S 04*>: You've never heard of the Earl of Derby?

<*S 02*>: No. Never fe=, I wouldn't know him if I fell over him.

<*S 01*>: Erm+

<*S 05*>: Drunk as a lord.

<*S 02*>: [laughs]

<*S 01*>: +and that is about, Oh erm Jason this might erm be interesting for you. Tomorrow eleven p.m. tomorrow is the deadline for an unclaimed lottery p= prize of nearly a hundred and ten thousand pounds. And they reckon the ticket was bought in Wirral.

<*S 03*>: Really.

<*S 02*>: Oh.

<*S 03*>: Oh it was me.

In the radio journalists' discourse a mutuality is achieved not dissimilar to that in the lifeguards' talk above. Even though the discourse is multiparty rather than two-party, there is clear evidence that information is provided in a listener-sensitive way and that efforts are made to achieve shared knowledge, to align perspectives and to establish agreement on the preferred action for the group as they decide on which stories are to run later that day. Footing shifts are evident again (e.g. . . ., *oh, . . ., what's this . . .?*), suggesting participants' sensitivity to the conversational frame. Overall, though, in this example mutuality is less collectively achieved than pre-established. There is less effort invested in aligning attitudes or in reinforcing points of view. Indeed, in this extract there is an altogether greater sense of ritual, resulting in part from the generic stability of such (presumably daily) professional meetings. The familiarity of the genre matches the familiarity of the participants with one another and with their own roles. An ambience is thus created in which roles can be more overtly performed. Creativity is relatively dense in this extract. It is co-produced but there is an altogether less marked sense of it emerging steadily and organically from the relationships between the participants in a particular encounter.

The differences between the two genres in the two examples may be important. The lifeguards' talk is predominantly professional collaborative idea (with 'socialising' tendencies); the journalists' talk is predominantly professional collaborative task (with 'socialising' and 'collaborative ideas' tendencies). The task-directed nature of their activity influences the contours of their talk; there is greater emphasis on transactional content and less emphasis on interpersonal relations. And the work-related setting is also a factor in inhibiting too overt a creative co-production of mutuality. Although acknowledgements (*yeah*), laughter and backchannelling are present, such features are generally less active. Creative uses of language include:

- Irony. For example, in reply to an earlier question concerning the visit of the Housing Minister, one of the journalists replies humorously *I just dropped him off. That was w= why I was late.* A question concerning the winning of a large lottery prize elicits another playful piece of fiction from another of the team: *It was me.* There are ironic functions here in the mock 'withholding' of news in a 'newsroom'.
- Imaginative play with shared knowledge. This results in a creation of impossible, fictional worlds. For example, in the case of the discussion of the (now dead) British writer of fiction for children Beatrix Potter, one of the journalists imaginatively projects a situation in which tourists visit the writer's house even though it is known that the house was not established as a tourist attraction until after her death. *All those bleeding tourists going round her house she didn't like.* A similarly creative play with intertextual reference makes real and embeds in the current discourse the fictional mice which inhabit Beatrix Potter's stories (*It was all them mice wasn't it.*) The fictional mice are assumed to be real mice which make her life in her house in London unhappy.
- Mock interest or mock excitement: *Phew!*
- Puns and wordplay. For example, with reference to the Earl of Derby as a possible source for a story, one of the speakers quips *I wouldn't know him if I fell over him* which elicits a punning play with the institutionalised simile *Drunk as a Lord.*
- Mutual co-construction as speakers pattern and echo across turn boundaries: the reference to the *Earl of Derby* <S 04> is taken up by <S 02> *I wouldn't know him if I fell over him* which is in turn developed by <S 05> *Drunk as a Lord.* There is no sense here of creativity as simply an individual entity.
- Repetition and other kinds of pattern forming.

The journalists' discourse includes more banter and wordplay as a creative complement to the tasks in hand, serving almost as an element which undercuts the seriousness of the tasks discussed in the meeting. Overall, the creativity is directed more towards a topic or topics. It is more ideational and presentational (see chapter 2) than affective or interpersonal; it is more concerned to play with ideas rather than feelings or attitudes, though never, of course, exclusively. The creativity is co-produced but altogether more staged. The speakers achieve shared values and degrees of interpersonality but the discourse is constructed through individual performances, more overt display of the self (the *dramatis personae* in the humorous episodes projected in the last seven lines of the extract are the two speakers themselves) and the formation of individual and group identities. The journalists' use of the first person reference is not just a normal use of a personal pronoun but, in positioning themselves within the humorous episodes, may be seen as an example of what Harré (1988: 166), arguing the constructionist view, refers to as using pronouns to 'locate acts of speaking at locations in a social world'.

Different types of interaction and context are thus helpful in accounting for the varied and complex ways in which creativity is achieved and in identifying grounds and motivations for creativity. However, although creativity is pervasive in relation to a range of spoken discourses, there is none the less a danger that creative language use might be thought equally to impregnate all the above cells in the CANCODE generic framework. In fact, as we have begun to argue, no cell in the matrix can be excluded but tendencies are stronger in some contexts and in some types of interaction than others.

Further classifying and contextualising the data: credit security controllers, flatmates, student couple and teachers

I used to think I was a pair of curtains and then I pulled myself together.

Example 5.3 Credit security controllers

It is not possible to cite the full version of the following extract because it runs to several minutes of recording. Although some very minimal repetitions occur during this time, the transcript reveals no examples of creative language in over ten minutes of exchanges. The generic context is that of 'professional/transactional information provision' and the extract here occurs when the meeting is coming to a close.

[The primary purpose of the meeting is an examination of the legal particulars of documents relating to credit security. The participants are: <S 01> field officer: male (30s); <S 02> field officer: male (40); <S 03> manager: male (55).]

<S 03>: But the release now of savings is going to be an issue all right isn't it?

<S 02>: Yeah.

<S 01>: Yes.

<S 02>: How is it approved? And can the board delegate that authority to somebody? To to release erm can, yeah that's right. Can the board delegate it?

<S 03>: Well I [unintelligible] Well my reading of that would say that that is quite specific.

<S 02>: Yeah.

<S 03>: You don't know whether there's provision for the appointment of loans officers and credit officers and all this kind of.

<S 02>: Mm.

<S 03>: I wouldn't. There doesn't seem to be anything there except to say that the board must approve this.

<S 02>: But but in accordance with the registered rules.

<S 03>: [unintelligible]

<S 02>: That's the only pos=, so it's, the question is thirty two three B. What's the inter=, can that, can the board delegate its authority under that section Sean?

<*S 01*>: Yeah.
<*S 02*>: Thirty two three B.
<*S 03*>: Or I wonder is that a limit according to the registered rules. Monitoring of it.
<*S 01*>: [unintelligible]
<*S 03*>: [whistles]
<*S 02*>: I know.
<*S 01*>: I used to [unintelligible].
<*S 03*>: [unintelligible]
[laughter]
<*S 01*>: I used to think I was a pair of curtains but then I pulled myself together.
[laughter]
<*S 01*>: I used to think I was being ignored but nobody still talks to me.
<*S 02*>: [laughs]
<*S 01*>: Cowardly [unintelligible] this morning. What was in the tea? It's that s=, it's that bloody foreign coffee [laughs] that's what it is.
<*S 03*>: Foreign coffee?
<*S 01*>: That's that foreign coffee [unintelligible].

After such a long period of time in which documents are pored over and during which time the main purpose of the exchanges has been to transmit or obtain information, the speakers take a holiday from information transfer and manage conversational turns in order to joke and banter their way through to the end of the formal proceedings of the meeting (note the whistle, which suggests a different conversational frame has been or is being established). The business done, it seems, they are free to play with words and the labels for what is in their immediate environment. The context and interaction type have restricted opportunities for such engagements. An increase in creativity coincides for all the speakers with points of release from institutional identities in which information transfer is the main requisite. In short, they creatively recast themselves through the shift in topic and conversational frame.

Example 5.4 Flatmates

The next example involves a group of friends discussing their flat and partners. The genre here is 'intimate collaborative idea'.

[<S 01> secretary: female (31); <S 02> scientist: female (31); <S 03> unemployed: female (28); <S 04> production chemist: male (29). Speakers 03 and 04 are partners.]

<*S 03*>: I mean there's not room enough for two people in my kitchen. You're still brushing up against each other all the time. It's quite stressful when you're cooking.
[unintelligible]

<S 01>:   [unintelligible] making square pastry or something like that.
<S 03>:   [unintelligible] knock through into that shed. But it's still, I
          th=, I still think it's a good idea it's too much like hard work.
<S 02>:   Mm.
<S 03>:   I could just see if we're gonna do a great big massive thing like
          that it'll be years before we get any semblance of any decent
          kitchen.
<S 04>:   he thing to do is, when you g=, when you start making money
          is pay someone to do it.
<S 03>:   Yeah.
<S 01>:   Some things I think I definitely worth paying someone to do.
<S 03>:   Abso-bloody-lutely.
[unintelligible]
<S 01>:   [unintelligible] house-keeper.
[laughter]
[unintelligible]
<S 04>:   Yeah.
<S 03>:   Bloody too right.
<S 02>:   I would as well.
<S 01>:   That's the first I'd get.
[laughter]
<S 02>:   Me too. I would. Especially if I lived with Tom.
<S 03>:   He's not untidy is he?
<S 02>:   Oh God. He lives in total chaos.
<S 03>:   Well I do really.
<S 02>:   I've been on a campaign to sort him out.

In this example language choices are made to underscore more critical and
divergent-adversarial attitudes and the absence of repetition appears to reinforce this. The extract also involves a cluster of specific figures of speech (a
term, ironically, only rarely analysed with reference to speech), for example,
metaphor, idioms, slang and hyperbole all cluster within a relatively short
stretch. Metaphorical expressions such as the reference to being on a 'campaign' to sort out a boyfriend or 'brushing up' against somebody in a small
kitchen coexist with hyperbolic expressions (*in total chaos; great big massive thing;
it'll be years . . .*) and deliberately counterfactual statements (*there's not room
enough for two people in my kitchen*), wordplay by infixing (*abso-bloody-lutely*, which
also suggests a footing shift to a less serious mode of evaluation), deliberate
underplaying by simile (*it's too much like hard work*). The analysis here further
underlines how creative language is often related to the expression of emotion
and affect. But it also exposes the extent to which language analysis, founded in
the past century mainly on ideational, truth-conditional and decontextualised
referential approaches, needs to take fuller account of the relationship between
creativity and densities of emotion and identity-display.

A corpus always has limits

Scaredy cat, scaredy cat, don't know what you're playing at!!

In the last extract the language certainly serves a more creative-critical function in which creative choices are made mainly for affectively divergent purposes. But even here the two speakers seem largely to concur, and in CANCODE data generally there are few examples of overtly 'critical' creativity, involving people breaking generic boundaries or resisting norms in order to express rebellion, to underline a negative stance or to conflict with what is expected. Such elements form an important component of creativity but in this corpus creative language use is mainly for convergent purposes. Such data are, however, in evidence in other corpora and this feature is examined in the next chapter (see especially pp. 173 ff. below, as well as the section on humour in the workplace, pp. 163–4 below). It is important to continue to recognise the limitations inherent in any corpus and to seek ways of constructively augmenting that corpus by constantly re-evaluating its limits and limitations. It is one reason why, even on the basis of a representative 5-million word corpus, it is inadvisable to move too seamlessly to too generalised a set of claims about the nature of language or about the nature of creativity. (See also Appendix 1 for further discussion of issues of corpus analysis.)

Example 5.5 Student couple

The social and interactive context of the following exchange is less hierarchical and much less obviously concerned with the transfer and retrieval of information. The speakers are partners who are clearly very familiar with each other and who partake in a more symmetrical relationship. The speech genre is closest to that of 'intimate collaborative idea'.

[The couple in this extract reminisce about the time when they first met. The conversation starts off with a narrative by speaker <S 01> who talks about his drinking habits and this later develops into gossip about an acquaintance. <S 01> student: male (26); <S 02> student: female (22). The genre is 'socialising collaborative ideas'.]

> <S 01>: I'd wake up like in the middle of the night er er anything
>   disturbed me and I wake up feeling shit. I wouldn't be ill or
>   anything I'd just feel Oh God.
> <S 02>: Yeah.
> <S 01>: I'd fall back to sleep and then+
> <S 02>: [laughs]
> <S 01>: +maybe er I'll have shivers for about an hour.
> <S 02>: Oh God.
> <S 01>: Go back to sleep.
> <S 02>: You're a right alcoholic.
> <S 01>: And wake up fine. I know. [inaudible]

\<S 02\>: Just think that's what that's what you could be now.

\<S 01\>: I know. I could be eighteen stone.

\<S 02\>: Could have been Adam Potter with a massive pot pregnant belly.

\<S 01\>: I know. [tuts]

\<S 02\>: With heart disease and all+

\<S 01\>: I know.

\<S 02\>: +sorts of horrible liver conditions.

\<S 01\>: So easy to fall into though. I mean you like [inaudible] at dinner time and Kevin gets tanked up.

\<S 02\>: I know.

\<S 01\>: Then goes to work. But he don't get drunk you know he just gets tanked up.

\<S 02\>: But he drives as well.

\<S 01\>: I know. I thought he did.

\<S 02\>: Aye. You know and they're

\<S 01\>: I've not seen them for about a year now.

\<S 02\>: They're both still at home living with their mum aren't they.

\<S 01\>: I know. Bit weird family though aren't they.

\<S 02\>: Very. Very strange.

\<S 01\>: Strange old world.

\<S 02\>: I know. It's like I see his mum and dad up the street and I'm sure they must recognise me I've been there often enough and they+

\<S 01\>: Oh yeah.

\<S 02\>: +never speak.

\<S 01\>: I know. Mm. Odd. A strange family.

\<S 02\>: You know I'm like somebody to say hello to anybody who I vaguely know you know.

\<S 01\>: E=even if you do.

\<S 02\>: I even say hello to people I don't know. [laughs]

\<S 01\>: Even if you just say hello to them though they're like weird with it aren't they.

\<S 02\>: Yeah.

\<S 01\>: He's completely off his trolley.

\<S 02\>: Yeah. He's a bit barking i'n't he.

\<S 01\>: And she she's friendly enough. But she's

\<S 02\>: But I don't know when I go to their house I always feel like she doesn't want you there. That she's fed up of visitors and Can't you bog off or something.

\<S 01\>: Well they do have like twenty visitors a day don't they.

\<S 02\>: Oh. Yeah I think I'd been annoyed. And Dave just sits up there waiting for people to call doesn't he.

\<S 01\>: Yeah.

\<S 02\>: Don't think he moves from that room. Oh well.

\<S 01\>: [inaudible]

\<S 02\>: He's off our Christmas card list anyway.

In this extract the two speakers adopt a range of creative strategies. They engage in playful insults which are direct but clearly to be interpreted indirectly as banter; they deploy hyperbolic expressions (*with a massive pot pregnant belly; don't think he moves from that room; they do have like twenty visitors a day*); there is a liberal use of metaphoric and fixed expressions, some creatively extended (*he's completely off his trolley*), some deliberately ellipted (*he's a bit barking* (mad)); and there is a creative play with cultural allusions (*he's off our Christmas card list anyway*). Also noticeable is a particular strategy of 're-voicing' by creatively projecting other speakers' words for humorous effect (e.g. *that she's fed up of visitors and can't you bog off or something*). Such a strategy involves grammatical and discourse patterns more than it does specifically lexical or figure-of-speech patterns. It serves, however, to contribute to the marked density of creative formulation in the extract.

Example 5.6 Teachers

[Two primary school teachers are discussing arrangements for changing classes. <S 01> is female (30) and <S 02> is female (34). They are meeting to check on the availability of a room in order to accommodate a change of class. The genre is primarily 'professional collaborative ideas'.]

> <S 01>: So if Monday was clear which we need to check with+
> <S 02>: I teach Lenton on Monday
> <S 01>: Right.
> <S 02>: If they're not going on a trip or anything like that.
> <S 01>: Well they won't go on a trip for sure.
> <S 02>: So they should be here.
> <S 01>: So it could be Monday if the test's on Tuesday. Right.
> <S 02>: And that wouldn't upset any apple carts would it? No?
> <S 01>: I wish it did. I've got one or two bad apples in my class too.
> [both laugh]

These data illustrate the greater risks which attach to pattern re-forming choices as speaker <S 02> introduces an idiom (*upset any apple carts*) with which it is enquired whether any inconvenience or trouble would be caused by the suggested arrangement. The idiom is then transmuted by speaker <S 01> with reference to the idiomatic metaphor of bad apples, meaning that in any collection of things there can be one or two examples which do not fit in. The phrases of both speakers, but especially the response of <S 01>, risk being seen as inappropriately inventive, affective and lightening the tone amid the information transfer, though the informality and social symmetry of the context reduces attendant risks. However, alongside such pattern re-forming runs an extensive set of pattern forming echoes and repetitions which on another level create a mutuality and commonality conducive to the verbal play with the idioms. This is the case even though the main context for the relationship here is 'professional' and thus to some degree always more formal rather than more informal, especially when the teachers are making arrangements for the children in their charge.

Gender, humour and the workplace

To Love, Honour and OK!
> (*The Sun* newspaper, February 2003: a headline describing the
> purchase of rights to a celebrity wedding by *OK!* magazine)

The CANCODE corpus is generally lacking in examples of language used in the workplace and in the context of business organisations.[2] The following data do not belong within the CANCODE corpus but are used here because they provide, at an appropriate juncture in this chapter, an example of a genre of professional-collaborative task. The data were obtained as a result of research into the language of small business organisations (Mullany, 2003). The company is especially interesting because both men and women are involved in managing it, from managing director to middle-management levels. Particularly striking in the data is a frequent use of humour in the workplace context, a strategy which in this data is more commonly employed by female than male speakers and which bears out research first undertaken by Holmes and Marra (2002).

We have seen this kind of practice in the more media-based examples above (radio journalists) and at the closure of a meeting (credit controllers), where joking, banter and humour appear to be used mainly to reinforce collaborative working, to control turn taking or to negotiate or display identities. As noted above, it is always important to keep scrutinising data which are not in a corpus as well as data which are in the corpus. For example, it was noted that much of the CANCODE data shows language used widely for purposes of mutuality and solidarity. The data collected by Mullany illustrate workplace uses of humour which are more adversarial, showing contest as well as collaboration.

Example 5.7 Company meeting

[A mixed group of men and women managers have been discussing the poor performance of the company in selling a new product. <S 01> (female) and <S 02> (female) are equals in the institutional hierarchy. Michael (absent) (male) is <S 01>'s boss. Rosie (absent) is <S 02>'s boss. <S 03> (female), and <S 04> (male) are also present at the meeting which is chaired by <S 05> (male). All the speakers are in their thirties.]

<S 02>: It's just absolutely ridiculous . . . it makes me very sad.
<S 01>: We've just got to hope that now Michael is on board that somebody looking at sales and distribution.
<S 04>: Mm.
<S 01>: that you can look at the two together cos before you know well Rosie did distribution didn't she. Is that the +
<S 02>: yeah but
<S 01>: +hold up side?

<*S 02*>:   You really have come as him haven't you?

<*S 01*>:   Sorry?

<*S 02*>:   You really have come as Michael, haven't you?

<*S 03*>:   [laughs]

<*S 04*>:   [laughs]

<*S 05*>:   But here we are again but here we are again at yet another meeting talking about it yet again and yet again coming to no conclusion . . .

Humour is used here by <S 02> to challenge particular practices and the role of people higher in the company. It works by allowing a potentially literal statement to be made by non-literal means. It is an act of indirectness, as potentially serious underlying criticism is not explicit and can be denied (<S 02> can simply say that she was 'only joking'). But it is an effective creative strategy in that interactional goals are achieved, both tactically and tactfully. To a degree, too, the authority of the 'male' chair is also indirectly challenged in this episode.

Although a preliminary observation only, in CANCODE and related data, pattern forming seems to be more common in female talk than in male talk. (In constructing and co-constructing gender positions men seem to prefer to 'display' rehearsed joke telling and often rather stagey sexual puns and banter.) In fact, when compared with women, men are less spontaneously creative in talk, although women do very successfully manage sexual banter, especially in all-female company (see Eggins and Slade, 1997). This is an area in need of more extensive research in the workplace, where traditionally women are not seen to be openly contestive, adversarial or pattern re-forming in language use or to use humour strategically. It is also important to extend such research to a wider range of contexts involving both male–female as well as single-gender interactions.

Creativity clines: mapping language and social context

The examples analysed above illustrate points on a creativity cline or continuum and how those points along the clines are organically related to particular social contexts and relationships. The most creative language features, this research suggests, cluster reciprocally and interactively and are salient at both topic- and transaction-boundaries and in the interpersonal management of discourse evidenced in footing shifts, etc. As indicated in chapter 3, there are two main levels of 'creative' interactions. First, *pattern re-forming* features: more overt, presentational uses of figures of speech, open displays of metaphoric invention, punning, uses of idioms and departures from expected idiomatic formulations. Second, *pattern forming* features: less overt, maybe even subconscious and subliminal repetition; parallelisms, echoes and related matchings which regularly result in expressions of affective convergence, in implicit signals of intimacy and symmetries of feeling. But linguistic creativity is less likely to occur in those contexts which involve a one-way process of information provision or in those

Table 5.2 Mapping creativity and social interactional context.

Context type		Interaction type	
	Information provision	*Collaborative task*	*Collaborative idea*
Transactional	commentary by museum guide	choosing and buying a television	chatting with hairdresser
Professional	oral report at group meeting	colleagues window dressing	planning meeting at place of work
Socialising	telling jokes to friends	friends cooking together	reminiscing with friends
Intimate	partner relating the story of a film seen	couple decorating a room	siblings discussing their childhood

Key: light shading = less prone to creativity; dark shading = more prone to creativity.

of professional interaction in which the main purpose is transactional and where relations between participants in a particular context may be more asymmetrical. The more intimate the discourse and the more participants are involved in sharing experiences and ideas (collaborative ideas discourses, in particular), the more relationships are socially symmetrical, the more they may feel prompted to wordplay and creative invention.[3]

Table 5.2 attempts a provisional mapping of the CANCODE categories of speech genres with the kinds of evidence of creativity found in the different speech genres in the corpus. There is shading across all categories because creativity is possible within all genres. But the darker the shading the more such contexts are likely to be prone to creative language use. The categories are not wholly water-tight, of course. For example, there is much creativity in the more formal, 'professional task' encounter of the radio journalists above (which in any case contains an embedding of more 'socialising' and 'collaborative ideas' contexts). Although it would capture better the reality of creative language use in the data, the shading does not allow for different tendencies and possibilities within and across the cells; the shading is, however, true to the clinal and probabilistic nature of such uses of language.

As such data continue to be investigated, it also has to be acknowledged again that the data are interpreted from the point of view of an outsider, with the analyst ascribing to participants particular intentions, assigning to stretches of language particular functions, and framing accounts of effects and of emotional contours which may not accord with the value systems or observations of participants. None the less, though subject to ongoing evaluation, the categories do show different varieties and clines of creative talk within a broader semiotic of spoken discourse and do allow tendencies to be discerned.

The creativity continuum: conclusions

In previous chapters (see pp. 64 ff.) and previously in this chapter (p. 148) the scalar and probabilistic nature of creativity has been illustrated and underlined. And in both chapter 4 and the current chapter, different clines of affect (intimacy, evaluation and intensity), as manifested in lexical, grammatical and discoursal choices, have been shown to be closely related to instances of creativity and to pattern forming and pattern re-forming tendencies in particular. At several points in this book, most notably pp. 110 ff., creativity in language use has also been shown to be closely related to social context or 'context type' and to be manifest in certain contexts of interpersonal interaction or interaction types than others. This concluding section explores this notion further, with some additional scrutiny of data and another attempt to diagrammatise the probabalistic character of the relationship between creativity and social context.

The very probabilistic nature of the mapping of creativity onto social context means that the tendencies are not easy to capture diagrammatically and do not appear to allow for exceptions. This is not to say, of course, that a museum guide does not invest creatively in ensuring that a flow of information or a set of responses to questions is interactionally appropriate. It is also easy to imagine an encounter with a hairdresser which was replete with wordplay; or a collaborative task with an intimate or member of the family which was punctuated by silence or by only the most transactional of exchanges; or the relating of the content of a film which seemed more appropriate for a transactional rather than intimate context type and where in all three cases there did not seem to be any extra motivation for the break with expectations. And it should not be forgotten that deviations from expected contextual frames can be a schema-refreshing source of creativity.

Of course, the nature of the interaction and of the relationship constructed through that interaction is crucial. So creativity is likely to occur even in contexts of information provision if the social context has a relatively informal character; and by analogy, the fairly formal settings of discussion with a hairdresser which can involve the execution of instructions, or a service encounter in which goods are bought, are less likely to provide any sustained stimulus to creative uses of language. The example of collaborating to complete tasks would seem to engender a setting of mutuality and a shared context of partnership; but here the context and the nature of the relationship is a determining factor. For example, colleagues working together window-dressing in a department store would be more task-orientated, while partners decorating a room together may find that the intimacy of the relationship lightens the task to the point where the discourse became more densely populated with wordplay and creative uses of language.

Conclusions

If you don't strive, they won't thrive.
(SBC Radio, Singapore, horticultural discussion, May 2002)

• Creative language use or 'creativities' cannot be captured and described or evaluated wholly by formalistic definitions. Creative functions can vary according to speakers' evolving relationships, the nature of external task demands and the changing character of social contexts and speech genres.
• Creativity is probabilistic. Creative language use is more likely to occur in some contexts and in some kinds of interpersonal contact rather than in others. It can be defined with reference to an account of forms and functions but its purposes and uptake will depend on a dynamic of locally negotiated processes and specific instances. Such processes can be seen from the outside but its meanings can only be speculated upon, as it is the speakers and users in their contexts who produce or respond accordingly. In this sense, creativity is, paradoxically, a 'definitely' emergent, instantial category of language.
• Recognising creativity in context is valuable. But there are many factors which constitute a context, and different contextual frames can operate within a single 'context'. For example, humour can be a significant strategic feature which crosses categorial boundaries.
• Creativity seems to be best captured and discussed with reference to clines and continua, with due recognition that there are many points of overlap.

In the next chapter, the argument and data move, metaphorically and literally, forward and beyond: forward to a consideration of a wider range of social discourse, including a particular focus on professional and institutional encounters; and beyond to sets of data which encompass social contexts and practices which extend those collected as part of the CANCODE project. Among the discourses explored are those of computer-mediated communication, professional discourses such as law, psychiatry and medicine, and discourses of adolescents from different cultural and linguistic backgrounds. There is also an examination of the creative uses of English by non-native but expert users of the language. And there is consideration of some political and ideological bases to creative language use.

Chapters 5 and 6 belong together in their concern with social and cultural contexts. In chapter 6, however, there is also a re-evaluation of patterns of language use beyond the more immediately recognisable and common encounters of informal everyday talk. The creative use of language in chapter 6 is more generally uncommon, but is common to particular social practices and includes contexts in which the self is dramatised, fictionally constructed, and in specific respects creatively contested. At the end of this chapter the matrix presented at the end of chapter 5 (Table 5.1), in which creativity is mapped in relation to social contexts, is revisited and reworked and a more inclusive, dynamic and process-based paradigm proposed.

Notes

1   As indicated in Chapter 3, CANCODE stands for 'Cambridge and Nottingham Corpus of Discourse in English'. The corpus was developed at the University of Nottingham, UK, between 1994 and 2001, and was funded by Cambridge University Press ©, with whom sole copyright resides. The corpus conversations were recorded in a wide variety of mostly informal settings across the islands of Britain and Ireland, then transcribed and stored in computer-readable form. The corpus is designed with a particular aim of relating grammatical and lexical choice to variation in discourse context and is used in conjunction with a range of lexicographic, grammar and vocabulary teaching projects (Carter and McCarthy, 1995a; Carter *et al.* 2000). In spite of trends to ever larger, multimillion-word corpora and associated quantitative analysis, in the case of CANCODE the main global aim has been to construct a corpus which is contextually and interactively differentiated and which can allow more qualitative investigation. The data have been especially carefully collected with reference to a range of different speech genres and social contexts. In all cases, to safeguard against possible misinterpretation by the analyst, information on speaker relationships is provided in the majority of cases by the person contributing the data to the corpus. An assessment of speakers' own goals remains central to the analysis.

2   The situation is changing and in 2003 an extension to the CANCODE corpus was commissioned by Cambridge University Press. The CANBEC corpus (Cambridge and Nottingham Corpus of Business English Communication) was established, and at the time of writing was scheduled to complete initial data collection in 2004. Recordings have been made in a variety of companies, ranging from multinational financial institutions to self-employed accountants, to medium-sized IT companies, to car manufacturers. Types of recordings include informal meetings between managers, presentations to peers, formal meetings with clients, associates chatting about mutual concerns in the pub and manager/subordinate communication. The corpus will contain one million words of spoken business English. Research on creativity will also form a part of the analysis of this corpus.

3   Appendix 2 takes a number of points raised in this chapter and explores them further, with particular reference to the creative extension of the morphemes *-y* and *-ish*.

Exploring further

Several studies include analyses of talk in different settings and speech genres. See Drew and Heritage (1992), Tannen (1993) and Koester (2001) for illuminating studies of workplace talk; Hopper *et al.* (1981) offer a contrasting study of intimacy in talk; Hutchby (1999) writes on openings in radio talk shows; Ragan (2000) looks at contexts of health care discourse involving women; Drew and Chilton (2000) examine familiarity in telephone conversations. Lindenfeld (1990) studies discourse in markets. Spacks (1985) examines gossip. McCarthy (1998b) looks at linguistic resourcing in the CANCODE corpus in terms of 'the everyday conversation of everyday people'; Hopper (1992) provides a study of telephone conversations.

Shotter (1993) looks at the construction of everyday realities through conversation. Tracy and Coupland (1990) make a valuable contribution to the study of overlaps, multiple discourse goals and purposes in talk. Carter and McCarthy (1997a) research affective purposes in everyday talk.

For further exploration of the role of humour in the workplace and, more generally, of gender relations in the context of creative interactional strategies, see Coates (1989, 1996, 2000), Coates and Cameron (1989), Cox *et al.* (1990), Holmes (2000a and b) and Holmes and Marra (2002). Note also the role of creativity in the 'construction' of gender. See Benwell (2001) for discussions of language play in magazines for men and Bucholtz (2003) on gender and identity construction in conversational interactions of teenagers. Coates (2002) focuses on distinctive features of male–male talk. Norton (2001) offers a classic study of identity and gender with particular applications to the classroom and language teaching and learning.

The role of silence in conversation is a neglected aspect of conversational analysis and is generally underdescribed in this book. See Tannen (1990) and Jaworski (1993, 2000) for further analysis. For further discussion of the possibilities here, see chapter 6: epilogue.

6 Creativity, discourse and social practice

> We are thinking of the extraordinary creativity of the multitude of ways in which young people use, humanize, decorate and invest with meanings their common and immediate life space and social practices – personal styles and choice of clothes, selective and active use of music, TV, magazines, decoration of bedrooms; the rituals of romance and subcultural styles; the style, banter and drama of friendship groups, music-making and dance . . . There is work, even desperate work in their play.
>
> (Willis *et al.*, 1990: 1–2)

Introduction

We have seen from previous chapters that a range of insights into the nature of language and creativity can be generated by examining instances of language use in a corpus of everyday spoken discourse, and by close exploration of the contexts of interaction and speech genres in which creativity occurs. There are clear grounds for arguing that some contexts are more creativity-prone than others, that creativity is both a psychological and a sociocultural phenomenon, and that a range of different patterns of language, including parts of speech and related features of the grammar and vocabulary of English, play a key part in the establishment of creative effects. And the most basic observation is that creative language use is pervasive and ubiquitous in the CANCODE corpus of spoken discourse.

While the use of corpora allows a more thorough and systematic approach to evidence for demotic creativity and its functions, it is important not to forget that corpora provide no more than a snapshot of the language. Even multi-million word corpora, such as *The Bank of English* and *The British National Corpus*, now widely in use in the compilation of dictionaries and grammars, have their limitations and only give a picture of the language which the corpus sources provide. For example, although the situation has changed in recent years, early examples of corpora contained large bodies of newspaper data. Newspaper data are relatively easy to obtain and whole years' issues of some individual newspapers are now readily available on CD-Rom; but it skews the picture to argue that particular patterns of language are significant on account of frequency in such a corpus of newspaper language, for such a corpus becomes idealised and atypical of the language as a whole.

Extensive use of the CANCODE corpus for the purposes of this book has allowed examples to be drawn from many informal everyday interactions; but five million words, though large by the standards of many spoken corpora, does not by any means constitute a reliable data set for all the spoken English in currency. Its mainly British sources, if not handled sensitively, may also distort the evidence still further in favour of a particular geographical variety and its attendant cultures. The matrix used for the collection of the data has its limitations too, in that its composition reflects the primarily pedagogic purposes for which the corpus was constructed. For example, there are only limited examples of professional discourse or discourse involving other languages, or examples of the use of English by speakers whose first language is not English. In this chapter a wider range of data sources is consulted which goes beyond that collected as part of the CANCODE project. The matrix is also extended to include a wider sociolinguistic and sociocultural profile of use and users and a more dynamic account of social processes.

An extension of the range of sociocultural contexts simultaneously extends the range of purposes and goals for creativity. Previous chapters have underlined the ways in which, for example, creative language is used for ludic and aesthetic purposes, for purposes of relationship-building and for drawing attention, directly and indirectly, to key components of a message. The data examined in this chapter push our understanding of creativity beyond these boundaries. The framework used for the description of creativity is also reassessed in the light of these data. Frameworks are necessary heuristics by which initial hypotheses and understandings can be constructed and developed, but there is a danger that they may appear to make the object of investigation too pre-packaged. In this chapter the notions of pattern forming and pattern re-forming are also therefore subjected to further critical scrutiny.

In this chapter the more inclusive social and cultural focus allows further consideration of creativity as a social practice in relation to both individual and group identities. There is also a re-evaluation of patterns of language use beyond the more recognisable and commonly encountered contexts evoked in earlier chapters. As already indicated, the matrix presented at the end of chapter 5, in which creativity is mapped in relation to social contexts, is revisited and reworked with reference to the data expansion and development in the following pages and, accordingly, a relatively more inclusive and process-based paradigm proposed.

Interlingual creativity, crossings and identities

Because of the nature of the CANCODE corpus an impression may have been created in this book so far that there is a kind of linguistic purity to the language practices evidenced in our data, that creativity and language play reside within a single language, or that it can only be triggered in monolingual contexts. However, bilingual and multilingual communities have been especially rich in the production of creative artefacts, and there is some evidence to suggest that conditions of multilingualism and multiculturalism may favour creative production. In this section the data range is extended beyond the kinds of contexts preferred for the CANCODE project and a wider range of sociocultural processes and related sociolinguistic research explored.

For example, research by Rampton (1995) describes a phenomenon which he terms *crossing*: a feature of cross-lingual transfers and creative mixing of language codes which is distinctively oral rather than written in mode. The specific focus of language crossing in Rampton's studies is centred on multiracial urban adolescents in the South Midlands of Britain and concerns, as Rampton puts it, 'the use of Creole by adolescents of Asian and Anglo descent, the use of Panjabi by Anglos and Afro-Caribbeans and the use of stylised Indian English by all three' (Rampton, 1996: 89). Rampton's study is in a tradition of interactional sociolinguistics and is principally concerned to explore the relationship between language and social roles, with particular reference to race and ethnicity. However, the data also go a long way to illustrate the degree to which members of the groups studied engaged in crossing from one language to another and, most significantly, as part of day-to-day exchanges which are characterised by what is termed *liminality*. In Rampton's data, liminal exchanges take place in contexts which are socially fluid. They are fluid because normally ordered social life is loosened and normal social settings and interactions involving rules and purposes set by adults or by conventional social institutions do not apply.

Language crossing is therefore, according to Rampton, more likely to take place in settings in which young people come together without any overt goals. Typical contexts include: the playground; the school corridor; street corners; shopping malls; casual music sessions; anywhere groups casually assemble and communicative purposes are not pre-defined. Typical samples of data include contexts in which a 15-year-old Afro-Caribbean boy teases a classmate and a 15-year-old Asian girl is teased about her having an older boyfriend by using a stylised Asian English with marked Panjabi intonation in order to encourage her to engage in playful banter.

Most instances found by Rampton involve the use of Creole and of Creole crossing. In Rampton's data Creole is much more extensively integrated by all speakers into their own primary language codes, indicating the extent to which it is symbolic of all that is valued in the culture shared by the adolescents in the study. In the following example, two boys, one Anglo (Alan) and one Asian (Asif), both aged 15, are being held in detention at their school. The extract shows them speaking with an Anglo female teacher (Ms J) aged in her mid-twenties. She says why she is a little late for the supervision of the detention, explaining that she had to contact the headteacher and then further explaining why she now needs to go to fetch her lunch before the detention proper begins. The boys attempt to undermine her position and to criticise her by locking her into a sequence of question and answer. When she departs and the boys are left on their own, they mock her statements using a markedly Creole intonation, most obviously on the word 'lunch'.

Example 6.1

> *Ms J:* I had to go and see the headmaster.
> *Asif:* why?
> *Ms J* none of your business.
> *Alan:* a-about us?
> *Ms J:* no, I'll be back.
> *Asif:* hey how can you see the headmaster when he was in dinner?
> *Ms J:* that's precisely why I didn't see him.
> *Asif:* what?
> *Ms J:* I'll be back in a second with my lunch.
> *Asif:* NO, dat's sad man I'll be . . . I had to miss my play right I've gotta
>   go.
> *Alan:* with mine.
> *Asif:* LLunch . . . You don't need no . . .
> *Alan:* Llunch . . .
> *Asif:* Have you eat your lunch Alan?

These creative mixes indicate an underlying artistry in the appropriate handling of what are effectively two voices, a feature originally referred to by Bakhtin as *double-voicing*. However, the resulting hybrid discourse is not simply creative for its own sake. In many of Rampton's examples, this double-voicing is put to social use either for the purpose of criticism, for the kind of banter and verbal duelling which reinforces group values and affiliations, or simply in order to express identities and values which are separate from the dominant discourses and which could not be altogether articulated by a single voice. In many cases the choices are creative ones and the speakers learn to make them; the choices are, however, not merely aesthetic but are socially and culturally motivated (see also Bauman and Briggs, 1990, as well as discussion of Bakhtin and voicing in Chapter 2, p. 67). Notice, too, how the repetition of *lunch* here, normally seen as convergent pattern forming, functions for critical and adversarial purposes – another warning against seeing too narrow a link between forms and meanings.

Rampton (1995: 193) observes that 'language crossing was located in moments when the ordered flow of social life was loosened and normal social relations could not be taken for granted'. In other words, it is the existence of particular social processes that gives rise to particular language practices, and in this connection the conditions for liminality are especially indicative as potential sites for particular kinds of language use, including creative language use. Liminality is particularly significant in the case of adolescents. Indeed, the term is used in Turner's (1982) account to refer to initiation rites in agrarian societies and, most specifically, to a middle phase between childhood and adulthood in which there is a transition between one well-defined phase and another. Such phases of transition involve an inevitable adjustment and reworking of social, cultural and ethnic identities and take place against a background of fluid social roles and expectations. Such social spaces also entail experiments, as identities are conformed to or departed from, as positions are defended or dis-agreed with, and as new potential for identity marking is negotiated.

In a study of adolescents in Hong Kong (Candlin *et al.*, 2000) further evi-dence is found of a negotiation of discourse styles relative to the forging of identities. Although the community is largely homogenous with regard to language (they are Cantonese-speaking), examples of a range of different exper-iments with identity were located in the data collected. These experiments took the form of conformity and non-conformity with the adult world. In almost all instances the data collected are in liminal contexts when the adoles-cents are not in school or at home, when they are together with their peers and not engaged in serious activities designed and managed by adults.

In the following example two adolescent boys are working with a social worker while being observed by the research fieldworker. One of the boys (S 01) suggests that the fieldworker is sexually attracted to the social worker. When no response is forthcoming, the suggestion is pursued further, and then further corroborated by the second boy (S 03). The boys tease the fieldworker (S 02) through a series of sexual puns and innuendos, first saying that he is good at masturbating (lines 4 and 5) and that he wants a prostitute (line 7). (In colloquial Cantonese, playing a TV game is literally transliterated as 'hitting the machine' while masturbating is, literally 'hitting the airplane' — the simi-larity in meaning and sound accounting for the pun's dual meaning.) The continued teasing by reference to Kowloon Tong (a part of the city where there are numerous love hotels) further underscores the suggestion of illicit sexual relations.

Example 6.2

> <S 01>: Sir, very good at TV games, Sir, we will play TV games then.
> <S 02>: It's closed down.
> <S 01>: No.
> <S 03>: What? You did well in masturbating yesterday!
> <S 01>: You are very good at masturbating.
> <S 02>: How do you know?
> <S 01>: Of course, after you did that (laughing) I saw you are out from Kowloon Tong.
> <S 02>: I go there every day.
> <S 01>: No, there are 'Kowloon' two words, without that 'Tong' word.
> <S 02>: I work there.

The boys' creative language use here involves more pattern re-forming than pattern forming, with the reforming consolidating acts of divergence and dis-engagement. By saying something which it is forbidden to say in public, the boys are here testing how far they can go in the trespassing of social boundaries and exploring whether there will be any reaction. They do so by means of a wordplay which is used for social purposes. The creative facility which the ado-lescent boys exhibit is displayed not merely for its own sake but rather to assert and extend their own identities, to tease and criticise a representative of the 'authoritative' adult world, and to use these liminal social moments to try out or mark out a different social territory.

Code-mixing and online communication

The significance of the relationship between creative communication, language crossing and more intimate and fluid speech genres is further evidenced in a sub-corpus of emails and IRC (Internet Relay Chat) data collected in Notting-ham as a supplement to the CANCODE corpus. Several thousand emails and several hours of IRC data have been collected on a variety of topics in order to examine the continua between planned and unplanned discourse, the inter-penetration of spoken discourse features into written text, as well as the creativity manifest in these more informal, mixed-mode forms of communica-tion. The email data collected illustrate, in particular, the extent to which different languages can be creatively combined. The resulting hybrid is of course written rather than spoken, but, as in the manner of much email dis-course, is sufficiently informal, pervasive and everyday to count as 'demotic'.

In the following example of IRC transliterated Cantonese, text-messaging shorthand and standard English are used to mark out an interpersonal territory in which emotion and affect are expressed in a private discourse in which form and the meaning of form are overtly played with. The two writer/speakers, Viki and Sue, are girls and are both undergraduate students at the University of Nottingham, England. Viki is 21 years old; Sue is 22 years old.

Example 6.3

> *Viki:* it's snowing quite strong outside . . . be careful
> *Sue:* I will, thx
> *Viki:* wei wei . . . lei dim ar?
> *Sue:* ok, la, juz got bk from Amsterdam loh, how r u?
> *Viki:* ok la . . . I have 9 tmrw
> *Sue:* haha, I have 2–4 . . . soooooooooooo happy
> *Viki:* che . . . anyway . . . have your rash gone?
> *Sue:* yes, but I have scar oh . . . ho ugly ar!
> *Viki:* icic . . . ng gan yiu la . . . still a pretty girl, haha!!

[Cantonese translations: wei wei . . . lei dim ar — hi, how are you?; ng gan yiu la — it doesn't matter; ar, che, loh and la are discourse markers in Cantonese.]

Note here in particular the creative mixing of email/texting shorthand (*thx* = thanks), (*tmrow* = tomorrow), (*9, 2–4* = classes at 9 a.m. and 2–4 p.m.), (*icic* = I see, I see). There is also a creative play with voice and vocalisation (*soooooooooooo, haha*) and the constant inserting of interactive discourse markers from Cantonese.

In the following online exchange feelings and attitudes are more obviously in evidence as two girls, also both Nottingham university students from Hong Kong), discuss food, attitudes to university work and boy friends. Note in this exchange too that the greater nuancing of feeling results in the use of more 'emoticons', that is, graphic symbols such as smileys – :) and (: – alongside the usual linguistic and acronymic shorthand forms such as *u* (you) and *ic* (I see). Kerensa is 23 years old: Alice is 20 years old.

Example 6.4

> *Kerensa:* I'm full now.
> *Alice:* what did you have ar?
> *Kerensa:* some chicken ribs and rice.
> *Alice:* You ordered food from take away?
> *Kerensa:* yeah.
> *Alice:* I'm using the real icq ar . . .
> *Kerensa:* u bad person.
> *Alice:* mud yea ar!! what have you been doing tonight, apart from eating?
> *Kerensa:* copying 2 pages of notes
> *Alice:* :)
> *Kerensa:* (:
> *Alice:* why? Talking to your 'lo kung'?
> *Kerensa:* wai hahahah ng hai ar. He just went offline . . . he'll call later
>   gua. miss him so much . . . wanna mary him right no hehe
> *Alice:* hahaha ng gi chow la . . . ai
> *Kerensa:* hahaha yeah yeah

[Cantonese translations: mud yea ar? – what do you mean?; Lo kung – husband; ng gi chow – don't feel ashamed: ng hai ar – no, certainly not; gua, ar, wor, lei and la are discourse markers in Cantonese.]

Some may argue that such discourses underline the irreversible decline of standard English into a series of mutually unintelligible sub-languages; another way of seeing such exchanges is, however, to observe the richness and invention of which everyday users of English are capable and to praise the creative invention which results from the mixing. An even stronger interpretation would be to recognise the clear need the two girls have to appropriate a language which is not simply English but their own English and, for them, to develop a repertoire of mixed codes which enable them to give expression to their feelings of friendship, intimacy and involvement with each other's feelings and attitudes – a discourse which would not be to the same degree available to them through the medium of standard English. Here there is no overt expression of social critique as in the crossings into Creole made by many of the adolescent speakers captured by Rampton. But there is none the less an implicit recognition that standard English has no clear value for them for the purposes of daily intimate email exchange and accordingly new modes of speaking/writing are invented and developed. Both participants here creatively develop a discourse which is neither English nor Cantonese but is one which expresses for both a dual identity and a dual linguistic affinity (see also Fung, 2001).[1]

Discourse, social context and critique: a cautionary note

I have already commented above on problems of interpretation of this kind of data (see chapter 5, p. 148). But it must be underlined again here that I am interpreting data as an outsider, ascribing to participants particular intentions, assigning to stretches of language particular functions, and framing accounts of effects and of emotional contours which may not accord with the value systems of participants. The provisional nature of all interpretations of language use needs to be acknowledged. Researchers could seek to make contact with the participants of such exchanges themselves but even participants' own accounts of intentions and responses fall foul of a circular dialectic of relativity and the difficulties of interpreting intentions. Such points become especially acute when liminal social contexts and cross-lingual crossings are involved and the observer is even more markedly cast into an even more obviously outsider position. It is therefore accepted that categories of description and commentary here are provisional, that the analysis is necessarily largely qualitative, and that ethnographic participant-based analysis does not at this stage form part of the discussion of these contexts. These points have been very well put by Bauman and Briggs (1990: 68):

> The problem of false objectivity emerges from the positivistic character of most definitions of context. This equation of 'the context' with an 'objective' description of everything that surrounds a set of utterances has two important implications. First, since it is obviously impossible to point to all aspects of the context, the researcher becomes the judge of what merits inclusion. Second, positivistic definitions construe context as a set of discourse-external conditions that exist prior to and independently of the performance. This undermines the analyst's ability to discern how the participants themselves determine which aspects of the ongoing interaction are relevant. It also obscures the manner in which speech shapes the setting, often transforming social relations. Reifying 'the context' also implicitly preserves the premise that meaning essentially springs from context-free prepositional content which is then modified or clarified by 'the context'.

As we have seen in the previous chapters, especially in chapter 4, the fluid movement across styles and voices, the pushing out of resonant words and phrases, and the forging of associations with varying clines of intensity, formality and value also feature in the speech of monolinguals (and in that sense 'crossing' is a feature of language *per se*). What can, however, be concluded at this point is that, difficult though interpretations of meaning can be, there are interesting connections between creativity and liminality, that creativity and crossing can be linked with critical social purposes and particular discourse contexts, and that issues of identity play a significant part in the ways in which language can be creatively extended. Although there is a fascinating play with and across languages and cultures, the important point to underline is that the creativity in evidence is, not for the first time in this book, both ordinary and extraordinary.

Creativity and professional communication

In this section, there is also further consideration of social and cultural contexts which go beyond those considered within the framework of CANCODE data. In particular, there is particular reference to professional discourses and to creative problem-posing and problem-solving in professional encounters involving in particular professional/client interpersonal exchanges.

Much inspiration is taken here from several sources in the work of Candlin who, with his associates, has been instrumental in taking applied linguistic research into the domains of the workplace. Although there are valuable data in the CANCODE corpus involving professional context types, including pedagogic contexts, the extent of the data compiled by Candlin and others is unparalleled, involving both well-established genres such as those from law, psychiatry, communication disorder and healthcare delivery such as doctor and nurse/patient discourse but also less well-established ones from emergent social practices such as professional encounters in the fields of psychotherapy, workplace enterprise bargaining, family planning counselling, alternative dispute resolutions, work with aphasics and AIDS counselling. Such data allow important further insights into the relationship between language use, creativity and social practices, affording particular insights into discourses which are creatively constructed to meet new social and institutional demands.

A representative example of creativity at work in such contexts can be drawn from the following data of Garbutt (1996), in which a borderline personality disorder patient is engaged in a clinical consultation session with a psychiatrist.

Example 6.5

> *Patient:* I don't know, maybe it's sort of delusion, escape that I – y'know I just felt just this – it was just living and breathing was a little bit easier y'know, er,
> *Doctor:* mayb- living and breathing was easier.

The patient in this case, like many similar patients, finds great difficulty in isolating and giving expression to emotions. Accordingly, the discourse of such patients is often repetitive, with the same round of iterative statements recounting daily activities in a monotonous, prosodically flat voice seemingly disengaged from personal experience of the activities. In such instances the role of the psychiatrist is often to do no more than prompt further talk in a non-judgemental and non-directive way and to seek to create a convergent discourse in which there is emphasis on the relational and interpersonal nature of the discourse rather than on overtly transactional or ideational ways forward.

However, the extract also reveals a significant moment where the patient accounts for her situation by means of a less mundane, more metaphorical analogy and the psychiatrist does no more than repeat her utterance:

> *Patient:* it was just living and breathing was a little bit easier y'know, er,
> *Doctor:* mayb- living and breathing was easier

What appears on the surface to be no more than interpersonal talk or 'small talk' (Candlin, 2000; Coupland, 2000) is also strategically significant and marks out the creative competence of the psychiatrist, by simple but non-directive, pattern forming repetition of the patient's own discourse, in encouraging the patient to open up more. The patient refers to *escape* and to *breathing* (both words which can function literally and metaphorically), and this 'metaphorical' door in the discourse is also potentially an opening out for the patient into fuller contact with her own feelings. The creativity of the psychiatrist lies in recognising and reinforcing such an opening, in combining pattern forming and re-forming with language and content. In terms of treatment of a patient within such a clinical context the discourse is not simply one of locating and applying solutions but rather one in which a new discourse of patient-watchfulness is creatively patterned and then worked with, convergently and co-constructively.

Counselling and new discourses

A similar example is provided in Candlin (2000: xviii) by means of the following data drawn from recordings of interaction between a doctor and a patient with HIV/AIDS.

Example 6.6

> *Doctor:* I'll give you – this one here, Indinavir, is really easy to take. You take it before you eat.
> *Patient:* You reckon that's easy.
> *Doctor:* Right.
> *Patient:* Look at that, avoid food one hour before and two hours after taking it? Basically, if you were trying to do that, you'd never eat. I'd take it in the morning and then . . . two hours later I'd be able to have my breakfast?
> *Doctor:* That's right.
> *Patient:* It'd never work. Couldn't do it.
> *Doctor:* Couldn't do it. All right. OK.

In contrast to the more asymmetrical encounters familiar in most doctor–patient interactions, the doctor and patient are here working together in a kind of therapeutic alliance to solve the problems encountered by the patient. The doctor has no direct experience of the condition and has to co-construct solutions. This can often mean that the doctor does no more than echo the patient, providing support and a sense of alliance as they mutually explore and negotiate possibilities. The echoing and repetition by the doctor of the patient's words, which may on the surface appear to reflect a discourse which is going nowhere, are part of a process of problem-solving in which obtaining support for patient conformity to particular drugs regimes, in particular new regimes, is an important part of the process. Both doctor and patient are approaching the problem in a creatively co-constructed manner, with the doctor eager to assist in finding a way through, and in the process forming a new discourse in which interpersonal and negotiated chat forms an important component of the consultation. Such a newly created discourse – new because the territory of this kind of consultation and counselling is itself new territory, socially and culturally and historically – draws on pattern forming resources with which both participants are familiar from everyday talk. But these resources are creatively reformulated and 'transformed' here for new purposes and new institutional contexts (see also Candlin and Garbutt, 1996; Garbutt, 1996).

Such creatively evolving patterns are not always clearly homogenous, however. In a related data sample (Candlin *et al.*, 1998; Moore *et al.*, 2001) the discussion is between a female doctor and a female HIV patient and concerns antiretroviral treatment. The consultation involves a long and complex process during which the doctor takes the patient through several stages in a persuasive process, drawing on a range of significant medical evidence. The extent to which the doctor cites this authoritative evidence from the research literature and from her own participation in conferences is relatively risky in such a context, as it could be perceived by the patient to be no more than an exercise which simply invokes the doctor's medical knowledge and which fails to pay attention to the needs of the patient in an area where knowledge is frequently contested by patients themselves. The approach adopted by the doctor here is more distinctly directive and asymmetrical than non-directive and symmetrical. For example, there are a number of occasions in which she makes a direct appeal to outside authorities and is in a heavily persuasive mode.

Example 6.7

> *Doctor:* Yep. What appears to be true now, and there were a number of papers presented demonstrating what I'm saying to you, so this is not one per- this is all over the world people are coming out with information . . . The way it works is this. First of all . . . any- you should not be started on single treatment, that is bad medicine in 1996.
>
> *Patient:* Yeah . . .
>
> *Doctor:* You must be started on combination . . . and this is coming from a guy called John Sawyer, that they brought in from America to talk yesterday.
>
> *Patient:* Mm.
>
> *Doctor:* What he suggests is a good thing to do, is to start people on DOUBLE something . . .

At this point the patient who has followed the argument carefully intervenes more strongly:

> *Patient:* I just find it all so tedious. That is why I put it off as well as my lack of, y'know, beliefs.
> *Doctor:* Mm . . .
> *Patient:* Lack of belief, which is fair enough, but the rest of it's just like, I really don't know, and I just go AHHH (laughs), no, I can't keep up, I don't – I don't want to take any of this, it is BORING (laughs) . . .
> *Doctor:* There are two things that I think you have to think about. Okay? First thing is you actually have to get it into your head, that this makes YEARS of difference to your life.
> *Patient:* Mm-hmmm
> *Doctor:* Years of difference. Number two is, you've got to get serious about yourself. You tend to swan around. Y'know you tend to sort of just float around in your life.

Further discussion ensues, with the doctor recognising that the pills can cause initial discomfort but reinforcing the advantages of increased dosage and double combinations of pills, together with an argument that commitment and belief on the part of the patient can also be instrumental to an improved condition:

> *Doctor:* It really makes a difference.
> *Patient:* Okay.
> *Doctor:* Now if you like – you've already –I don't know whether you can or not this CIN3 –
> *Patient:* What you said before is – you were saying that I – I can get some potential back in my life as well.
> *Doctor:* That's right.
> *Patient:* You're not just saying that if I believe in this I can make myself well. You mean I can make myself well enough to . . . BELIEVE in something else, which is where my problem is.
> *Doctor:* That is. That is – that's-look, I – I have to tell you, I sat there listening to these guys and I – all I could think of was you. I had Joan Bradley in my brain.

The discourse here converges towards the end. Initially, this convergence is not as a result of any therapeutic alliance but rather as a result of a more directive and instrumentalist discursive practice on the part of the doctor. There is little creative pattern forming in the earlier phases. Each speaker adopts different verbal strategies and alignments, with only minimal verbal echoing of each other's position. The doctor departs from expectation by not taking the patient's own views into account and by appearing not to involve the patient. But in this final sequence the creativity of the exercise becomes more transparent as the patient is persuaded into an appraisal of her own condition and a better understanding and reassessment of her own values. The patient takes on the doctor's own projection of her condition and recycles the doctor's words, making them her own. There is thus both a convergence of values and a remarkable signal of the doctor's identification with her patient in her statement that *I had Joan Bradley in my brain.*

The creative discursive competence of the doctor here lies in an assessment which is different from the situation described in example 6.5 above. The doctor here judges that the patient needs persuasion, evidence and a direct appeal to a different cast of mind, a different attitude to her condition, *before* any convergence is possible. In other words, the mutuality of values expressed at the end has been worked for but is as creative an achievement as an approach which requires creative co-construction throughout. The shift in the doctor's discourse, from appeal to the evidence of the 'we' community of medical experts to the attested 'I' experience of identification with her patient (Joan Bradley), is essentially an act of creative problem-solving and as a result stands a good chance of ensuring both compliance with the medication on the part of the patient and a renewal of belief in her own potential.

The example reinforces the creative processes manifest in counselling at different levels, and shows how there is a deeper underlying insight in recognising that different creative processes are required in different situations and by different patient needs. Counsellor creativity within counselling is related not simply to the amount of information processed but also to how the information is processed and combined in novel yet effective ways. Creative therapists have well-differentiated road maps of the counselling process for different types of clients.

The example is, of course, to some degree different from a number of the exchanges examined in the previous two chapters in which there are more overt instances of wordplay and patterning, but it is creativity at work none the less, directed in particular at practical problem-solving procedures as part of an interpersonally sensitive professional practice.

Alternative dispute resolution: creativity and interdiscursivity

The creation of new discourses specific to new cultural contexts is also illustrated, Candlin and others argue, by the example of another professional discourse: alternative dispute resolution (Maley *et al.*, 1995; Candlin and Maley, 1997). The practice involves parties who are brought together so that they may avoid recourse to a court of law. The practice of dispute resolution out of court has become increasingly common. But it is a new situation, in which the previously more institutionally fixed roles of lawyer and client are subject to re-evaluation.

The new situation demands new modes of discourse to meet the tension produced by two alternative and to an extent competing discourses: that of the court of law and that of what might at times be more properly termed therapeutic counselling. Candlin and Maley illustrate how those involved professionally in alternative dispute resolution seek creatively to combine and fuse these two different discourse styles into a new schema-refreshing discourse to meet the requirements of a new social and institutional practice, in the process also creatively evidencing the emergence of new orders of discourse. At times the professional adjudicators will adopt the more confrontational and adversarial styles of a court of law; at other times they will adopt the more conciliatory and symmetrical styles of a counselling session.

The point to underline here is that there is a significant professionally based creativity involved in strategically blending the separate and in some respects oppositional discourses into a new practice. The term *interdiscursivity* captures a process in which a new discourse emerges to meet particular sociocultural goals and purposes; but the new hybrid discourse emerges by drawing, interdiscursively, on what already exists (adjudicatory and therapeutic discourses), further referring to, utilising and exploiting texts and discourses which are already socially and culturally in commerce. In the process, too, professionals create a new discourse identity to realise their new profession.

A post-modern 'critical' creative practice

There is a sense too in which, as a result of these studies, counselling can be seen as a distinctively post-modern social practice, in that conventional or previously understood authority structures do not obtain. In many of the instances discussed above, counselling takes place without any clear generic framework. Indeed, a kind of generic hybridity emerges in which there are constantly changing alignments in relationship and counselling practice. For example, in therapeutic counselling, the therapist often needs to follow the client's own discourse shifts, and in HIV/AIDS counselling the patient at times counsels the doctor as new treatment territories are occupied, abandoned and modified. In the case of HIV/AIDS counselling the absence of any clearly hierarchised role or authority or knowledge relationship means that often what Turner (see above) calls liminal social spaces are occupied, and it is within these spaces that some of the most creative counselling practices take place. The creative counsellor occupies these liminal spaces by realigning expectations and outcomes, by widening, narrowing, altering or completely replacing existing frames. Rather than provide solutions themselves, sometimes the counsellor has to prompt patients to draw inferences; sometimes the counsellor has to allow sequences of talk without any apparent connection because it is in such sequences that the most creative insights emerge; and sometimes the achievement of concord between therapist and patient – what was referred to above as a therapeutic alliance – is the most likely way in which understandings can be grounded.

In this respect, within the domains of counselling and professional advice-giving illustrated above, creativity is critical. This is not critical in the kinds of senses in which it occurs in some instances of language crossing or in using language for divergent, oppositional and non-consensual criticism of an existing order or practices. It is instead also *critical*, as Chris Candlin (personal communication) has pointed out, as a result of occurring at a 'critical' moment in a professional exchange when the resources of all involved are being critically tested. And it is also *critical* in a wider sense of being at a critical moment in a crucial site in the sociohistorical emergence, evolution and development of new social discourses. (See Candlin, 1987, for a core statement regarding criticality in applied linguistic research.)

Postgraduate supervisory session

The following sample from the pedagogic component of the CANCODE corpus is extracted from a supervisory session between a doctoral research student and her supervisor. Both work in a department of English literature in a UK university. The student has completed two years of study and is entering her third and (normally) final year. The discussion ranges over a number of academic issues to do with the organisation of the thesis, but the focus is on the relationship between the topic of the thesis and its critical apparatus. At this point in the deliberations, supervisor and student discuss the selection of an appropriate external examiner for the thesis. A final decision over such selection normally rests with the supervisor, or in some cases with a departmental committee. Students are normally brought into the discussion in a more informal way. It can be a time when the student is understandably apprehensive.

What is interesting in this extract is the equilibrium achieved by both parties in the process of problem-posing and decision-making. Clearly, the relationship between supervisor and student has been negotiated during the course of several previous meetings into one in which possibilities are jointly explored and decisions are made through a process of consensus. The symmetry between student and supervisor allows a potentially sensitive topic to be openly discussed without any appeal to authority structures. The situation created is relaxed and becomes increasingly characterised by jokes and humorous anecdotes. This is particularly apparent when a particular well-known academic author is suggested who is known to be no longer alive, and again on the part of the supervisor who recounts one of his own experiences when an assigned examiner died during the examining process. The increasing jokiness and banter coincide in part with the end of the session, after the main supervisory business has been done, but the interaction is none the less underscored by a mutuality which allows the research student an important degree of ownership of the decision-making process.

Example 6.8

> <S 01>: Well I've thought of Richard [inaudible] but he's not very well
>   disposed to critical theory [inaudible].
> <S 02>: Well that might be a bad idea then.
> <S 01>: Mm.
> <S 02>: But I thi= I'd still rather go for a [inaudible] than a critical
>   theorist I think.
> <S 01>: Yeah. Yeah.
> <S 02>: Because that's a sort of minefield the whole critical theory.

\<*S 01*>: Mm. [inaudible] John Searle? No. [laughs] No. I don't think so. Esling? [laughs]

\<*S 02*>: [inaudible] A wave. A wave [inaudible] you know. Esling would be wonderful, bring him back. All is forgiven.

\<*S 01*>: [laughs]

\<*S 02*>: Yes. Yes [inaudible] technically impossible to have an external examiner who was dead [inaudible] underground you can wheel them into your room.

\<*S 01*>: Mm. Mm.

\<*S 02*>: Their expenses would be sort of from the mortuary rather than from first class rail travel you know.

\<*S 01*>: [laughs] [inaudible] Yeah.

\<*S 02*>: Long as they were present+

\<*S 01*>: Put them out the back. [laughs]

\<*S 02*>: + they were present present in the room at the time you know. I've actually killed my external examiner [inaudible] writing. Well

\<*S 01*>: Did you?

\<*S 02*>: Mm. [inaudible] killed as he was em, he began reading and dropped dead.

\<*S 01*>: [laughs]

\<*S 02*>: I didn't know this and I had to find someone else.

\<*S 01*>: [laughs]

\<*S 02*>: So I am personally responsible for the death of one of the major scholars of my time.

\<*S 01*>: That's awful.

\<*S 02*>: Mm. He had a heart attack.

\<*S 01*>: What lots of attacks?

\<*S 02*>: It was never explained to me+

\<*S 01*>: Mm.

\<*S 02*>: +the relation between the heart attack and reading my thesis. Whether the you know.

\<*S 01*>: It must have been so exciting.

\<*S 02*>: It might have been that. Might have been a rage.

\<*S 01*>: [laughs]

\<*S 02*>: It might have been nothing to do with me at all. I never knew any of this. You know all I knew was that an awful sort of gap opened up and I+

\<*S 01*>: Mm.

\<*S 02*>: +heard nothing for months. And then he wrote to my supervisor saying what's happened and it was explained to me that the external had died [inaudible].

\<*S 01*>: [laughs]

\<*S 02*>: Anyway so

\<*S 01*>: Anyway. [laughs]

\<*S 02*>: Another reason not to make your thesis too controversial.

<*S 01*>: [laughs]

<*S 02*>: You know. [laughs] We couldn't afford to have another one.

<*S 01*>: [laughs] . . .

<*S 02*>: Good. And er er increasingly I mean section one again section [inaudible] three.

<*S 01*>: Mm.

<*S 02*>: Em I will be a bad reader of clipped [inaudible] incidentally. I mean noticing spelling mistakes and noticing places where it seems to be dull or noticing places where it seems to be confusing.

<*S 01*>: Mm. Mm.

<*S 02*>: I won't actually give you any good advice cos here you're on your own I think.

The degree of discoursal creativity on the part of the supervisor in initiating and encouraging the tone of the encounter is of a different order from some of the relationships discussed above or from the more institutionalised roles of lecturer–student discourse which are normally characterised by more conventionally distinct hierarchies. By the time a doctoral student reaches the third year of a course of study, they rightly have a degree of autonomy and self-determination which is different from that enjoyed at earlier stages in their educational career, for example at school or even as an undergraduate. The shift in symmetry achieved by the supervisor here is thus less markedly creative than the interdiscursivity brought about by highly skilled psychotherapists or HIV/AIDS counsellors facing new social and cultural contexts. Assessments with reference to clines of the kind established in chapter 5 inevitably come into play here. But the supervisor has none the less created a professional context in which greater equilibrium is conducive to greater involvement.

Creativity at the supermarket checkout

The final example in this section involves another instance of creativity within a professional context. Here the context and the worker involved are not ones to which the term professional is normally ascribed; the example shows a routine workplace activity which is skilfully utilised by a checkout operator in a supermarket. The data represent an example of what has been termed *small talk*, a category of language use which has conventionally been seen in derogatory terms as something highly formulaic and superficial. In a collection of papers with the title *Small Talk* (Coupland, 2000) a number of studies set out deliberately to blur distinctions between what may or may not be significant in talk encounters. Many of the examples used involve sensitive management of everyday spoken interaction for the achievement of social purposes, both private and public. The contexts range from telephone talk, family dinner party conversations, driving instruction and more institutionalised contexts such as a hospice meeting and interaction in a government office.

In this instance *small talk* occurs in a context normally connected in our minds with a highly routinised, ritualistic activity and in a context more readily associated with a production-line of assembly workers in which there are limited frames of expectation on the part of all participants. On the face of it, it may seem as if supermarket checkout operators have limited opportunity to break out of ritualistic exchanges about the weather, about being busy or about the nature of the financial transactions. One contribution to the *Small Talk* collection demonstrates otherwise, however. In a study in a number of supermarkets in New Zealand, Kuiper and Flindall (2000) show how different operatives are able to put their own distinctive and individual imprint on these seemingly insignificant and ephemeral exchanges, in each case breaking from the more predictable routines. The following extract highlights the creative skills of one of the most distinctive of the operatives:

Example 6.9

> *Operative:* Good morning.
> *Customer:* Morning.
> *Operative:* How are you?
> *Customer:* I'm fine, thanks.
> *Operative:* You look well. You look nice.
> *Customer:* . . . had – had ten days in hospital.
> *Operative:* Oh, did you? You feeling better?
> *Customer:* I've had a new hip put in.
> *Operative:* Oh, well good for you. As – is – you going well with it?
> *Customer:* Yep.
> *Operative:* Super.
> *Customer:* Down to – ah – one crutch.
> *Operative:* Good for you.
> *Customer:* On my right side. Tell me, the Sheba pet food. You've got beef cuts, beef and kidney but no turkey in. Turkey's the popular one.
> *Operative:* Let me ask Murray for it – 'scuse me, Murray – in the Sheba line of catfood will we be getting turkey?
> *Murray:* We'd like to think so . . . problems with the shipping . . . from America.
> *Customer:* I see you've got beef and kidney. It's just come in – It was it's just come in.
> *Customer:* Well it must have, cos I didn't see it on Friday.
> *Murray:* No . . . only just arrived. In fact, I didn't even realise that myself.
> *Customer:* Yeah, well. So I wanted to buy turkey.
> *Operative:* Yeah. Should be coming in very shortly. I'll know on Tuesday.
> *Customer:* Okay, I'll go home and tell him.
> *Operative:* Four dollar fifty, thanks. Thanks.
> *Customer:* Sorry. . . . been out a lot
> *Operative:* That's your cat's favourite, is it?
> *Customer:* Yes.

Operative: They all have their favourites.
Customer: . . . might be other cats also like it.
Operative: That's why we're out.
Customer: Yeah. Thank you. Okay.

(Kuiper and Flindall's data)

The checkout operator in this extract, whose name is Dusty and who comes from North America, has the ability to combine the routine utterance with the more overtly and genuinely interpersonal insert. By quickly dispensing with the more routine and phatic small talk, she is able to build a more 'relational' small talk which serves to make her discourse less superficial and more interactive and interpersonal. For example, her enquiry after the customer's operation is not simply a one-turn routine but contains follow up questions. The closure of the negative talk concerning the stocking of the wrong variety of catfood is not left at the purely transactional level but is followed up with an enquiry about the customer's cat. Dusty's engagement with the customer goes beyond the limits of checkout discourse and achieves a measure of mutual participation in a work encounter not normally associated with this kind of personal involvement.

Initial conclusions

The following preliminary conclusions might be drawn from discussions in this chapter so far.

*   Exploration of a wider range of social contexts from the liminal discourses of adolescents to professional therapy and supermarket encounters confirms the significance of creativity as a social practice. The creativity at work here is different from that examined in the immediately preceding chapters; it is to some extent closer to creativity as problem-solving of the kind described in chapter 1, pp. 31 ff. and cannot be described simply in terms of language 'play'. It involves speakers in the creative co-construction of relationships, but in more formal and professional encounters of the kind not normally seen as sites for creative language use.
*   Examining creativity in terms of patternings at word, phrase and sentence level reveals much; but to restrict analysis to such levels fails to account for the kinds of creativity which operate across speaking turns, or for the ways in which new discourse styles can be creatively constructed in response to evolving social and professional practices. Interdiscursivity involves creative practices – a creative blending of discourses not too far removed from a parallel conceptual blending discussed in chapter 4, pp. 122–4.
*   Creativity is not unconnected with issues of social and cultural identity and is emergent in different forms of intra- and cross-cultural communication. Such creativity can be deployed for socially accommodating purposes but by contrast for critical and socially distancing purposes too.
*   Creativity is *critical* in more than one sense. It can be used for critical purposes in that an existing social order is resisted, challenged and critiqued.

Creativity is also 'critical' as a result of occurring at a critical moment in a crucial site in the evolution and development of social discourses.

One aspect of creativity and of creative discourses which has not so far been examined is the question of the creation of alternative worlds. When in chapter 2 questions of literature and literariness were discussed, the fictional, non-literal nature of language was explored. And in chapter 5 the creation of alternative, fictionalised worlds was seen in some of the exchanges. The next section focuses on some technological changes which have facilitated the creation and participation in alternative worlds. As in the previous sections in this chapter, here the emphasis on new discourses means that there is a corresponding move towards longer stretches of text and to effects which go beyond single words and phrases, important though such features continue to be.

Creativity and Internet discourse

> In general the arts establishment connives to keep alive the myth of the special, creative individual artist holding out against passive mass consumerism . . . Against this we insist that there is a vibrant symbolic life and symbolic creativity current in everyday life, everyday activity and expression – even if it is sometimes invisible, looked down on or spurned. We don't want to invent it or propose it. We want to recognise it – literally re-cognise it.
>
> (Willis *et al.*, 1990: 1–2)

The general term computer-mediated communication (CMC) refers to all the interactions human beings have via computer terminals. In this section various CMCs are examined, with an emphasis on the ways in which a new communicative medium is responded to and different linguistic challenges are met. Although attention is given here to the word- and phrase-generating capacity of these responses, the main focus is on creative acts which are revealed at the level of discourse interaction and its attendant patterns and in those contexts in which personal and interpersonal identities are foregrounded.

Among the most obvious of developments occasioned by the explosion of information and communication technologies in the past twenty years is the rapid increase in the lexicon, as new words appear which refer to new communicative activities. Among the most striking innovations are those in which a basic form is creatively extended into a range of new formations and contexts. For example the prefix *e-* used as a shorthand for *electronic* in compounds such as *e-commerce* has proliferated to the point where the following extensions are in common use: *e-bank*, *e-loan*, *e-newsletters*, *e-tailers* (referring to Internet-based shopping and retailing), *e-books*, *e-conferences*, *e-cards*, *e-management*, *e-therapy*. Similar frequent and relatively obvious creative extensions, often for eye-catching and playfully creative purposes, include the address symbol @ which is extended as a replacement for the preposition *at* or simply the letters A and T as, for example, in *Business @ the Speed of Thought* (the title of a book by the head of the Microsoft organisation, Bill Gates), @ Home (domestic appliance store), *The Where It's @ Bar, All the latest @tractions* (respectively, the name of a business; newspaper advertising slogan). Similar extensions occur with dot.com and other CMC and Internet-related language or what has come to be called Netspeak (see Crystal, 2001: ch. 2). Even *netizen* is now used to describe a citizen of the global CMC community.

However, above all the medium has provided an impulse towards new text types and new forms of creative interaction, in which a new interface has been created between spoken and written language. Also central to these discourses is the way in which new spaces are created for the expression of new identities. And we might note in this connection how identities may be constructed more markedly on-line, where communication is non-visual and is not obviously related to the class, race, gender or sex of the participant.

IRC: interfacing spoken and written discourse

Computer interactions are principally written communications, but recent analysis (Crystal, 2001) has begun to underline the extent to which typically spoken forms can be represented in web-sites, in email communication and in particular in Internet Relay Chat (IRC). For many users standard email communication has evolved as a markedly informal mode of communication; and there is clearly a sense in which email exchanges are used as if a conversation were taking place. However, in email communication the medium is written, the communication process is slowed down by a keyboard, there is a time lag in replies, and the electronic nature of the communication ensures that the keeping of records and copies is different from that involving paper and similar documents. The normal email communication is not face-to-face and communication not only is not spontaneous and therefore is more detached, but also lacks any of the prosodic features which accompany normal conversational interchange.

Yet in emails the conventional concern for accuracy in written communication is often suspended, or at least relaxed, especially with regard to spelling and punctuation; some messages, such as those used for arranging meetings often take, similar to spoken discourse, the form of one-word responses; messages are often copied with replies inserted in the body of the original message with the result that the interactive character of spoken exchanges is preserved; and, although the medium is constantly evolving, there is a distinctly temporary and provisional character about it, which has led to comparisons with casual conversations such as telephone calls. The language of email is certainly associated with informality in communication and the language used for such communication is often a reflection of this mode (see Baron, 2000 for a fuller discussion).

Internet Relay Chat (IRC) is a form of computer communication which makes use of facilities for a greater degree of synchronicity or real time in electronic communication. IRC can take place synchronously (in real time) or asynchronously (in which responses are delayed or deliberately postponed). IRC is an innovation which has changed the communicative landscape, especially in the sense of requiring users to orientate themselves to a new set of circumstances. Indeed, as is the case with email communication, the data examined often require not only some redefinition of what is meant by speech and writing but also some questioning of standard terms such as formal and informal communication. The growth of real-time 'chat-lines' for both two- and multiparty communication has also extended a number of 'spoken' creative possibilities.

Working with such language data requires us therefore to suspend or at least question some of the traditional notions held about the channels of speech and writing. For example, IRC is a written medium in the sense of being composed of visual marks on a screen, but a variety of features, mainly resulting from the medium's synchronicity, have led many commentators to compare it with the spoken language (Werry, 1996; Rintel and Pittam, 1997; Jones, 2002), although the only use of sound in many chat-pages is the 'door chime' that lets participants know that someone new has entered the room. Other commentators have pointed out that evolving 'hybrids' such as IRC cause problems for our notions of binary contrast between speech and writing. Such explanatory contrasts do not hold when most IRC data are examined, since IRC is both 'interactive *and* edited' (Ferrara *et al.*, 1991: 24).

Chat-lines

I came, I saw, I logged on.

For the most part, email exchanges take place between participants who know each other. Witness, for example the extent to which email communication is now a standard feature of communication within an office or within a professional or business organisation. Communication takes place within certain known and knowable parameters. Chat-lines, on the other hand, may involve both familiar and less familiar characters and participants. Conversations may involve relationships which have been built up over a period of time; or they may involve participants who arrive in a virtual space or 'room', often with an assumed name or identity, one which may obscure the age, gender and social or ethnic background of the participant. (And the very metaphor of the 'room' suggests a face-to-face conversation rather than a spatially displaced communication.) We shall begin with a semi-anonymous exchange, in which the participants have already been introduced, before moving to examples of exchanges in which identity needs to be more directly negotiated.

The following transcript (extracted from Carter *et al.*, 2001: 277) is of an IRC interaction between two people with the log-in names of Cato and Regent. Before examining the language data, some contextual explanations are required both of features referred to or responded to by the participants or of features embedded within the transcription itself. In this particular chat-room the software technology allows the creation of a 'buddy' list which participants can store electronically; it also sends a 'clanging' message every time a new chatter enters the chat-room; and a warn button is available by which participants can send each other warnings if they use offensive language. Excessive use of offensive language can mean that the offender is automatically removed from the chat-room.

Example 6.10

> *Cato:* hi buddy!!!;-)
> *Regent:* hiya, wassup?
> *Cato:* I been working SOOOO HARD!
> *Regent:* did you know that your warning level is 0%
> *Cato:* well when I was on with Julia she gave me a 20% warning
> *Regent:* what does it mean?
> *Cato:* if someone misbehaves you can send them a warning
> *Cato:* try it – pretend I said a rude word
> *Regent:* for tea I'm having toad int hole with cabbage
> *Cato:* yum yum, you really know how to live well
> *Regent:* you just said a rude word you naughty thing
> *Cato:* what – yum, yum?
> *Regent:* no you said to pretend you said a naughty word so I did
> *Cato:* durrr!
> *Regent:* ok how do you do it
> *Cato:* click on the warn button
> *Cato:* have you died or something?
> *Regent:* all right hold your horses stop rushing me
> *Cato:* sorry ;-)
> *Regent:* SLOW DOWN
> *Cato:* ok, *slow*
> *Regent:* slooooooooow dn
> *Cato:* *sssssllllllooooooowwwwww*
> . . .
> *Regent:* bye everyone, bye bye
> *Cato:* tarra luv!
> *Regent:* good init?
> *Cato:* yeh hehehe
> Regent: ;-)
> *Cato:* hooorah!
> *Regent:* amazing
> *Regent:* silly tune aint it
> *Cato:* you can go now you passed the smiley test
> *Regent:* bye
> *Cato:* byyyyyeeeee.

[The use of an ellipsis (. . .) indicates that the dialogue has been edited for reasons of overall length.]

Although the medium used is written and responses are typed on a keyboard, a number of features of the chat-room language used by the participants here blur easy distinctions between written forms as both Cato and Regent work hard to approximate spoken forms of language. For example, a 'smiley' is used to create a facial gesture; laughter is represented (*hehehe*); spelling is creatively manipulated in order to reproduce particular sounds, familiar intonation patterns (e.g. *SLOW DOWN*, *SOOOO*) and vocalised backchannels and salutations/sign-offs such as *durrr* and *byyyyeeeee*; punctuation, in particular, is used to act as a channel for the expression of feelings. Capitalisation, asterisks and exclamation marks are exploited to underline what both participants frame as a type of interaction which cannot pass without an overt expression of emotion or uses of voicing. Furthermore, the informal nature of the encounter is clearly perceived and reinforced by both participants to the extent that deliberately regional forms of language are utilised. Examples of such 'regional' forms would be: *aint it*, *innit* (isn't it?), *tarra luv* (goodbye, love), *wassup* (what's up?), *toad int hole* (toad-in-the-hole, a regional dish).

The text produced is also marked not only by the easy informality of the encounter but also by its relatively playful and creative character, for many of the forms listed as marking the presence of the spoken voice involve creative, grapho-phonemic manipulations of the language system. Asterisks are even used to mark out a point of view in which the participants quote themselves almost as if they were characters in a fictional encounter. The resources available lead to very particular dramatisations of the self; it is almost as if the detached, somewhat anonymous and non-visual nature of the encounter leads to a need for excessive self-presentation and to a need to establish and anchor individual presence. It is clearly a context in which the participants feel that more personal signs need to be made manifest.

However, in terms of language use, the communicative exchanges are still produced in written language and are bound by such limitations of written discourse as the relative slowness of composition (to the point where Cato is told to slow down and, because Regent is so comparatively slow, Cato enquires whether Regent's silence indicates that he might not still be alive).

If we see IRC simply as a written genre, then according to the large body of research, IRC should be characterised by the 'detachment' thought characteristic of writing, rather than the 'involvement' thought integral to speech; however, research literature on CMC is awash with references to participants' strongly emotional behaviour, for example in episodes of 'flaming' (Baron, 2000). It is clear that simple notions of involvement or engagement based on the physicality of face-to-face dialogue (such as non-verbal signals, prosodics and paralinguistic effects) that have been the mainstay of linguistic accounts of dyadic exchanges do not take us very far in this new communication context. More useful here, perhaps, is the way some computer scientists have been characterising the quality of engagement as 'presence', and regarding this not simply as physical visibility or even geographical location, but as various degrees or aspects of force or effect – in other words, impressions of agency. Stone (1995), for example, suggests that 'narrow-bandwidth' communication (e.g. computer-based communication in its present form) can produce a more intensive experience of engagement – a more heightened sense of 'presence' – than the 'wide bandwidth' variety (i.e. face-to-face interaction).

> The effect of narrowing bandwidth is to engage more of the participants'
> interpretive faculties . . . Frequently in narrow-bandwidth communication
> the interpretive faculties of one participant or another are powerfully, even
> obsessively, engaged.
>
> (Stone, 1995: 93)

Discussion has also embraced the playfulness of IRC (e.g. Laurel, 1993; Daisley, 1994) as well as the theatricality of computer-mediated spaces for communication (Danet, 1995).

The focus for this section of the chapter is more on creative language play as an integral part of more routine exchanges and it draws in particular on significant research in this domain by Angela Goddard, involving data she has collected as course manager/tutor of an Internet-based communications studies module at Manchester Metropolitan University, UK (Goddard, 2004). During the course of her work with the programme she had unique access to the 'chatters' who produced the course chatlogs which were an integral component of the course module. In many research papers (e.g. Werry, 1996; Rintel and Pittam, 1997), analysts have no contact with their informants and so no way of checking out their own 'researcher' interpretations of online contributions.

Creativity, the self and multiparty discourse: Goddard's case study

> Many conversations between friends and intimates contain little informa-
> tion and may be regarded as instances of play and banter. These discourses
> are not used to solve a practical problem. They are not 'task-based'. They
> are language for enjoyment, for the self, for its own sake. And they are
> often fantasies – not about the real world, but about a fictional one in
> which there are no practical outcomes.
>
> (Cook, 1996: 230)

Goddard's data (2004) are work-in-progress and consist of the chatlogs of two groups of undergraduate students – one UK group, one Swedish group – who were working collaboratively on an online course during the academic year 1998–9, plus face-to-face interviews with the UK student 'chatters' who featured most frequently in the chatlogs. There were 60 students involved in total. They were registered on a course entitled 'Language, Culture and Communication', where the main task was to analyse a range of texts from the different cultural standpoints and where chat-room interactions were designed to clarify ideas and agree approaches. At no point did the students meet their European partners face-to-face in the traditional sense, although at two points during the course, video conferencing sessions were held in order for participants to see one another and to have some spoken interaction. In total, there are 35 chat-room interactions of varied duration, from a few seconds to one hour, consisting of approximately 6,000 words. An interaction has been defined here as beginning with the first user logging on (even if that user is alone) and ending at the point where the last user logs out. Most of the interactions involve multi-party communication. Before the collaborative intercultural work started, the UK students spent some time familiarising themselves with the 'chat' tool. This meant that the project produced data where the UK students were engaged some of the time in 'chat' with their UK peers as well as with their Swedish partners. The data used in this chapter section indicate which groups the students are from.[2]

Metaphors of space and place

> *I txt there4 I am.*

(17-year-old's text message to a friend)

Something of the sense of occupying new territory and of being in a different kind of communicative space is inscribed in a wide range of metaphorical references in Goddard's data, suggesting, in particular, that participants are exploring what Stone (1995) calls 'the architecture of elsewhere' (see also Gillen and Goddard, 2000). Examples 1–3 below, all produced by Goddard's UK students, show how the chat-room is given ontological reality via playful descriptions of its interior:

Example 6.11

1   *it's a bit cold in here*
2   *no furniture here*
3   *nice room, huh?*

In examples 4–6, chat-rooms are constructed as spaces involving a journey or simply underlining how easily the participants record that they have lost their bearings and become disorientated. This metaphor set was regularly used by both groups of students:

4   *maybe they got lost*
5   *we have been looking for you*
6   *there you are*
    no, I'm not there, I'm here

Participants regularly reflect on their own physical presence, questioning the extent to which what they have just typed and sent is where they actually are. Meanings are elusive in expressions such as these, making them flexible in their application. They can set up echoes, within a general theme, that may well reverberate differently for different groups of people, exemplifying, as indicated in chapter 2, Bakhtin's (1981) notion of utterances existing in a framework of intertextual and dialogic echoes.

7   *is there anybody there?*
8   *is there anybody out there?*
9   *do not fear, there is someone here*

Goffman (1974) describes participants in everyday conversations as regularly setting up 'frames' in interactions which are used to project notions of their identity and of the situation they find themselves in. This common conversational practice is translated into the medium of IRC by means of a particular 'story' of an event or type of relationship between participants in which analogies are drawn with familiar everyday practices and familiar social frames:

10   *I thought I would bring a friend*
11   *did you kick me out?*
      you just found yourself bounced?
12   *hello hello hello*
13   *morning campers*
14   *England calling*

Goddard comments as follows:

> Examples 10 and 11 both playfully turn technical hitches into cultural events: example 10, uttered when a participant arrived with 'clones' produced by the software as a result of clicking more than once on the entry button, frames the event as a genteel party; example 11, framing the event as an ejection from a night club, occurs when the software inexplicably closes the window of a user. The examples below, all 'broadcast messages' like examples 7–9, also carry strong connotations of British cultural events and figures: example 12 is the stereotypical utterance of a British policeman (the full version of which would be 'hello hello hello, what's going on here then?'), while examples 13 and 14 suggest holiday camp public address systems and radio transmissions, respectively. All three examples frame the experience of new technology via romantic, rather sentimental images of former times – holiday camp loud hailers, valve radio and the faithful British bobby pounding his beat. As well as invoking humour by the contrast of 'modern' with 'quaint', these references are interestingly apposite to the exploration of the new communication context of the participants: the policeman's comment frames the idea of people up to no good in secret, hidden places and thereby suggests the invisibility (and therefore criminal potential) of cyberspaces; the holiday camp public address and the radio transmission are constructions of voices disseminated afar, to large numbers of people simultaneously – a not inappropriate image for a situation where one student might be 'talking' to a large group of foreign partners. The examples all illustrate Bakhtin's concept of language as polyvocalic, and of utterances as items shaped from existing resources to suit the needs of the moment: 'The word in language is half someone else's' (Bakhtin, 1981: 293).

(Goddard, 2004)

It can be seen here that events and participants are being routinely represented or choose to represent themselves as if they were fictional or literary creations with individual 'presence' marked out in highly addressive and dialogic ways. And the literariness extends too to the extent to which cultural intertextual references are deployed.

The self as a dramatic effect

It has been observed on a number of occasions in this chapter how the detached and impersonal nature of friendly interpersonal exchanges leads participants into self-dramatisation. Goddard underlines that the work of Goffman is especially useful here, and indeed his notion of 'footing' has been applied to conversational data on a number of occasions (see chapter 5, p. 155). In his psychosociological studies over the past three decades he has sought to examine how the self is presented and received in a series of daily encounters; and his work applies with particular relevance to encounters in the new medium of IRC. For example, Goffman (1969) sees the self as a staging exercise, where a successful production of self entails a regularity and consistency of dramatic details. The chatlog interactions are particularly interesting at the opening and closing stages, where, to use Goffman's dramaturgical metaphor, performers make their 'entrances' and 'exits', an observation which parallels the creativity noted in previous chapters as occurring in turn-taking and in the management of turns.

Lack of space here prevents a detailed analysis of all such routines, but what is worthy of note is the regularity with which both groups of participants use grapho-phonemic play with vocalisation and voicing in order to give their utterances more of a pattern-reforming flourish. For example:

15   (Swedish student) *helloooooo!*
16   (UK student) *HIIIIIIIIII!*
17   (Swedish student) *byeee*
18   (UK student) *baaabaaa*

Goddard illustrates how, in Bakhtin's (1981) terms, these voices, in departing from the more standardised written form, are setting up heteroglossic relationships: in these cases, with speech and with other written texts, such as comics. Goffman (1981) points out some of the complex intertextual relationships that obtain between speech and writing when he talks about 'response cries', where the written form may have arisen because of an onomatopoeic relationship with speech noises, but where we may now say the written form because that has become the 'conventionalised blurting': an example of this would be 'eek'.

The IRC data contain many such examples of what Goffman terms 'blurtings', showing participants not only to be using onomatopoeia, but also to be commenting on it metalinguistically. Goddard's example 19 below first names the source of the noise, then 'produces' the noise itself – that of the chat-room entry 'chime', which in reality is very metallic-sounding; in example 20, one of the participants humorously dramatises his own embarrassment via a conventionalised 'clearing of the throat'. Both examples involve UK students talking amongst themselves:

19
entry clank
clank a lank

20
(D has invited S over to watch football on TV)
S: will you feed me?
D: I can try, just don't expect miracles!!!
D or cleanliness
D: ahem

Goffman (1981) stresses the dramatic nature of all response cries, in that they are all designed for an audience's appreciation and are all self-regarding: for example, if we trip over a paving stone and have no obvious addressee, we still utter a noise in case we are being observed having lost our cool. The response cry is then a signal that we have regained control. Similar face-saving moves to register the regaining of control can be observed in the IRC data: for example, when participants make mistakes in typing or when the technical environment plays up, participants utter what Goffman calls a 'spill cry' such as 'oops' or a 'threat startle' such as 'aargh'. In happier situations, participants symbolise other kinds of loss of control, for example via 'audible glee' in expressions such as 'HURRRRRAAAYYYYYYYYYYYY!!!' and 'WWHHHHEEEEEEE'; and even via mock-sexual noises such as 'MMMMMMMMMMbaby'.

Self-dramatisation, however, can also appear in the form of extensive aesthetic orchestrations, invoking directly Bakhtin's (1981) concept (with reference to the novel) of 'heteroglossia', where narrator's and characters' voices have important *intra*textual relationships as well as intertextual ones. For example, the extract below (example 21) shows an attention to syntactic and lexical parallelism across contributions that would be worthy of any literary author. Within this pattern, Hana, the only Swedish student in this interaction, could be seen as prompting the performance of the UK students, who seem determined to live up to her designation of them. Interestingly, though, in carrying out their performance, they establish solidarity as 'players' while she becomes most definitely the audience for their group orchestration:

21
Hana: I'll have you as my private entertainers . . .
Dave: Steve can sing too . . .
Helen: and he does a fabulous bellydance
Steven: and Helen is a mudwrestler
Dave: Tiggy does some fantastic things with fruit . . .

Tiggy: put them together and what do you get
Steven: and let's not even talk about what she can do with a jar of
         marmite and a toilet brush

All Goddard's examples used so far show qualities of heteroglossia, either through referring intertextually, connecting with dialogic threads outside the text, or through establishing intratextual patterns between the linguistic items of different speakers in multiparty talk. However, there is a further form of self-presentation where a participant constructs a variety of voices within one utterance. Here is an example:

22
(Swedish student)
Hana: thanks, I'm not offended . . . not a bit *very offended*

This 'speaker', Goddard observes, seems to be going beyond ideas of external spatio-temporal description to construct a kind of alternative voice akin to that of a narrator commenting on a character's interior feelings and motivation. The voices and messages carried are highly contradictory (as they often are in novels that express complexity), but act arguably as an entirely appropriate response to the complexity of the situation – where one of the UK students 'corrected' her spelling of 'okey' to 'okay' then immediately apologised for attempting the correction in the first place.

   Discussions in previous chapters of this book have focused for the most part on perceived instances of creativity involving instances of language at the levels of words, including figures of speech, and sentences, including, of course, the ways in which sentences link and cohere with one another. We have seen how in this chapter the ground has shifted a little towards higher levels of language and discourse organisation, with creative instances being located and redefined in relation to social contexts and different cultural frames and formations. The explorations of Internet discourse, for example, have introduced consideration of the part played by whole modes of language organisation such as speech and writing and of the ways in which a new discourse requires such modes to be both extended and fused for creative purposes. Goddard's research is seminal in all these respects.

Creativity: performing the self and constructing identities

Creativity in language is not unconnected with the search for and expression of identities. Identity is not simply a personal construct nor is it an entity which is pre-existent, singular, fixed and unchanging. It is multiple and plural and is constructed through language in social, cultural and ethnic contexts of interaction. It is dynamic and mobile and emergent, and is not normally something passively received or assumed. On the occasions in this chapter when the question of identity/ies has been raised, it has been pursued in relation to dynamically changing contexts, in relation to newly evolving media or frames of expectation or in those liminal or newly developing social contexts in which normal rules and conventions are suspended.

Thus, in contexts of professional interaction such as psychotherapy or HIV/AIDS counselling (where new linguistic frames are evolving) or in changing sociocultural contexts (such as Internet communication, where new styles are evolving) or in the adolescent transition between child and adult worlds (where crossings between languages mark out degrees of affiliation and disaffiliation), questions of identity and the creation of identities are very much to the fore. It is striking how in such circumstances the strength of the search to mark out a personal imprint is paralleled in interactive exchanges by a linguistic marking which is often creatively realised in schema-refreshing ways.

It is also interesting that the kinds of search for identity associated with these mobile, dynamic and liminal social contexts often take the form of response to a total, holistic act of speech. It is essentially creativity at a level of discourse and discourse patterning. In several of the instances recorded, the linguistic creativity works alongside the creation of the self as a dramatic artefact, a creative act which is almost in the manner of someone trying on different styles of dress – so that the voices assumed, experimented with, rejected or consolidated become acts of identity. And the contexts in which they occur become instrumental to our understanding of the sociocultural conditions of their formation. These fascinating but complex questions will be pursued further at the end of this chapter when previous frameworks and matrices designed to capture creativity in relation to social contexts will be revisited.

The next step to be taken at this stage, however, is to look more closely at those contexts which are more markedly *fictional* and which provide opportunities for a different form of identity display, most particularly within contexts closer to what are conventionally understood as literary. This leads us into the world of MUD communication.

Creating fictions and alternative realities: MUD communication

> As participants adjust to the prevailing conditions of anonymity and to the potentially disconcerting experience of being reduced to a detached voice floating in an amorphous electronic void, they become adept as well at reconstituting the faceless words around them into bodies, histories, lives . . . Acts of creative reading . . . can and do stand in for physical presence in these online encounters.
>
> (Porter, 1996)

A: Are you telling porkies?
B: What?
A: Porkies. Pork pies? Lies!

In this chapter so far we have examined contexts of Internet communication such as chat-lines in which real-time exchanges are possible and we have considered the extent to which email and similar communicative modes allow exchanges which, though composed in a written format, approximate the ongoing nature of spoken discourse interaction. In all of these contexts too the communication has involved people operating for the most part recognisably in their own identities or in identities close to their own and referring to a real-world subject matter of meetings, topics of argument, gossip about mutual acquaintances and so on.

In this section our attention turns to alternative realities, to virtual worlds and to subject matter which is totally imaginary. The term most commonly used in conjunction with these worlds is MUD. The term MUD stands for Multi-User Dungeon, although it is now more commonly used to stand for Multi-User Dimension (or Domain). It had its origins in the 1970s in role-play and similar computer adventure games such as 'Dungeons and Dragons'. The origin of MUDs in games means that the worlds which are inhabited in MUD communication include: horror stories, science fiction, historical romances and all kinds of fantasy projections involving treasure hunts, battles between good and evil, mythic sequences and so on. The format is a relatively standard one. An imaginary context is defined by a Game Master, and each player in the game, which may number up to 20 at any one time, is assigned a character with particular skills and attributes and with particular characteristics, particular clothing and weapons, and in some games a particular persona which has to be maintained for the duration of the game. 'Characters' here also do not necessarily denote human characters and can be robots, humanoid, animal, vegetable or alien creations. MUDs have mainly belonged to the domain of recreational games and social activity but they are also increasingly deployed in role-playing for training and educational purposes within educational, professional and commercial contexts, and in such circumstances may involve a partial, fictional re-creation of familiar features of the real world in that environment. The MUD users occupy a room, or virtual space, such as a castle or space station or cave or planet or even a simple room within an ordinary house, in much the same way as participants interact in a chat-room, but the crucial difference is that the reality which is created is a function of the participants and does not exist independently of them. As Crystal puts it (2001: 179), 'probably no other domain within the Internet offers such possibilities for creative, idiosyncratic, imaginative expression, and the likelihood that this situation will produce a distinctive linguistic variety', the creative potential being motivated above all by the *alternative* realities which such worlds entail and project.

A derivation of MUDs is MOO. MOO stands for 'MUD Object Oriented' and refers in particular to the objects such as roads, furniture, weapons, clothing, tools which can be utilised and deployed within the interactional environment by the MUD users. In a detailed study Cherny (1999) examined the linguistic character of the ElseMOO, a chat-group which could in theory have up to 100 or so users connected but which was normally characterised by a group of around 30 users conversing at any one time. Players or users can come and go, and unlike IRC, the world continues to move on once an individual has ceased to be involved.

Cherny's detailed stylistic analysis of the MUD register (Cherny, 1999: ch. 3) is valuable in accounting for the options available to the ElseMOO community and thus in allowing a measure of the extent to which individual participants chose to conform to or to depart from the norms of the community of users. A main conclusion drawn from Cherny's examination is that the group guarded its own stylistic practices carefully and took a measure of pride both in its distinctiveness and in the group's own awareness of its collective personality. For example, Cherny quotes Henry, one of the ElseMOO (also referred to as EM) participants, in the following terms:

> What good is it having a personality if you're just going to explain it to everyone? . . . By handing anyone who wants it a complete list of everything which makes EM unique you're threatening the uniqueness . . . I can see explaining some things . . . like obscure acronyms and such . . . but coming out and explaining ROLL CALL and 'losses' and things like that . . . little inside jokes and personality traits of EM . . . is just silly, in my opinion.

The quotation here underlines the rules of the game which the ElseMOO community has constructed, developed and preserved. Cherny's book and Crystal's study (2001: ch. 4) specify these rules in detail. The main aim here is not to catalogue the register features but to isolate the particular features which underscore the creative practices of the MUD group.

The user has two main options when taking a 'speaking turn': *saying* and *emoting*. A character, here Lynn, can be made to speak when the participant types >*say hello* and on screen the programme converts the command into *Lynn says 'hello'*. *Emoting* allows a character to express a range of emotions, actions, facial expressions and gestures, and can be produced on screen by means of a simple emote command such as >*emote smile* or >*emote glare*. Emotes have some resemblance to the emoticons in general IRC communication. Among the range of emote possibilities, Cherny notes the most frequent to be: *smile, laugh, wave, greet, grin, bow, nod, hug, guess, glare, poke* and *kill*. The emote commands are converted into a third person simple present form of the verb so that if the character Lynn types >*emote glare*, the on-screen conversion produces *Lynn glares*. The emote can be more specifically directed at other individual participants so that if Lynn were to type >*emote glare Ray* it would be correspondingly translated as *Lynn glares at Ray*. Within some MUD communities emotes are made more distinctive by abbreviations and word-class conversions (for example, >*emote oh boy* can become *Lynn ohboys*) and by reduplication (for example, *Jim glaresglaresglaresRay*), a process which also serves to intensify the emotional statement. In this connection some groups evolve their own forms of social disapproval and warmth with a matching, usually invented linguistic expression. For example, in EM a *whuggle* denotes an action closely resembling a hug, an action which is used sparingly and with marked gender associations. Cherny reports that it is more widely employed by female than by male participants.

Here is a typical piece of text preserved from an ElseMOO interaction

sequence and quoted as data in Cherny's analysis. Four characters are involved
in an imaginary game with a Christmas tree object. The tree has commands
attached to it such as 'shake' or 'clap' which can result in objects randomly
falling from the tree. One of the objects is a piece of Lego which resembles
Tom, one of the participating characters, and a discourse then develops in
which two 'toms' are simultaneously referred to. The server is unable to distinguish the two referents and the exchanges evolve into a sequence of
extended language play which illustrates the EM register but at the same time
underscores the power of the system for individual and group creativity:

Example 6.12

> Ray walks up to the tree and SHAKES IT VIOLENTLY.
> The tree shakes and shivers, and Tom just falls off onto the floor
> Ray giggles
> Penfold: You see no 'tom at ray' here.
> Lynn laughs too
> Ray says, 'now we have a problem',
> Ray: you haven't specified which 'tom' you mean
> Lynn: Which tom do you mean?
> Penfold: argh
> Ray: you see no 'tom ornament' here.
> Lynn says, 'too many toms!'
> Ray picks up Tom . . .
> Penfold says, 'lego my Lego Tom'
> Bonny eyes Ray warily
> Lynn [to Penfold]: hrmph
> Ray puts the annoying electronic bell in the Christmas tree.
> Penfold: ornament.
> Robin claps at the Christmas tree. Clap. Clap!
> The lights on the Christmas tree burst to life.

Some of the actions described here (for example, those described in the final
four lines in the sequence) are the direct outcome of programming skills on the
part of some of the participants. However, a number of typographic and stylistic conventions are also deployed here for particular expressive effects, serving
to reinforce the message or to allow attitudes to be formed towards the referential content of the mutual activity. For example, capitalisation for emotive
emphasis, conventional emotes such as *giggles* or *laughs too*, and EM-specific
emotes such as the *eyes warily*, a particular phrase which allows this group of
participants to construct statements which convey an ironic, quizzical and self-
conscious play with points of view and attitudes. The wordplay on *lego* and *Lego*
(the phrase 'let go' and the construction toy 'Lego') is the most overt instance
of pattern-reforming wordplay, but there is throughout a heterogeneous mix of
styles, allusions, attitudes and actions which to some degree resist any easy classification but which do signal the identity of this group of users at this particular

time. Membershipping within this group occurs over a period of time by careful and increasingly skilled assimilation of the conventions. The creativity in evidence here is exclusive as well as inclusive. It can be for internal consumption as well as for public display. It can be used to establish a sense of group identity as much as it can be used to establish an individual's own distinctive imprint, and, as discussed in chapter 2 (pp. 61, 76 ff.), it can involve a range of displaced, non-pragmatic, fictional and creative speech acts.

Mimicry, voicing and discourse intonation: a note

And I went 'WoW!' and he was like 'You're not? Are you?'

There have been a number of references in this chapter so far to issues of personal voice. They have been especially marked in connection with CMC where at the interface of the spoken and written medium participants have attempted to impart to their contributions a specific intonational contour and prosodic identity. The connections between a personal voice and identity remind us that phonology in discourse in particular is a key element in the projection of voice and voicings. It is impossible to do justice to all levels of language organisation but the focus on lexico-grammar, figures of speech and discourse organisation should not obscure consideration of the importance of prosodic features.

For example, many language users possess an inherent and creative capacity for mimicry and parody (see, for example, p. 106 above). Writers seeking to convey a particular identity also exploit the written medium in creative ways, and we have already seen in this chapter some of the ways in which writers make use of a range of punctuation devices (including asterisks, quotation and exclamation marks, capitalisation and particular emoticons) in order to add a spoken and interactive dimension and to give expression to an affective side of the message. And Bakhtin (1981) has reminded us how speakers utilise a range of strategies to repeat the words of others, embedding them in their own discourse and in the process utilising the quotation as part of their own statement, sometimes for intensifying and evaluative purposes, and often mocking or otherwise sending up the original.

> The transmission and assessment of the speech of others, the discourse of another, is one of the most widespread and fundamental topics of human speech. In all areas of life and ideological activity, our speech is filled to overflowing with other people's words which are transmitted with highly varied degrees of accuracy and impartiality . . . The topic of a speaking person has enormous importance in everyday life. In real life we hear speech about speakers and their discourse at every step. We can go so far as to say that in real life people talk most of all about what others talk about – they transmit, recall, weigh, and pass judgement on other people's words, opinions, assertions, information; people are upset by others' words, or agree with them, refer to them and so forth.
>
> (Bakhtin, 1981: 337–8)

Although writing in a context of literary representation in the novel, Bakhtin underlines how speakers in everyday conversations make use of polyphonic strategies and produce many-voiced texts in which there is a multiple layering of different speaking styles. In each case the principal means by which this is done is prosodic. The whole process also raises a further question valuably raised by Couper-Kuhlen (1996), who also reminds us that practices may be culturally variable:

> What counts as proper quoting of another's prosody? And what are the limits which determine how much copying is socially acceptable in a given culture or speech community?

To quote someone else's utterances for purposes of mockery or parody inevitably entails a recontextualisation of the original utterance. And very often speakers (and writers) go to particular lengths to align or distance themselves from the original, either by means of verbatim prosodic repetition or by means of deliberate prosodic distortion, although it is frequently difficult to determine where quotation starts and mimicry stops.[3] In terms adopted throughout this book, it is pattern-forming for pattern-reforming purposes.

More inclusive interpretation of discourse contexts needs to include reference to a wider social semiotic which embraces but also goes beyond language. Such factors as kinesics and proxemics, gesture and the whole visual component to a communicative situation are needed further to contextualise the analyses undertaken in this book. Such a recognition does not in any way invalidate the approach adopted here; nor does it invalidate the analyses provided at this stage. But it does suggest, as with all studies which have particular foci, that there are inevitable limitations attendant on any such a focus.

The creativity continuum revisited

In chapter 5 (p. 166) the scalar and clinal nature of creativity was discussed and its significance underlined, with particular reference to patterns and figures of speech. The argument has been further underscored in this chapter, with particular reference to categories of discourse and other patterns and levels of language organisation.

In previous chapters the scalar and probabilistic nature of creativity has been illustrated and underlined. And in both chapter 4 and the current chapter, different clines of affect (intimacy, evaluation and intensity), as manifested in lexical, grammatical and discoursal choices, have been shown to be closely related to instances of creativity and to pattern forming and pattern re-forming tendencies in particular. I have also argued at several points in this book, most notably in chapter 5, that creativity in language use is also closely related to social context or 'context type' and that it is more normally manifest in certain contexts of interpersonal interaction or 'interaction types' than others. This section explores this notion with some further scrutiny of data, and further attempts to diagrammatise the probabilistic character of the relationship between

Table 6.1 Mapping creativity and social interactional context: Matrix 1.

Context type	Interaction type		
	Information provision	*Collaborative task*	*Collaborative idea*
Transactional	commentary by museum guide	choosing and buying a television	chatting with hairdresser
Professional	oral report at group meeting	colleagues window dressing	planning meeting at place of work
Sociocultural	telling jokes to friends	friends cooking together	reminiscing with friends
Intimate	partner relating the story of a film seen	couple decorating a room	siblings discussing their childhood

Note: verbal creativity is potentially present in all zones but is more likely in the more heavily shaded zones.

creativity and social context which takes account of the kind of data introduced in this chapter. The more discourse-based data examined here forces, I argue, some re-evaluation of the kinds of mapping of creativity in relation to social context proposed at the end of chapter 5.[4]

Table 6.1, reintroduced here from chapter 5, attempts a provisional mapping of the CANCODE categories of speech genres with the kinds of evidence of creativity found in the different generic types in the corpus.

The conclusions from an examination of the CANCODE corpus were that linguistic creativity is less likely to occur in those contexts which involve one-dimensional information provision or in those contexts of professional interaction in which the main purpose is transactional. The more intimate the discourse and the more participants are involved in sharing experiences and ideas (collaborative ideas discourses, in particular), the more they may feel prompted to the kinds of wordplay and creative invention marked by pattern re-forming tendencies in the language. The nature of the interaction and of the relationship constructed through that interaction is crucial.

The creativity continuum: remapping creativity and social context

The data and context types explored in this chapter force a number of further questions upon us. The most central question is probably: to what extent can the model as developed (Matrix 1) accommodate both extensions to the data and an enlarged set of interaction types and an enriched range of social discourses and practices? Among the wider range of examples of creative language explored in this chapter are:

Table 6.2 Mapping creativity and social interactional context: Matrix 2.

Context type (*communication varies according to cultural and language affiliation*)		**Interaction type** (*including hybrid forms and embedding for creative purposes*)	
	Information provision	*Collaborative task*	*Collaborative idea*
Transactional	commentary by museum guide	choosing and buying a television	chatting with hairdresser
Professional	oral report at group meeting	colleagues window dressing	planning meeting at place of work; therapist or counsellor problem-solving with a patient
Sociocultural	telling jokes to friends	friends cooking together; on-line communication in a MUD game	reminiscing with friends; adolescents insulting an adult authority figure
Intimate	partner relating the story of a film seen	couple decorating a room	siblings discussing their childhood: Hong Kong Chinese friends emailing in English and in mixed code

- examples of multilingual and multicultural crossings in interactions involving adolescents, especially those which test the limits of the adult world and are critical of it, often face-to-face with the interlocutor;
- mixed-language code emails and text messages from the CANCODE email corpus, involving Cantonese-speakers;
- online chat at the interface of spoken and written discourse;
- the therapeutic alliances between a psychiatrist and a patient or between a doctor and an AIDS/HIV patient;
- the multiparty interactions between MUD participants in a created, fictional world.

The following features of the matrix have therefore been reconfigured in Table 6.2.

- The covert assumption that interactions are in a monolingual and monocultural context has been modified. New sample interactive contexts are therefore inserted into the boxes in the matrix. For example, the matrix embraces the possibilities of creative interaction in mixed-code or mixed-language emails in intimate context types.
- The relationship between the creative and the critical is also acknowledged. For example, adolescents in liminal situations play with language, in some

cases via crossings, subversively to test how far they can push authority figures.

- The spoken/written character of online communication is recognised in further insertions of sample context and interaction types. For example, 'collaborative task' interaction types include not simply friends cooking together but also participants in a game in a MUD chat-room.
- The embedding of and shifts between hybrid forms of interaction types (capturing the nature of interdiscursivity in specific discourses) are indicated. For example, more professional encounters are included. A therapist or counsellor engaged in a 'collaborative ideas' exchange with a patient is included alongside the kinds of joking and banter that may occur in a business meeting.
- The extent to which discoursal creativity is manifest in emergent professional contexts is accommodated in more prominent shading at the intersection between collaborative ideas and professional contexts. Such a point on the continuum was not allowed for in the matrix as designed at Tables 5.2 and 6.1.

Conclusion

The problem remains, of course, that, as with all on-the-page representations such as this, the matrix at Table 6.2 looks to be a static, product-based model which does not allow for the trying on and out of new identities or for more dynamically evolving interpersonal relations. To some extent this point has to be conceded. The matrix does not adequately capture the shifting and overlapping nature of discourse creativity of the kind captured in more liminal or IRC communications or in the newly emergent discourses of professional interaction which have been explored in this chapter. Shading attempts to represent such continua but it cannot be wholly achieved.

However, the model as designed at Table 6.2 is more inclusive than that in Table 6.1 and also indicates a variety of contexts and interactions which are not fully represented in the CANCODE corpus. It admits cross-lingual, cross-cultural discourse as well as interdiscursivity as sites for creative language use, as well as further acknowledging sites in which overt fictions are established as part of normal exchanges. And the patterns observed in the data in this chapter, particularly in critical therapeutic encounters, involve not simply pattern forming or pattern re-forming language structures but also genuinely *transforming* patterns, in which new ways of seeing problems are engendered as a result of changes in the discourse itself or as a result of the evolution of new discourses ranging from new therapeutic encounters to new modes of Internet communication. In this respect creativity is, as Candlin has pointed out, also *critical* as a result of occurring at a 'critical' moment in a crucial site in the evolution and development of social discourses.

The model still underlines the basic insights established in this study that the social contexts in which language use can be co-constructed and co-created are more likely to be informal and centred on more intimate relationships between speakers, that creativity is instantial and emergent, and that it is pervasive across a very wide range of discourses, cultural encounters and contexts. Creativity remains, however, culturally relative in that it can be valued only in relation to the moment-by-moment experiences of the participants. In this respect it also remains fundamentally clinal. Creativity embraces creativities.

Epilogue

> Thus respecting the ordinary language of ordinary people is not an act of trendy academicism, but recognition of the fact that those ordinary people will increasingly be using their ordinary voices to act in this extraordinary global village of ours. In the past, the only voices we could study were those of the powerful and the literate. Our apparently humble gadgetry of recording Walkman and lapel microphone has revolutionised all that: we can now listen to everybody's voice. The computer does not filter out the powerless, the old, the rich, the middle-of-the-road, but simply looks at . . . the whole gamut of speakers; it is that which we cannot ignore or stigmatise.
>
> (McCarthy, 1998b: 126)

> We have lived through a revolution. Yet now that we are all through it, we can see that our new readiness to say Yes to life . . . is now not so new after all. It is abundantly anticipated in common speech, in dozens of idioms and etymological connections that we've always been familiar with. It is as if the speech of ordinary people was always much wiser and craftier than our official creeds and philosophies: as if ordinary people always reckoned that life is a great blessing even though they knew perfectly well that it is disorderly and random, with no antecedently-built Plan or moral order or meaning whatsoever. Once again, truth has always been more democratic than we have been.
>
> (Cupitt, 1998: 43)

This final part of the book draws together some conclusions and points to some main directions for further research. The suggestions for further research are divided into three main parts: a focus on descriptions of language and descriptive frameworks for analysis; extensions to the work described and reported in this book where the main focus is on contexts of language use; and a third focus on specific application, here with particular reference to applications to teaching and learning.

Conclusions

In this book I hope to have demonstrated at least the following:

*   Creativity is present in many everyday spoken language exchanges. Creativity is not the exclusive preserve of the individual genius or the

pathological outsider. It is preferable to regard linguistic creativity as a common property.

- Ordinary, demotic, common talk is frequently both artful and art. Common talk has continuities with and exists along clines with forms that are valued by societies as art. The values which are attached to the art of common talk will vary according to context, time and place.
- Creativity is an act of mind but is also a contextual act, probabilistically related to certain types of interaction and certain speech genres.
- Creativity is always contextually framed and conditioned. Social and cultural contexts play a significant part as sites for creative language use.
- Creative language use is not simply ornamental but is fundamentally purposeful.
- Creativity emerges from interactional language encounters. It is often contingent and instantial.
- Creativity involves the breaking and establishing of patterns in a process of forming and consolidating, re-forming and transforming. Alternative worlds and different (sometimes fictionalised) ways of seeing can be created by words which refer to, represent and perform different voices, identities and perspectives.
- Creativity can be a contentious and confrontational as well as a cooperative and collaborative act. It is connected to the expression of emotions and to varying forms of intimacy.
- Creativity is closely related to language play and to games which may and often do frequently involve humour for both light and serious purposes.
- An extensive spoken corpus can be of real value in studying manifestations of spoken creativity, though the conclusions will always be bound by the limits of the corpus. Studying large stretches of text in a corpus reinforces the case for viewing creativity as a social and discourse practice.

Suggestions for further research

Describing language patterns

Accounts of creative language patterns can be considerably tightened up and made more replicable. This book has done no more than lay out initial points of departure. Most crucially, the norms against which deviations or departures from norms can be measured need to be more fully described. In syntax this is to some extent less problematic, as accounts of standard grammar are comprehensive. In the case of spoken grammar, however, data have only begun to be assembled relatively recently and descriptions are only beginning to emerge. Noting the more salient aspect of spoken grammar and the extent to which pattern forming and re-forming tendencies are manifest would be a starting point.

With regard to vocabulary, too, the notion of core vocabulary is confined for the most part to single orthographic words. Can patterning be fully accounted for without some extension of the framework to embrace multiword units?

Creative play with idioms and routinised chunks of language also needs to be included and that requires again tighter specification of the most likely basic patterns before effects can be located with any precision. The increased development of computer software to search in a corpus for multiword units will greatly assist this process, although frequency of pattern is of course only one component in the working out of norms, and frequency is likely to vary generically and contextually.

Even given such potentially improved accounts there are further descriptive and ethnographic research challenges: for example, determining the balance between scripted and improvised talk in speech encounters and in the process deciding what constitutes the script and the nature of the rehearsals that produce the script. This is an elusive process and may involve: much more empirical fieldwork; interviewing participants; researchers reflexively reviewing our own interactional linguistic practice and experimenting with different models for becoming a participant in the research process. In many ways such processes move us beyond language form and into domains in which language forms and norms intersect with scripts for social behaviour and mentalistic, memory-based speech performance. In terms of the refinement of the descriptive clines proposed in this book, valuable research can be undertaken both back and forth and along and across clines involving script to improvisation, formulae to invention, constraint to creativity.

Voicings

More can be made of the phenomenon of voicing. This is a large area for potential research, continuing from and moving beyond the parameters of analysis outlined at several points in the book. It is worth noting that almost all everyday speech reporting is creative, that is, it is a creative reconstruction of what the original speaker said and involves reports with varying degrees of dramatisation. There are descriptive challenges here in accounting for the prosodic features of voicing. The phenomenon includes projecting or throwing of the voice by an individual or by pairs or small groups of speakers, and revoicings (when the voices of others are reproduced). There are challenges in accounting for the creative functions of voicing which in the case of revoicing, in particular, can involve accounting in varying degrees for comic parodies, for reaccenting and ventriloquising the voice of others in different types of representation and misrepresentation, and for the use of revoicing for purposes of polemic and critique. And there are further challenges in identifying voice features when things are said in order to be deliberately overheard by others. There are also interesting research directions with reference to the creative presentation and stylisation of the voice in written text, including speech reporting in the novel, a topic already covered in some detail in work by Bakhtin, and in work in stylistics more generally. A computer search in any spoken corpus on the word *voice* is both revealing and suggestive. The whole phenomenon of voicing is marked in spoken narratives and anecdotes and can be especially marked at the openings and closings of such speech events.

Multimodality

This is another key direction for further research. This book has focused on language as a system in isolation from non-verbal communicative systems. The development of video-corpora to supplement and extend audio-tape recording will necessitate changes in focus. Creativity in spoken language is never simply a matter of words. Words are accompanied by gestures, eye-contact and gaze, body language, pauses and uses of silence, all of which may be creatively realised. And the communication is often even more acute in the case of the listener who, while not speaking much, may contribute even more (creatively) to a communication through channels of non-verbal feedback. In this connection, and although it is often verbal, there are possibilities for examining varying degrees of creativity in phatic communion.

The meaning of context

There has been a focus in this book on the interrelations between creativity and social context, facilitated in part by a corpus that is sociolinguistically profiled and differentiated contextually and generically. Developing further understanding of the connections between creativity and context offers real possibilities not only for tighter specification of the fit between creative language use, and the type of interaction and social roles engaged in by speakers; the process also underlines the need for a fuller description of context in terms of relations of power, gender, social class, ethnicity, age and identity of the interactants in creative processes.

So, further scrutiny of yet more naturally occurring spoken data is required. For example, among the issues raised in this book, in relation to which further consideration and research is needed, are:

- the relationship between creative language use and particular topics, together with the relationship between creativity, topic shifts, turn boundaries and turn allocations;
- the connection between such patterns and gender roles;
- the relationship between creative language use and particular genres (thus, is creativity more or less likely in spoken narrative than in multi-party discussion?).
- Is creativity negotiated in mixed gender talk so that particular kinds of display and presentationality are allowed or particular identities promoted or constrained?
- Is the use of creative language connected to the exercise of power in particular contexts?
- Does creativity confer power and conversational control among interlocutors?
- Is such power related to the gender or ethnicity of the speaker?

These questions are just a few among those which might be posed and pursued in relation to CANCODE and similar data. All require further inspection of the meaning of context and creativity.

In terms of context, too, it is a not unreasonable criticism of this book to comment how frequently the interactions involve younger and middle-aged speakers. Older speakers may have different speech styles, involving, for example, longer turns and a greater reliance on narrative for the communication of meaning and on self-portraiture through personal anecdote. And speakers of English as an additional language may be different again.

Creativity and the language classroom

Discussions of creativity in relation to language teaching and learning have been extensive and continue to be a very major point of application of a wide range of theories of creativity.

For example, the teaching of literature in a variety of cultural contexts may be better informed by understandings of the pervasively creative character of everyday language, supporting attempts by some practitioners (see Brumfit and Carter, 1986; Pope, 1994; Carter and McRae, 1996; Cook, 2000: part 3) to establish continuities between literary and everyday language and establish stronger bridges between language and literature teaching. The idea that creativity exists in a remote world of literary 'genius' can be demotivating to the apprentice student of literature, especially in contexts where a second or foreign language literature is taught. Appreciation of literary and broader cultural variation can also be stimulated by reference to what learners already understand and can do in much everyday interaction rather than by more deficit-related pedagogic paradigms. Interpreting alien cultural events is, after all, a part of most people's daily lives, especially in an increasingly globalised community.

The challenges of interpretation of conversations embedded in contexts and cultures are similar to those of the interpretation of literary texts, and pedagogy has never shied away from the literary challenge. Kramsch (1993) constantly reminds us that the learner is someone struggling not just with lexico-grammar and pronunciation, but with moving from one cultural context (the classroom) to another (the target culture), in search of that third place in between, where a transformed identity is forged. This is not to say, of course, that reading a conversational transcript is the same as reading a novel by George Eliot, but it is to say that there are continuities between such reading practices.

But it is not only in the teaching of literature and culture where research into learners' exposure to more open-ended and creative aspects of language may be developed. One criticism of notional-functional and task-based approaches to second and foreign language teaching and learning is a tendency towards focusing on the transactional and on the transfer of information, with the danger that language use comes to be seen only as utilitarian and mechanistic. While learners undoubtedly have survival needs, and while a language such as English has indeed become a utilitarian object for many of its world-wide users, learners in many contexts around the world relatively quickly pass from purely utilitarian motivations towards goals associated with expressing their social and cultural selves (Widdowson, 2000), and seek that kind of liberation of expression which they enjoy in their first language. In these respects method-ologies which build on *I* (*illustration*) *I* (*interaction*) *I* (*induction*) structures, as illustrated by Carter and McCarthy (1995a), may help learners better to inter-nalise and appreciate relationships between creative patterns of language and purposes and contexts which can foster both literary appreciation and greater language understanding. Aston (1988) nicely refers to 'learning comity' (as in the book's title) as a desirable response to the transactional bias of contempo-rary language pedagogy, and much of his argumentation centres round bridging 'interactional' gaps (and the development of interactional competence tasks), as opposed to the transactional information gaps so beloved of communicative pedagogy. There are numerous possibilities for empirical classroom research into these more pedagogically focused aspects of creativity.

Understanding and appreciating the poetry of spoken discourse requires attention to materials development which fosters reflection on different types of creative discourse, the relationship between creativity and different socio-cultural contexts, and the ways in which verbal art and language play are manifested in different cultures (Brumfit, 1985; Kramsch and Sullivan, 1996). 'Learning' such creativity in behaviourist terms is not the goal, but much good, humanistic language teaching is concerned with helping the learner to present him/herself in the desired way in the target language; and the work of socio-linguists and sociologists of language which underlines how speakers construct and position themselves in social space by their rhetorical actions, utilising the lexico-grammatical resources of the language (see Harré, 1985, for example, on 'situational rhetorics'), may be substantiated in the observation and analysis of everyday language, and is clearly relevant to the learner's engagement with the resources and meaning potential of the target language.

Final final word

No matter. Try again. Fail again. Fail better.

(Samuel Beckett)

One final thought about the extent of creativity revealed in this book is the apparent paradox of pointing out how exceptional people are when being cre-ative at the same time as underlining how pervasive is the phenomenon of people being creative. It leads to the intriguing idea that our systems for describing language may need to be realigned to account for the fact that cre-ative language may be a default condition, a norm of use from which ordinary, routine 'non-creative' exchanges constitute an abnormal departure. Such a hypothesis needs much more rigorous testing and further exploration; it requires much better definition than we have at present concerning norms of use, not just in written language but particularly in spoken language; and it requires more spoken data from more speakers in more interpersonal contexts of everyday use. But it does raise questions about models of language which are built too narrowly on written data, on single sentences produced by a single user and without full reference to a dynamic of social and cultural contexts. It requires us to ask more fundamental questions about creativity in interaction and dialogue, and to extend our data range to include more examples of newly emerging professional and other discourses. Even more fundamentally, it means that instead of asking what does a study of spoken language tell us about creativity, we ask what does a study of spoken creativity tell us about the nature of language.

The research in this book into a range of contexts underlines the extent and significance of creativity in everyday spoken language. Research still has a long way to go but it reveals an interplay of complex patterns and choices relative to particular speech genres and particular social contexts. It provides a stimulus to explore more fully how speakers perform a variety of functions in particular contexts of interaction. As a linguistic phenomenon, spoken creativity is clinal; people are not always creative to the same degree. It is also probabilistic in that it is more likely to occur in intimate and collaborative dialogic conditions. It involves both senders and receivers in its formation and does not exist wholly for aesthetic purposes; it is typically co-produced and regularly clusters in and is emergent from particular interpersonal and affective platforms. Creative language is not a capacity of special people but a special capacity of all people. It shows speakers as language makers and not simply as language users. And that seems as a good a place as any to have a final word.

Notes

1   My colleague, Zoltán Dörnyei, has reported to me examples of relatively everyday 'bilingual' family conversations. Zoltán is Hungarian and his wife, Sarah, is English but Hungarian speaking. Their two sons are, at the time of writing, aged 6 and 4. Zoltán writes: 'We used to say (not any more, though): "Kitchenbe goni", which meant, "Let's go to the kitchen" or "I'm going to the kitchen". The "be" suffix attached to "kitchen" is the Hungarian preposition "in/into" (and prepositions in Hungarian are added to the nouns in a good agglutinating manner). The "ni" bit after "go" is the infinitive marker for Hungarian verbs. So the phrase is: "kitchen-in to-go". Interestingly, the grammatical structure doesn't come from either Hungarian or English, that is, in Hungarian we would say the "let's go" bit differently and "kitchen" would follow the verb in these cases. However, the phrase "to go to the kitchen" would translate literally "kitchen-in to-go", so I presume this is where the formula comes from. And to top it off, we then further varied this and would even say, "Kitchenbe wentni" – referring to the past ("I went to the kitchen"), which would be literally translated into English as "Kitchen-in to-went" . . . I hasten to add that we sometimes do have real, grammatical conversations as well!!!' The special family discourse illustrated here, Zoltán tells me, gave enormous pleasure to the children who knew it was a hybrid, made-up language but who responded appropriately to the creation of linguistic fictions.

2   Students were aware that their interactions were being recorded, as a notice to this effect was posted on the chat-page and was brought up each time users

logged on. There was an alternative room where interactions were not
recorded, and this was freely accessible to all students. Interestingly, there are
several occasions in the data where students arrange to go to this room in order
to continue their chat. This is stated because the situation was one where students had no option but to be recorded. However, after the data were
collected, the permission of students was sought on an individual basis. Of particular interest to Goddard was the extent to which students' language choices
might encode how they responded to the medium both as a mode of learning
and as a mode of interaction with fellow-students.

3   For detailed analysis see Couper-Kuhlen (1996), who includes particular con-
    sideration of pitch levels and registers; Couper-Kuhlen and Selting (1996), who
    offer an interactional perspective on prosody; Guenther (1999), studying
    reported dialogues based on informal (German) dinner-party conversations;
    Dienhart (1999) who makes a linguistic-anthropological study of riddles in
    terms of phonetic and semantic triggers; and Rossen-Knill and Henry (1997),
    who give an account of verbal parody based on real data in which repetition
    and re-presentation are key components.

4   Michael McCarthy (personal communication) notes here that the instances of
    discourse creativity are, for him, of a markedly different order from some of
    the instances of creative tropes and wordplay illustrated in earlier chapters and
    suggests that a broader historical sweep may help to underline these differ-
    ences. He writes 'For example, the invention of printing and the spread of
    literacy mean that you can have something called a novel, which can be very,
    very long, longer than oral story-telling could last, and which people can read
    at their leisure and convenience. So along come Fielding and Defoe, etc. Then
    in this century we have radio and TV and phones, so we can combine them cre-
    atively and have radio phone-ins with all the new discourse forms they bring.'
    Therefore new discourses, such as the therapeutic and email discourse,
    perhaps, Mike suggests, need to be seen in this historical context of evolving
    discourse types, not least because a creative pun in Shakespeare is not funda-
    mentally different from a modern-day pun.

Exploring further

Classical cross-cultural studies of verbal play for collaborative and non-consensual
purposes include: Hewitt 1997; Basso's anthropological study (1979); Abrahams's
work on 'playing the dozens' (1962); Labov's study of ritual insults (1972). Other
contributions to this formative tradition are by Dundes et al. (1972/86), Gossen
(1976) on poetic duelling, and Bowen (1989).

   Further studies of liminality and crossings at key social and cultural moments in
the formation of beliefs and identities include those by Mechling (1984), Le Page
and Tabouet-Keller (1985), Schave and Schave (1989), Eckert (1990) and Rampton
(1999). Maybin (2003) offers a valuable study with reference to voicings and vocalisation in the context of adolescent development in a school context. Eckert
(1990) and Buchholtz (2003) write with particular reference to girls' talk. In this
connection Harré (1985, 1988) offers insightful accounts of the use of pronouns as
a rhetorical strategy for self-presentation.

   On creativity and interdiscursivity in professional contexts, see work by Sarangi and Roberts (1999) as well as Koester (2001) and Mullany (2003), as indicated in chapter 5, for accounts of the ways in which workplace talk straddles transactional and relational/interpersonal modes.

Among further studies of patterning in 'small talk' is work by Cheepen (2000), Coupland *et al.* (1992) and Drew and Chilton (2002). For particular reference to phatic communion see Schneider (1988, 1989).

Exploring further: epilogue

On creativity in educational contexts, with particular reference to first language contexts, see Pope (1994, 2002, forthcoming). Nash and Stacey (1997) give a classic account of creativity in the light of compositional processes. Nash (1998) contains a range of illuminating insights into creative writing.

In the field of second and foreign language teaching and learning, Cook (2000: part 3) proposes a range of ideas complemented by studies by Lantolf (1997) and Sullivan (2000). Research by Broner and Tarone (2001) underlines the creative problem-solving capacities of learners on- and off-task. Otto (1998) offers a valuable first-base study of learner creativity and language learning with a focus on individual learner differences.

On the development of interactional competence, drawing on insights from creative meaning co-construction and with reflections on and practical applications to the language classroom, see Aston (1988) for a comprehensive study.

Finnegan (2002: part 3) contains rich ideas for a more multimodal approach to creative communication. For an interesting philosophical discussion of many of the issues raised in this book, see Cupitt (1998, 1999).

Appendix 1

A note on transcription and corpus analysis

Working with a spoken corpus: warning notes

Multimillion word corpora are now widely in use in linguistic research. There is little doubt that work in corpus linguistics has led to considerably enhanced insights into the nature of language, not least because a linguist is now able to corroborate intuitions about key lexico-grammatical patterns with evidence from computer searches which go beyond what any one individual brain can retain and 'compute'. It is argued in this book that a computer corpus of spoken English can deepen our understanding of the nature of creativity since it makes available a range of data, related to context and interaction type, which would not otherwise be retrievable in such quantities.

Most computer corpora have been established in order to undertake quantitative analysis. But it still remains the case that qualitative judgements and assessments are necessary and are even, it is argued in the case of this book, often preferable. In spite of recognition of the potential afforded by computational analysis, it is also necessary to be aware of the limitations which attend these research practices. Although several of these points are taken up at different points of this book, these are listed here.

- The data are only ever as useful as the transcription of those data. And transcription varies from one transcriber to another. Although transcribers of the CANCODE corpus received a uniform training, how something is heard and, crucially, how it is interpreted and then transcribed remain key variables.
- The analyst works with a written version of a spoken corpus, and written versions are only ever a simulacrum of the data. Although audio-tapes are available and are regularly consulted, it is important to use words and phrases such as 'real speech' both confidently and cautiously.
- The speech is only ever 'real' to the participants of a speech event. And even for them, there are varying degrees of reality. Speakers perform differently according to whether they know about the recording or if they suspect that there may be a hidden microphone. CANCODE data were collected for the most part with speakers knowing of the existence of

Table A1.1 Transcription codes.

Transcription convention	Symbol	Explanation
Speaker codes	<S 01>, <S 02>, etc.	Each speaker is numbered <S 01>, <S 02>, etc.
Extralinguistic information	[ ]	This includes things like laughter, coughing and inaudible speech on the tape. Pauses or length of pauses are not normally indicated.
Interrupted sentence	+	These instances are marked by a + at the point where one speaker's utterance is interrupted and are followed by another + when the speaker resumes his or her utterance: <S 01>: I think I would like+ <S 02>: Right. <S 03>: + to teach. These interruptions may overlap with the previous speaker's utterance or occupy an individual turn after which the interrupted speaker resumes his or her turn. Or these interruptions occupy turns by themselves and do not overlap with the utterance that has been interrupted.
Backchannel	( )	Backchannel items tend to overlap with the turn of the current speaker and are therefore inserted into his or her utterance, e.g.: <S 01>: I think I would like (<S 02>: Right) to teach.
Unfinished words	=	Speakers not only change their course in mid-sentence but also in the middle of individual words which has been marked as follows: <S 01>: I wouldn't ha=, I wouldn't have thought so.
Punctuation	. ? ,	A full stop or question mark is used to mark the end of a sentence (depending on intonation). 'Sentences' are anything that is felt to be a complete utterance such as: <S 01>: What did you think of the film? <S 02>: Lovely. 'Lovely' is considered as a sentence here. A comma indicates that the speaker has re-cast what he/she was saying, including false starts, e.g.: <S 01>: I bet, is that supposed to be straight?

microphones. It is clear that in some cases speakers relax into the speech event and operate less self-consciously but that is by no means universally the case.

- The data will be differently interpreted according to whether the analyst was a participant in or an observer of the speech event.
- The assignment of a stretch of spoken language to a particular type or category of speech remains a matter of subjective judgement which may vary from one analyst to another, and in any case the presence of multiple categories and functions makes the assignment of a text to a single category problematic.
- As mentioned at several points throughout the book, the existence of patterns such as 'pattern forming' structures, of which participants may be less consciously aware, means that the analyst comments on language use from a different perspective. Even more overt pattern re-forming moves can lead to different insider and outsider interpretations. Methodologically, more work is needed in order to find appropriate ways of researching participants' responses.
- The CANCODE corpus itself is characterised by the generally consensual and collaborative nature of the exchanges. There is only minimal evidence of contestation and adversarial dialogue. Such styles may be a feature of the methods of recording, the selection of participants, the contexts for recordings and so on. As has been remarked on a number of occasions throughout the book, a corpus needs to be read for what is not there as well as what is there and to be supplemented wherever necessary.

For further discussion of these and related issues see McCarthy (1998b, 2001a) and a number of the papers published as part of the CANCODE project and listed in Appendix 3.

Notes to Table A1.1

• The transcription codes used by the professional transcribers of the corpus indicate a broad rather than narrow approach to the data, resulting in part from the pedagogic design of the CANCODE project – the production of grammars and dictionaries. Narrower transcription is undertaken in the case of those extracts in the book where segmental and suprasegmental features of voicing, intonation and rhythm are of significance for the analysis of language and creativity. In such cases original taped recordings have, where possible, been revisited and the data retranscribed.

• The use of ellipses in the data extracts (. . .) indicates that there is a break in the sequence of data. This feature is rare as most extracts are taken as complete speech sequences.

• Speech overlaps are not indicated in the data unless such a feature is judged to be of significance for analysis. Backchannels are, however, indicated, as above.

• Names in the transcripts have been anonymised as appropriate.

Appendix 2

New words for old

This appendix is included to underline the evidence presented in chapter 5, in particular that creative language play is more likely to occur in certain social and interpersonal contexts than in others, and that the *-y* and *-ish* suffixes are both especially creativity-prone and regularly co-occur with such contexts. The data also underline the points made in chapter 4 about *core vocabulary* being a semantic and structural base for creative extension and derivation. The research is essentially quantitative.

-y and *-ish* words

The following words have been located in the CANCODE corpus using searches for the morphemes *-y* and *-ish* as word endings. The words are judged to be 'new' in so far as they may not as yet have established places in most dictionaries of English. Some are of course more striking to some people than others and the strikingness depends as always on the dynamic of the particular context of use.

Selected new words

The list shows the file extensions which mirror the CANCODE categorisation scheme (see Table A2.1 for the key to these as well as p. 150 above for a more detailed description). The number in brackets indicates the number of occurrences in the corpus.

> **arsey** (2) dmx, dcx; **beigey** (1) dmx, **blokey** (1) dmx; **bluey** (5) kmx, dcx, kfx, dmx, dcx; **cubey** (1) dcx; **divey** (1) dmx; **echoey** (1) dcx; **hidey** (1) dcx; **holey** (1) dcx; **housey** (3) dmx, dmx, dmx; **jokey** (2) dmx, dfx; **lookey likey** (2) dcx, dcx; **mousey** (1) dmx; **nicey** (1) dcx; **olivey** (2) dcx; **orangey** (4) kmx, kmx, kmx, kmx; **sciencey** (1) dcx; **servicey** (2) inx, inx; **slidey** (2) dpx, dmx; **tomatoey** (2) dcx, dmx; **wedgey** (2) kfx, dmx; **amateurish** (2) dcx, dcx; **babyish** (1) dcx; **biggish** (5) dnx, kcx, dmx, inx, inx; **blondish** (1) dnx; **bluish** (1) kcx; **blueish** (1) dcx; **chilliish** (3) kmx, kmx, kmx; **comfortableish** (1) dmx; **coolish** (2) dnx, knx; **cowboyish** (1) dcx; **eighteenish** (1) dmx;

eightish (7) dcx, dcx, ipx, ipx, ipx, ipx, ipx; **elevenish** (2) dcx; **essay-ish** (1) dpx; **eveningish** (1) dcx; **fifteenish** (1) dfx; **fiveish** (4) dcx, dcx, dcx, dcx; **fourish** (4) dpx, knx, dmx, dnx; girlish (2) kfx, kcx; **highish** (1) dnx; **hellish** (1) inx; **hottish** (1) dcx; **latish** (1) inx; **longish** (3) kfx, dcx, dcx; **maroonish** (1) inx; **newish** (2) dmx, dmx; **niceish** (3) dmx, dmx, dmx; **oldish** (1) dnx; **paperboyish** (1) dmx; **pinkish** (1) dmx; **poorish** (2) dcx, dcx; **quietish** (1) inx; **rogueish** (1) inx; **scarecrowish** (2) dcx, dcx; **septemberish** (1) inx; **seventeenish** (1) dcx; **Sharonish** (1) dcx; **shortish** (4) dcx, dcx, dmx, kfx; **sixish** (5) dmx, dmx, dcx, dcx, kmx; **sixtyish** (1) dmx; **slobbish** (2) dcx, dcx; **sweetish** (1) dmx; **teatimeish** (1) inx; **thirtyish** (2) imx, dcx; **three-ish** (3) dmx, dmx, dfx; **threeish** (1) dcx; **tomboyish** (1) dfx; **twelvish** (1) dcx; **twoish** (1) dcx; **waspish** (1) dcx; **weakish** (1) dmx; **youngish** (6) dmx, dmx, dmx, dmx, dfx, dcx.

Words and content

The table below illustrates the relationship between the file extension and CANCODE categories. It also shows the number of occurrences of the words listed above, according to category. Note that for this piece of research the 'pedagogic' files (used mainly to support the study of English in classroom contexts) are included, although they have not been included as data elsewhere in the book.

Words and categories

Here the new words involving *-y* and *-ish* are grouped together into the following core lexico-semantic categories. In keeping with observations made throughout chapter 4 (especially pp. 115 ff.), it is interesting to note that core vocabulary plays a formative part in creating a framework for creative language use.

Sample data

Below are some prototypical extracts from the corpus which illustrate words from the list above in their discourse context. Both the illustrative examples are drawn from intimate contexts within the corpus examples.

[Two girl friends are trying on clothes for a party. Both speakers are in their mid-twenties. The genre is intimate collaborative task.]

    <S 01>: No.
    <S 02>: Really. I mean I thought to myself really we should be ashamed of each other. [coughs] But em er when I pop it on just over the bra without the dress like I tried it on with her over a dress there's something goes wrong at the side of my bust. It kind of sticks out the shaping isn't quite right. But I mean I love the

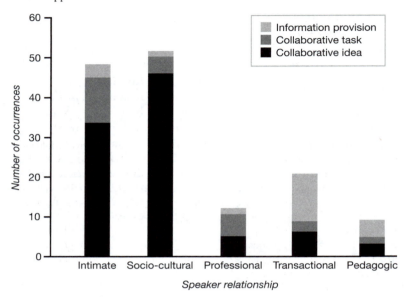

Figure A2.1 Distribution of new words.

collar and the sh= short turn-up sleeves. You may see them in there in your one pink deep pink and er this beautiful *bluey* turquoise and a *beigey* colour which I can't wear. If they'd had white I might have tried the whi= [unintelligible] Well it still would have stuck out.

[Four friends are discussing fabrics for the purpose of decorating a kitchen. <S 01> (male) is in his early thirties; the other speakers are all female and in their late twenties. <S 02> and <S 04> are flat mates.]

<S 01>:   Yeah. That's all it's going to get you though.
<S 03>:   Yeah. That's the problem. If it was blue orange I'd be really well.
<S 02>:   That's red not orange.
<S 03>:   It's orange.
<S 02>:   Well why did you say you can make the red stand out if there isn't any red? It's blue green red and yellow isn't it.
<S 01>:   Well it's a kind of *orangey* red isn't it.
<S 03>:   Yeah.
<S 04>:   Or is it a *reddy* orange?
<S 02>:   It's not a *reddy* orange.
<S 01>:   *Orangey* red.
<S 03>:   Or *reddish*.
<S 02>:   No. It's *orangey red* not *reddy orange*.
<S 03>:   That's good. [laughter]

Table A2.1 Distribution of new words.

	Transactional	Socialising	Pedagogic	Intimate	Professional
Information provision	Inx (12)	Icx (1)	Ipx (6)	Imx (2)	Ifx (1)
Collaborative ideas	Dnx (7)	Dcx (48)	Dpx (4)	Dmx (37)	Dfx (6)
Collaborative tasks	Knx (3)	Kcx (4)	Kpx (1)	Kmx (10)	Kfx (6)

Table A2.2 Creative morphemes and categories.

Time/age/season /number	Size/shape	Colour	Taste	Personal attributes
eighteenish (1)	cubey (1)	beigey (1)	nicey (1)	blokey (1)
eightish (7)	wedgey (2)	bluey (5)	olivey (2)	mousey (1)
elevenish (2)	biggish (5)	bluish (1)	orangey (4)	amateurish (2)
eveningish (1)	highish (1)	blueish (1)	tomatoey (2)	babyish (1)
fifteenish (1)	longish (3)	maroonish (1)	chilliish (3)	blondish (1)
fiveish (4)	shortish (4)	pinkish (1)	hottish (1)	coolish (2)
fourish (4)			sweetish (1)	cowboyish (1)
lateish (1)				girlish (2)
newish (2)				niceish (3)
oldish (1)				paper-boyish (1)
Septemberish (1)				roguish (1)
seventeenish (1)				scarecrowish (2)
sixish (5)				slobbish (2)
sixtyish (1)				tomboyish (1)
tea-timeish (1)				weakish (1)
thirtyish (2)				
threeish (4)				
twelveish (1)				
twoish (1)				
youngish (6)				

Further research

This very initial search confirms the existence of creative extensions involving -*y* and -*ish* morphemes and the concentration of such forms within more intimate and sociocultural contexts and within certain types of interaction. The data confirm a number of the hypotheses advanced in the book but further research could be undertaken in order to search more extensively in different social contexts, paying particular attention, for example, to gender relations, age and ethnicity of the speakers, whether the speakers were first language speakers of English, considering whether the creative uses were in pairs or groups, and providing therefore a more precise description of a wider dynamic of sociocultural uses of words and new word formations.

Appendix 3
CANCODE publications 1994–2003

The following items have all been published as part of the CANCODE project.

Adolphs, S. and Carter, R. A. (2003) 'Corpus stylistics: point of view and semantic prosodies in To The Lighthouse', Poetica 58: 7–20.

Carter, R. A. (1997) 'Grammar, the spoken language and ELT', in Hill, D. A. (ed.) Milan 95: English Language Teaching, Rome: The British Council: 26–32.

Carter, R. A. (1997) Investigating English Discourse: Language, Literacy and Literature, London: Routledge.

Carter, R. A. (1997) 'Speaking Englishes, speaking cultures, using CANCODE', Prospect 12, 2: 4–11.

Carter, R. A. (1998) 'Orders of reality: CANCODE, communication and culture', ELT Journal 52, 1: 43–56.

Carter, R. A. (1999) 'Common language: corpus, creativity and cognition', Language and Literature 8, 3: 195–216.

Carter, R. A. (1999) 'Standard grammars, standard Englishes: some educational implications', in Bex, A. R. and Watts, R. (eds) Standard English: The Continuing Debate, London: Routledge: 149–68.

Carter, R. A. (2002) 'Recognising creativity', IH Journal of Language and Development 13, 9: 14.

Carter, R. A. (2002) 'Spoken English, grammar and the classroom', in Hughes, R. (ed.) At Full Stretch: Spoken English and the National Curriculum, London: Qualifications and Curriculum Authority. Published at http://www.qca.org.uk.

Carter, R. A. (2004) Language and Creativity: The Art of Common Talk, London: Routledge.

Carter, R. A. and Adolphs, S. (2003) 'Creativity and a corpus of spoken English', in Goodman, S., Lillis, T., Maybin, J. and Mercer, N. (eds) Language, Literacy and Education: A Reader, Stoke-on-Trent: Trentham Books: 247–62.

Carter, R. A. and Adolphs, S. (2003) 'And she's like "it's terrible like": spoken discourse, grammar and corpus analysis', International Journal of English Studies, 3, 1: 45–57.

Carter, R. A. and McCarthy, M. J. (1995) 'Discourse and creativity: bridging the gap between language and literature', in Cook, G. and Seidlhofer, B. (eds) Principle and Practice in Applied Linguistics, Oxford: Oxford University Press: 303–21.

Carter, R. A. and McCarthy, M. J. (1995) 'Grammar and the spoken language', Applied Linguistics 16, 2: 141–58.

Carter, R. A. and McCarthy, M. J. (1997) Exploring Spoken English, Cambridge: Cambridge University Press.

Carter, R. A. and McCarthy, M. J. (1997) 'Written and spoken vocabulary', in Schmitt, N. and McCarthy, M. J. (eds) *Vocabulary: Description, Acquisition, Pedagogy*, Cambridge: Cambridge University Press: 20–39.

Carter, R. A. and McCarthy, M. J. (1999) 'The English get-passive in spoken discourse: description and implications for an interpersonal grammar', *English Language and Linguistics* 3, 1: 41–58.

Carter, R. A. and McCarthy, M. J. (2001) 'Designing the discourse syllabus', in Hall, D. and Hewings, A. (eds), *Innovation in English Language Teaching*, London: Routledge: 55–63.

Carter, R. A. and McCarthy, M. J. (2001) 'Size isn't everything: spoken English, corpus and the classroom', in Research Issues, *TESOL Quarterly* (July): 337–40.

Carter, R. A. and McCarthy, M. J. (forthcoming, 2004) 'If you ever hear a native speaker, please let us know!' *IATEFL Journal*.

Carter, R. A. and McCarthy, M. J. (2004) 'Talking, creating: interactional language, creativity and context', *Applied Linguistics*, 25, 1: 62–88.

Carter, R. A. and McCarthy, M. J. (forthcoming) *The Cambridge Advanced Learners' Grammar of the English Language*, Cambridge: Cambridge University Press.

Carter, R. A., Hughes, R. and McCarthy, M. J. (1998) 'Telling tails: grammar, the spoken language and materials development', in Tomlinson, B. (ed.) *Materials Development in L2 Teaching*, Cambridge: Cambridge University Press: 45–68.

Carter, R. A., Hughes, R. and McCarthy, M. J. (2000) *Exploring Grammar in Context*, Cambridge: Cambridge University Press.

Hughes, R., Carter, R. A. and McCarthy, M. J. (1995) 'Discourse context as a predictor of grammatical choice', in Graddol, D. and Thomas, S. (eds) *Language in a Changing Europe*, Clevedon: BAAL/Multilingual Matters: 47–54.

Hughes, R. and McCarthy, M. J. (1998) 'From sentence to grammar: discourse grammar and English language teaching', *TESOL Quarterly* 32, 2: 263–87.

McCarthy, M. J. (1994) 'Vocabulary and the spoken language', in Longo, H. P. (ed.) *Atti del seminario internazionale di studi sul lessico*, Bologna: Clueb: 119–30.

McCarthy, M. J. (1994) 'What should we teach about the spoken language?', *Australian Review of Applied Linguistics* 2: 104–20.

McCarthy. M. J. (1995). 'Conversation and literature: tense and aspect', in Payne, J. (ed.) *Linguistic Approaches to Literature*, Birmingham: University of Birmingham English Language Research: 58–73.

McCarthy, M. J. (1998) *Spoken Language and Applied Linguistics*, Cambridge: Cambridge University Press.

McCarthy, M. J. (1998) 'Talking their heads off: the everyday conversation of everyday people', SELL 10: 107–28.

McCarthy, M. J. (1998) 'Taming the spoken language: genre theory and pedagogy', *The Language Teacher* 22, 9: 21–3.

McCarthy, M. J. (1999) 'Turning numbers into thoughts: making sense of language corpora technology and observing language', *The Language Teacher* 23, 6: 25-7.

McCarthy, M. J. (1999) 'What constitutes a basic vocabulary for spoken communication?', *SELL* 11: 233–49.

McCarthy, M. J. (1999) 'What is a basic spoken vocabulary?', *FELT Newsletter* 1, 4: 7–9.

McCarthy, M. J. (2000) 'Mutually captive audiences: small talk and the genre of close-contact service encounters', in Coupland, J. (ed.) *Small Talk*, Harlow: Longman: 84–109.

McCarthy, M. J. (2001) 'Discourse', in Carter, R. A. and Nunan, D. (eds) *The Cam-*

bridge Guide to Teaching English to Speakers of Other Languages. Cambridge: Cambridge University Press: 48–55.

McCarthy, M. J. (2001) *Issues in Applied Linguistics*. Cambridge: Cambridge University Press.

McCarthy, M. J. (2002) 'Good listenership made plain: British and American non-minimal response tokens in everyday conversation', in Biber, D., Fitzpatrick, S. and Reppen, R. (eds) *Using Corpora to Explore Linguistic Variation*, Amsterdam: John Benjamins: 49–71.

McCarthy, M. J. (2002) 'What is an advanced vocabulary?' *SELL* 3: 149–63. Reprinted in Tan, M. (ed.), *Corpus Studies in Language Education*, Bangkok: IELE Press: 15–29.

McCarthy, M. J. (2003) 'Talking back: "small" interactional response tokens in everyday conversation', in Coupland, J. (ed.) *Research on Language and Social Interaction* 36, 1 (special issue on *Small Talk*): 33–63.

McCarthy, M. J. and Carter, R. A. (1994) *Language as Discourse: Perspectives for Language Teaching*, Harlow: Longman.

McCarthy, M. J. and Carter, R. A. (1995) 'Spoken grammar: what is it and how do we teach it?', *ELT Journal* 49, 3: 207–18.

McCarthy, M. J. and Carter, R. A. (1997) 'Grammar, tails and affect: constructing expressive choices in discourse', *Text* 17, 3: 231–52.

McCarthy, M. J. and Carter, R. A. (2001) 'Ten criteria for a spoken grammar', in Hinkel, E. and Fotos, S. (eds) *New Perspectives on Grammar Teaching in Second Language Classrooms*, Mahwah, NJ: Lawrence Erlbaum Associates: 51–75.

McCarthy, M. J. and Carter, R. A. (2002) 'From conversation to corpus: a dual analysis of a broadcast political interview', in Sánchez-Macarro, A. (ed.) *Windows on the World: Media Discourse in English*, Valencia: University of Valencia Press: 15–39.

McCarthy, M. J. and Carter, R. A. (forthcoming) '"There's millions of them": hyperbole in everyday conversation', *Journal of Pragmatics*.

McCarthy, M. J. and Carter, R. A. (forthcoming) '"This, that and the other": Multiword clusters in spoken English as visible patterns of interaction', *TEANGA*.

McCarthy, M. J., Matthiessen, C.and Slade, D. (2001) 'Discourse analysis', in Schmitt, N. (ed.) *An Introduction to Applied Linguistics*, London: Edward Arnold: 55–73.

McCarthy, M. J. and O'Dell, F. (1999) *English Vocabulary in Use, Elementary Level*, Cambridge: Cambridge University Press.

McCarthy, M. J. and O'Dell, F. (2002) *English Idioms in Use, Upper Intermediate Level*, Cambridge: Cambridge University Press.

McCarthy, M. J. and O'Dell, F. (2002), *English Vocabulary in Use, Advanced Level*, Cambridge: Cambridge University Press.

McCarthy, M. J. and O'Dell, F. (forthcoming) *English Phrasal Verbs in Use, Intermediate Level*, Cambridge: Cambridge University Press.

McCarthy, M. J. and O'Keeffe, A. (2003). '"What's in a name?" – vocatives in casual conversations and radio phone-in calls', in Meyer, C. and Leistyna, P. (eds) *Corpus Analysis: Language Structure and Language Use*, Amsterdam: Rodopi: 153–85.

McCarthy, M. J. and Slade, D. (forthcoming) 'Extending our understanding of spoken discourse', in Cummins, J. and Davison, C. (eds) *Kluwer Handbook on English Language Teaching*, Dordrecht: Kluwer Academic Publishers.

McCarthy, M. J. and Spöttl, C. (forthcoming) 'Formulaic utterances in the multilingual context', in Cenoz, J., Jessner, U. and Hufeisen, B. (eds), *The Multilingual Lexicon*, Dordrecht: Kluwer Academic Publishers.

McCarthy, M. J. and Tao, H. (2001) 'Understanding non-restrictive *which*-clauses in spoken English, which is not an easy thing', *Language Sciences* 23: 651–77.

McCarthy, M. J. and Walsh, S. (2003) 'Discourse', in Nunan, D. (ed.) *Practical English Language Teaching*, New York: McGraw-Hill: 173–95.

Stanfield, C. (1996) 'English as she is spoke' (conversation with CANCODE researcher Jean Hudson), *Cambridge Language Reference News* 2: 2.

References

Abrahams, R. D. (1962) 'Playing the dozens', *Journal of American Folklore* 75: 209–20.

Aijmer, K. (1996) *Conversational Routines in English: Convention and Creativity*, London and New York: Longman.

Alexander, R. (1997) *Aspects of Verbal Humour in English*, Tübingen: G. Narr.

Amabile, T. (1983) *The Social Psychology of Creativity*, New York: Springer Verlag.

Anderson, L.-G. and Trudgill, P. (1992) *Bad Language*, Harmondsworth: Penguin.

Antaki, C. and Widdicombe, S. (1998) 'Identity as an achievement and as a tool', in Antaki, C. and Widdicombe, S. (eds) *Identities in Talk*, London: Sage: 1–14.

Armstrong, I. (2000) *The Radical Aesthetic*, Oxford: Blackwell.

Aston, G. (1988) *Learning Comity*, Bologna: Editrice Clueb.

Aston, G. and Burnard, L. (1998) *The BNC Handbook: Exploring the British National Corpus Using SARA*, Edinburgh: Edinburgh University Press.

Attridge, D. (1988) *Peculiar Language: Literature as Difference from the Renaissance to James Joyce*, London: Methuen.

Babcock, B. A. (1993) 'At home, no women are storytellers: ceramic creativity and the politics of the discourse in Cochiti Pueblo', in Biebuyck, D. P. (ed.) *Tradition and Creativity in Tribal Art*, Berkeley: University of California Press: 70–99.

Bakhtin, M. (1981) 'Discourse in the novel', in *The Dialogic Imagination*, Austin: University of Texas Press.

Bakhtin, M. (1986) 'The problem of speech genres', in *Speech Genres and Other Late Essays*, trans. V. W. McGee, Austin: University of Texas Press.

Barnbrook, G. (1996) *Language and Computers*, Edinburgh: Edinburgh University Press.

Baron, N. (2000) *Alphabet to Email: How Written English Evolved and Where It's Heading*, London: Routledge.

Basso, K. (1979) *Portraits of 'the Whiteman': Linguistic Play and Cultural Symbols among the Western Apache*, Cambridge: Cambridge University Press.

Bateson, G. (1972) 'A theory of play and fantasy', in *Steps to an Ecology of Mind*, New York: Ballantine: 177–93.

Bauman, R. (1977) *Verbal Art as Performance*, Boston, MA: Newbury House.

Bauman, R. (1986) *Story, Performance and Event: Contextual Studies of Oral Narrative*, Cambridge: Cambridge University Press.

Bauman, R. and Briggs, C. L. (1990) 'Poetics and performance as critical perspectives on language and social life', *Annual Review of Anthropology* 19: 59–88.

Bayer, P. (1997) *Art Deco Interiors*, London: Thames and Hudson.

Becker, J. A. (1994) '"Sneak-shoes", "sworders" and "nose-beards": a case study of lexical innovation', *First Language* 14: 195–211.

Bennett, T. (1990) *Outside Literature*, London: Routledge.

Benwell, B. (2001) 'Male gossip and language play in the letters page of men's lifestyle magazines', *Journal of Popular Culture* 34, 4: 19–33.

Berliner, P. (1994) *Thinking in Jazz: The Infinite Art of Improvisation*, Chicago: University of Chicago Press.

Berlyne, D. (1971) *Aesthetics and Psychobiology*, New York: Appleton-Century-Crofts.

Bever, T. G. (1986) 'The aesthetic basis for cognitive structures', in Brand, M. and Harnish, R. (eds) *The Representation of Knowledge and Belief*, Tucson: University of Arizona Press: 314–56.

Bhaya, R. (1985) 'Telling lies: some literary and other violations of Grice's maxim of quality', *Nottingham Linguistic Circular* 14: 53–71.

Bhaya, R., Carter, R. and Toolan, M. (1988) 'Clines of metaphoricity and creative metaphors as situated risk taking', *Journal of Literary Semantics* 17, 1: 20–40.

Biber, D., Conrad, S. and Reppen, R. (1998) *Corpus Linguistics: Investigating Language Structure and Use*, Cambridge: Cambridge University Press.

Birdsong, D. (1995) 'Iconicity, markedness, and processing constraints in frozen locutions', in Landsberg, M. (ed.) *Syntactic Iconicity and Linguistic Freezes: The Human Dimension*, Berlin: Mouton de Gruyter: 31–45.

Bloom, H. (2002) *Genius: A Mosaic of One Hundred Exemplary Creative Minds*, London: Fourth Estate.

Bloomfield, L. (1935) *Language*, London: George Allen and Unwin.

Blum-Kulka, S. (1997) *Dinner Talk: Cultural Patterns of Sociability and Socialization in Family Discourse*, Mahwah, NJ: Lawrence Erlbaum Associates.

Blum-Kulka, S. (2000) 'Gossipy events at family dinners: negotiating sociability, presence and the moral order', in Coupland, J. (ed.) *Small Talk*, Harlow: Longman.

Boden, M. (1990) *The Creative Mind: Myths and Mechanisms*, London: Weidenfeld and Nicolson.

Boden, M. (ed.) (1994) *Dimensions of Creativity*, Boston: MIT Press.

Boden, M. (1999) 'Computer models of creativity', in Sternberg, R. J. (ed.) *Handbook of Creativity*, Cambridge: Cambridge University Press: 351–72.

Bohm, D. and Nichol, L. (eds) (1998) *On Creativity*, London: Routledge.

Bohm, D. and Peat, D. (eds) (2000) *Science, Order and Creativity*, London: Routledge.

Bolinger, D. (1950) 'Rime, assonance and morpheme analysis', *Word* 6: 117–36.

Bowen, J. R. (1989) 'Poetic duels and political change in the Gayo highlands of Sumatra', *American Anthropologist* 91: 25–40.

Boxer, D. and Cortes-Conde, F. (1997) 'From bonding to biting: conversational joking and identity display', *Journal of Pragmatics* 27: 275–94.

Broner, M. and Tarone, E. (2001) '"Is it fun?" Language play in a fifth-grade Spanish immersion classroom', *The Modern Language Journal* 85, 3.

Brown, G. and Yule, G. (1983) *Discourse Analysis*, Cambridge: Cambridge University Press.

Brumfit, C. J. (1985) 'Creativity and constraint in the language classroom', in Quirk, R. and Widdowson, H. G. (eds) *English in the World: Teaching and Learning the Language and Literatures*, Cambridge: Cambridge University Press: 148–57.

Brumfit, C. J. and Carter, R. A. (eds) (1986) *Literature and Language Teaching*, Oxford: Oxford University Press.

Bruner, J. S., Jolly, A. and Sylva, K. (eds) (1976) *Play: Its Role in Development and Evolution*, Harmondsworth: Penguin.

Bublitz, W. (1988) *Supportive Fellow-speakers and Cooperative Conversations: Discourse Topics and Topical Actions, Participant Roles and 'Recipient Action' in a Particular Type of Everyday Conversation*, Amsterdam: John Benjamins.

Bucholtz, M. (2003) '"Why be normal?" Language and identity practices in a community of nerd girls', in Goodman, S., Lillis, T., Maybin, J. and Mercer, N. (eds) *Language, Literacy and Education: A Reader*, Stoke-on-Trent: Trentham Books: 141–58.

Burke, P. (1945) *Metaphor and Philosophy*, New York: Harcourt Brace.

Burke, P. (1993) *The Art of Conversation*, Ithaca, NY: Cornell University Press.

Caillois, R. (1969 [1955]) *Man, Play and Games* (trans. Meyer Barash), New York: Free Press of Glencoe.

Cameron, D. (2000) *Good to Talk?* London: Sage.

Cameron, L. (2002) *Metaphor in Educational Discourse*, London: Continuum.

Cameron, L. (1999) 'Identifying and describing metaphor in spoken discourse data', in Cameron, L. and Low, G. (eds) *Researching and Applying Metaphor*, Cambridge: Cambridge University Press: 105–33.

Cameron, L. and Deignan, A. (2003) 'Combining large and small corpora to investigate tuning devices in spoken discourse', *Metaphor and Symbol* 18: 149–60.

Cameron, L. and Low, G. (1999) (eds) *Researching and Applying Metaphor*, Cambridge: Cambridge University Press.

Candlin, C. (1987) 'What happens when applied linguistics goes critical?', in Halliday, M. A. K., Gibbons, J. and Nicholas, H. (eds) *Learning, Keeping and Using Language: Selected Papers from the 8th World Congress of Applied Linguistics*, Amsterdam: John Benjamins: 461–86.

Candlin, C. (2000) 'General editor's preface' to Coupland, J. (ed.) *Small Talk*, Harlow: Longman, xiii–xx.

Candlin, C. and Garbutt, M. (1996) 'Voices: presenting and constructing the self in psychotherapy', paper presented at the Australian Applied Linguistics Association, Sydney, October, 1996.

Candlin, C., Lin, A., Lo, T. W., Lee, M. and Chu, K. (2000) 'The social significance of voices and verbal play: exploring group membership and identity in the discourses of Hong Kong youth', in *The Discourse of Adolescents in Hong Kong*, Centre for Language Education and Communication Research, City University of Hong Kong Research Report.

Candlin, C. and Maley, Y. (1997) 'Intertextuality and interdiscursivity in the discourse of alternative dispute resolution', in Gunnarsson, B.-L., Linell, P. and Nordberg, B. (eds) *The Construction of Professional Discourse*, Harlow: Longman.

Candlin, C., Moore, A. and Plum, G. (1998) 'From compliance to concordance: shifting discourses in HIV medicine', paper presented at the International Pragmatics Association Conference, Rheims, France (July).

Carter, R. A. (1987a) 'Is there a core vocabulary? Some implications for language teaching', *Applied Linguistics*, 8, 2: 64–72.

Carter, R. A. (1987b) 'Is there a literary language? Theoretical and pedagogical perspectives', in Steele, R. and Threadgold, T. (eds) *Language Topics: Essays presented to Michael Halliday*, vol. 2, Amsterdam: John Benjamins: 431–50.

Carter, R. (1995) *Keywords in Language and Literacy*, London: Routledge.

Carter, R. (1997) *Investigating English Discourse: Language, Literacy, Literature*, London: Routledge.

Carter, R. (1998) *Vocabulary: Applied Linguistic Perspectives* (2nd edn), London: Routledge.

Carter, R. (1999) 'Common language: corpus, creativity and cognition', *Language and Literature* 8, 3: 195–216.

Carter, R. and Adolphs, A. (2003) 'Creativity and a corpus of spoken English', in Goodman, S., Lillis, T., Maybin, J. and Mercer, N. (eds) *Language, Literacy and Education: A Reader*, Stoke-on-Trent: Trentham Books: 247–62.

Carter, R., Hughes, R. and McCarthy, M. (2000) *Exploring Grammar in Context*, Cambridge: Cambridge University Press.

Carter, R. and McCarthy, M. (1995a) 'Grammar and the spoken language', *Applied Linguistics* 16, 2: 141–58.

Carter, R. and McCarthy, M. (1995b) 'Discourse and creativity: bridging the gap between language and literature', in Cook, G. and Seidlhofer, B. (eds) *Principle and Practice in Applied Linguistics,* Oxford: Oxford University Press: 303–21.

Carter, R. and McCarthy, M. (1997a) 'Grammar, tails and affect: constructing expressive choices in discourse', *Text* 17, 3: 205–29.

Carter, R. and McCarthy, M. (1997b) *Exploring Spoken English*, Cambridge: Cambridge University Press.

Carter, R. and McCarthy, M. (2004) 'Talking, creating: interactional language, creativity and context', *Applied Linguistics*, 25, 1: 62–88.

Carter, R. A. and McCarthy, M. J. (forthcoming) *The Cambridge Advanced Learners' Grammar of the English Language*, Cambridge: Cambridge University Press.

Carter, R. and McRae, J. (1996) *Language, Literature and the Learner: Creative Classroom Practice*, Harlow: Longman.

Carter, R. and Nash, W. (1990) *Seeing through Language: Styles of English Writing*, Oxford: Blackwell.

Carter, R., Goddard, A., Bowring, M., Reah, D. and Sanger, K. (2001) *Working with Texts: A Core Book in Language Analysis*, London: Routledge.

Cattell, R. B. (1971) *Abilities: Their Structure, Growth and Action*, Boston, MA: Houghton Mifflin.

Cernak, F. (1994) 'Idiomatics', in Luellsdorff, P. A. (ed.) *The Prague School of Structural and Functional Linguistics: A Short Introduction*, Amsterdam: John Benjamins: 185–95.

Chafe, W. (1994) *Discourse, Consciousness and Time: The Flow and Displacement of Conscious Experience in Speaking and Writing*, Chicago: University of Chicago Press.

Channell, J. (1994) *Vague Language*, Oxford: Oxford University Press.

Cheepen, C. (1988) *The Predictability of Informal Conversation*, London: Pinter.

Cheepen, C. (2000) 'Small talk in service dialogues: the conversational aspects of transactional telephone talk', in Coupland, J. (ed.) *Small Talk*, Harlow: Longman.

Cheepen, C. and Monaghan, J. (1990) *Spoken English: A Practical Guide*, London: Pinter.

Cherny, L. (1999) *Conversation and Community: Chat in a Virtual World*, Stanford, CA: CSLI Publications.

Chiaro, D. (1992) *The Language of Jokes: Analysing Verbal Play*, London: Routledge.

Chomsky, N. (1964) *Current Issues in Linguistic Theory*, The Hague: Mouton.

Choul, J.-C. (1982) 'Si mouve, ma non troppo: an inquiry into the non-metaphorical status of idioms and phrases', in Herzfeld, M. and Lenhart, M. (eds) *Semiotics*, New York: Plenum: 89–98.

Chu, Y.-K. (1970) 'Oriental views of creativity', in Angoff, A. and Shapiro, B. (eds) *Psi Factors in Creativity*, New York: Parapsychology Foundation: 35–50.

Chukovsky, K. (1963 [1928]) *From Two to Five* (trans. and ed. Miriam Morton), Berkeley: University of California Press.

Clark, T. (1997) *The Theory of Inspiration: Composition as a Crisis of Subjectivity in Romantic and Post-Romantic Writing*, Manchester: Manchester University Press.

Clift, R. (1999) 'Irony in conversation', *Language in Society* 28: 523–53.

Coates, J. (1989) 'Gossip revisited: an analysis of all-female discourse', in Coates, J. and Cameron, D. (eds) *Women in Their Speech Communities*, London: Longman: 94–122.

Coates, J. (1996) *Women Talk: Conversation between Women Friends*, Oxford: Blackwell.

Coates, J. (2000) 'Small talk and subversion: female speakers backstage', in Coupland, J. (ed.) *Small Talk*, Harlow: Longman: 241–63.

Coates, J. (2002) *Men Talk*, Oxford: Blackwell.

Coates, J. and Cameron, D. (eds) (1989) *Women in Their Speech Communities*, Harlow: Longman.

Cohen, D. (1974) *Intelligence: What Is It?* New York: Evans.

Cohen, D. (1977) *Creativity: What Is It?* New York: Evans.

Colligan, J. (1983) 'Musical creativity and social rules in four cultures', *Creative Child and Adult Quarterly* 8, 1: 39–47.

Collins, M. A. and Amabile, T. (1999) 'Motivation and creativity', in Sternberg, R. J. (ed.) *Handbook of Creativity*, Cambridge: Cambridge University Press: 297–312.

Cook, G. (1994) *Discourse and Literature: The Interplay of Form and Mind*, Oxford: Oxford University Press.

Cook, G. (1995) 'Genes, memes, rhymes: conscious poetic deviation in linguistic, psychological and evolutionary theory', *Language and Communication* 15, 4: 375–91.

Cook, G. (1996) 'Language play in English', in Maybin, J. and Mercer, N. (eds) *Using English: From Conversation to Canon*, London: Routledge: 198–234.

Cook, G. (2000) *Language Play, Language Learning*, Oxford: Oxford University Press.

Cook, G. (2002) *The Discourse of Advertising*, London: Routledge.

Cornbleet, S. and Carter, R. (2001) *The Language of Speech and Writing*, London: Routledge.

Coulmas, F. (ed.) (1981) *Conversational Routines: Explorations in Standardized Communication Situations and Prepatterned Speech*, The Hague: Mouton.

Couper-Kuhlen, E. (1996) 'The prosody of repetition: on quoting and mimcry', in Couper-Kuhlen, E. and Selting, M. (eds) *Prosody in Conversation: International Studies*, Cambridge: Cambridge University Press: 366–405.

Couper-Kuhlen, E. and Selting, M. (eds) (1996) *Prosody in Conversation: International Studies*, Cambridge: Cambridge University Press.

Coupland, J. (2000) (ed.) *Small Talk*, Harlow: Longman.

Coupland, J., Coupland, N. and Robinson, J. (1992) 'How are you? Negotiating phatic communication', *Language in Society* 21, 2: 207–30.

Cowie, A. P. (1988) 'Stable and creative aspects of vocabulary use', in Carter, R. and McCarthy, M. (eds) *Vocabulary and Language Teaching*, Harlow: Longman: 126–39.

Cowie, A. P. (ed.) (2001) *Phraseology: Theory, Analysis and Applications*, Oxford: Clarendon Press.

Cox, J. L., Read, L. and Van Auken, P. (1990) 'Male–female differences in communicating job-related humour', *Humor* 3, 3: 287–95.

Crystal, D. (1995) *The Cambridge Encyclopaedia of the English Language*, Cambridge: Cambridge University Press.

Crystal, D. (1998) *Language Play*, Harmondsworth: Penguin.

Crystal, D. (2001) *Language and the Internet*, Cambridge: Cambridge University Press.

Csikszentmihalyi, M. (1988) 'Society, culture and person: a systems view of creativity', in Sternberg, R. J. (ed.) *The Nature of Creativity*, Cambridge: Cambridge University Press: 325–39.

Csikszentmihalyi, M. (1996) *Creativity: Flow and the Psychology of Discovery and Invention*, New York: HarperCollins.

Csikszentmihalyi, M. (1999) 'Implications of a systems perspective for the study of creativity', in Sternberg, R. J. (ed.) *Handbook of Creativity*, Cambridge: Cambridge University Press: 313–35.

Culler, J. (1988) *On Puns: The Foundation of Letters*, Oxford: Blackwell.

Culpeper, J. and Semino, E. (eds) (2002) *Cognitive Stylistics: Language and Cognition in Text Analysis*, Amsterdam: John Benjamins.

Cupitt, D. (1998) *The Religion of Being*, London: SCM Press.

Cupitt, D. (1999) *The Meaning of it All in Everyday Speech*, London: SCM Press.

Daisley, M. (1994) 'The game of literacy: the meaning of play in computer-mediated communication', *Computers and Composition* 2: 107–19.

Danet, B. (1995) 'General introduction: playful expressivity and artfulness in computer-mediated communication', in Danet, B. (ed.) *Journal of Computer-Mediated Communication* (Special Issue on Play and Performance). Also at www.ascusc.org/jcmc/vol1/issue2/

de Bono, E. (1992) *Serious Creativity: Using the Power of Lateral Thinking to Create New Ideas*, New York and London: HarperCollins.

Deignan, A. (1995) *Collins COBUILD English Guides 7: Metaphor*, London: HarperCollins.

Deignan, A. (1999) 'Corpus-based research into metaphor', in Cameron, L. and Low, G. (eds) *Researching and Applying Metaphor*, Cambridge: Cambridge University Press: 177–201.

Derrida, J. (1978) *Writing and Difference* (trans. Alan Bass), London: Routledge.

Dienhart, J. M. (1999) 'A linguistic look at riddles', *Journal of Pragmatics* 31: 95–125.

Dirven, R. (1985) 'Metaphor as a basic means of extending the lexicon', in Paprotte, W. and Dirven, R. (eds) *The Ubiquity of Metaphor*, Amsterdam: John Benjamins: 85–121.

Dirven, R. (1993) 'Dividing up physical and mental space into conceptual categories by means of English prepositions', in Zelinsky-Wibbelt, C. (ed.) *The Semantics of Prepositions: From Mental Processing to Natural Language Processing*, Berlin: Mouton de Gruyter: 73–97.

Dörnyei, Z. and Thurrell, S. (1992). *Conversation and Dialogues in Action*, Hemel Hempstead: Prentice Hall.

Drew, P. and Chilton, K. (2000) 'Calling just to keep in touch: regular and habitualised telephone calls as an environment for small talk', in Coupland, J. (ed.) *Small Talk*, Harlow: Longman: 137–62.

Drew, P. and Heritage, J. (1992) *Talk at Work: Interaction in Institutional Settings* (Studies in Interactional Sociolinguistics 8), Cambridge: Cambridge University Press.

Drew, P. and Holt, E. (1995) 'Idiomatic expressions and their role in the organisation of topic transition in conversation', in Everaert, M., van der Linden, E.-J., Schenk, A. and Schreuder, R. (eds) *Idioms: Structural and Psychological Perspectives*, Hillsdale, NJ: Lawrence Erlbaum Associates: 117–32.

Drew, P. and Holt, E. (1998) 'Figures of speech: figurative expressions and the management of topic transition in conversation', *Language in Society* 27: 495–522.

Dunbar, R. (1996) *Grooming, Gossip and the Evolution of Language*, London and Boston: Faber.

Dundes, A. L., Leach, J. W. and Ozkok, B. (1970) 'The strategies of Turkish boys' verbal dueling rhymes', *Journal of American Folklore*, 83: 325–49.

Duranti, A. (1997) *Linguistic Anthropology*, Cambridge: Cambridge University Press.

Eagleton, T. (1983) *Literary Theory: An Introduction*, Oxford: Blackwell.

Eckert, P. (1990) 'Cooperative competition in adolescent "girl talk"', *Discourse Processes* 13: 91–122.

Eggins, S. and Slade, D. (1997) *Analysing Casual Conversation*, London: Cassell.

Emerson, C. 1983. 'The outer world and inner speech: Bakhtin, Vygotsky and the internalization of language', *Critical Inquiry* 10, 2: 245–64.

Fabb, N. (1997) *Linguistics and Literature*, Oxford: Blackwell.

Fairclough, N. (1995) *Critical Discourse Analysis*, Harlow: Longman.

Farb, P. (1974) *Word Play*, London: Cape.

Fauconnier, G. and Turner, M. (2002) *The Way We Think: Conceptual Blending and the Mind's Hidden Complexities*, New York: Basic Books.

Fernandez, J. W. (ed.) (1991) *Beyond Metaphor: The Theory of Tropes in Anthropology*, Stanford, CA: Stanford University Press.

Fernando, C. (1996) *Idioms and Idiomaticity*, Oxford: Oxford University Press.

Ferrara, K., Brunner, H., and Whittemore, G. (1991) 'Interactive written discourse as an emergent register', *Written Communication*, 8, 1: 8–34.

Finke, R. (1990) *Creative Imagery: Discoveries and Inventions in Visualization*, Hillsdale, NJ: Laurence Erlbaum Associates.

Finnegan, R. (2002) *Communicating: The Multiple Modes of Human Understanding*, London: Routledge.

Fish, S. (1973) 'How ordinary is ordinary language?', *New Literary History* 5, 1: 41–54 (reprinted in *Is There a Text in This Class?* Cambridge, MA: Harvard University Press, 1980).

Fleming, D. (1995) 'The search for an integrational account of language: Roy Harris and conversation analysis', *Language Sciences* 17, 1: 73–98.

Freeman, D. (1993) '"According to my bond": King Lear and re-cognition', *Language and Literature* 2, 1: 1–18.

Friedrich, P. (1979) 'Poetic language and the imagination: a reformulation of the Sapir Hypothesis', in *Language, Context and the Imagination: Essays by Paul Friedrich*, Stanford, CA: Stanford University Press: 441–512.

Friedrich, P. (1986) *The Language Parallax: Linguistic Relativism and Poetic Indeterminacy*, Austin: University of Texas Press.

Fung, L. (2001) 'E-chat and new Englishes', mimeo, School of English Studies, University of Nottingham.

Galton, F. (1869) *Hereditary Genius: An Inquiry into Its Laws and Consequences*, London: Macmillan.

Garbutt, M. (1996) 'Figure talk: reported speech and thought in the discourse of psychotherapy', unpublished PhD thesis, Department of Linguistics. Macquarie University, Sydney.

Gardner, H. (1993a) *Frames of Mind: A Framework for the Study of Creativity*, New York: Praeger.

Gardner, H. (1993b) *Multiple Intelligences: The Theory in Practice*, London: HarperCollins.

Gardner, H. (1993c) *Creating Minds: An Anatomy of Creativity as Seen through the Lives of Freud, Einstein, Picasso, Stravinsky, Eliot, Graham and Gandhi*, London: HarperCollins.

Gardner, H. (1995) 'Creativity', *RSA Journal* 143, 5,459, May: 33–42.

Gavins, J. and Steen, G. (eds) (2003) *Cognitive Poetics in Practice*, London: Routledge.

Gerrig, R. J. and Bortfield, H. (1999) 'Sense creation in and out of discourse contexts', *Journal of Memory and Language* 41: 457–68.

Gibbon, D. (1981) 'Idiomaticity and functional variation: a case study of international amateur radio talk', *Language in Society* 10, 1: 21–42.

Gibbs, R. W. (1994) *The Poetics of Mind: Figurative Thought, Language and Understanding*, Cambridge: Cambridge University Press.

Gibbs, R. W. (1999a) *Intentions in the Experience of Meaning*, Cambridge: Cambridge University Press.

Gibbs, R. W. (1999b) 'Researching metaphor', in Cameron, L. and Low, G. (eds) *Researching and Applying Metaphor*, Cambridge: Cambridge University Press: 29–47.

Gibbs, R. (2001) 'Proverbial themes we live by', *Poetics* 29: 167–88.

Gibbs, R. W. (2002) 'Feeling moved by metaphor', in Csábi, S. and Zerkowitz, J. (eds) *Textual Secrets*, Budapest: Eötvös Loránd University: 13–28.

Gillen, J. and Goddard, A. (2000) '"Is there anybody out there?": creative language play and "literariness" in internet relay chat (IRC)', mimeo, Centre for Language and Communication, Manchester Metropolitan University.

Giora, R. (1999) 'On the priority of salient meanings: studies of literal and figurative language', *Journal of Pragmatics* 31: 919–29.

Glover, J., Reynolds, C. R. and Ronning, R. R. (eds) (1989) *Handbook of Creativity*, New York: Plenum Press.

Glucksberg, S. (2001) *Understanding Figurative Language: From Metaphors to Idiom*, Oxford: Oxford University Press.

Goatly, A. (1997) *The Language of Metaphors*, London: Routledge.

Goddard, A. (1996) 'Tall stories: the metaphorical nature of everyday talk', *English in Education* 30, 2: 4–12.

Goddard, A. (2004) 'Being online: linguistic strategies in interactive written discourse', work in progress for PhD thesis, University of Nottingham.

Goffman, E. (1969) *The Presentation of Self in Everyday Life*, New York: Anchor Books (repr. 1971, Harmondsworth: Penguin).

Goffman, E. (1974) *Frame Analysis*, Harmondsworth: Penguin.

Goffman, E. (1979) 'Footing', *Semiotica* 25: 1–29.

Goffman, E. (1981) *Forms of Talk*, Oxford: Blackwell.

Goodwin, M. (1988) 'Cooperation and competition across girls' play activities', in Dundas Todd, A. and Fisher, S. (eds) *Gender and Discourse: The Power of Talk*, Norwood, NJ: Ablex: 55–9.

Gordon, D. (1983) 'Hospital slang for patients: crocks, gomers, gorks and others', *Language in Society* 12: 173–85.

Gossen, G. H. (1976) 'Verbal duelling in Chamula', in Kirschenblatt-Gimblett, B. (ed.) *Speech Play*, Philadelphia: University of Pennsylvania Press.

Graves, R. (1966) *The White Goddess: A Historical Grammar of Poetic Myth*, New York: Noonday Press.

Guenther, S. (1999) 'Polyphony and the "layering of voices" in reported dialogues: an analysis of the use of prosodic devices in everyday reported speech', *Journal of Pragmatics* 31: 685–708.

Guilford, J. P. (1950) 'Creativity', *American Psychologist* 5: 444–54.

Hall, G. (2001) 'The poetics of everyday life', in McRae, J. (ed.) *Reading beyond Text: Processes and Skills* (Revista de Filologia y Su Didactica 24), Seville: University of Seville: 69–86.

Halliday, M. A. K. (1989) *Spoken and Written Language*, Oxford: Oxford University Press.

Halliday, M. A. K. (1994) *An Introduction to Functional Grammar*, London: Edward Arnold.

Hallman, R. J. (1970) 'Toward a Hindu theory of creativity', *Educational Theory* 14: 133–43.

Hanks, W. F. (1996) *Language and Communicative Practices*, Boulder, CO: Westview Press.

Harré, R. (1985) 'Situational rhetoric and self-presentation', in Forgas, J. (ed.) *Language and Social Situations*, New York: Springer Verlag: 175–86.

Harré, R. (1988) 'Accountability within a social order: the role of pronouns', in Antaki, C. (ed.) *Analysing Everyday Explanation*, London: Sage: 156–67.

Harrington, I. (1990) 'The ecology of human creativity', in Runco, M. and Albert, R. (eds) *Theories of Creativity*, London: Sage: 143–69.

Harris, R. (1980) *The Language Makers*, London: Duckworth.

Harris, R. (1998) *Introduction to Integrational Linguistics*, Oxford: Pergamon.

Havranek, B. (1932) 'The functional differentiation of standard language', in Garvin, P. (ed.) *Prague School Reader in Esthetics, Literary Structure and Style*, Georgetown: Georgetown University Press.

Hayakawa, S. (1941) *Language in Action*, New York: Harcourt Brace.

Herrnstein-Smith, B. (1978) *On the Margins of Discourse: The Relation of Language and Literature*, Chicago: University of Chicago Press.

Herrnstein-Smith, B. (1988) *Contingencies of Value: Alternative Perspectives for Critical Theory*, Chicago: University of Chicago Press.

Hill, J. (1985) 'The grammar of consciousness and the consciousness of grammar', *American Ethnologist* 12: 725–37.

Holliday, A. (1999) 'Small cultures', *Applied Linguistics* 20, 2: 237–64.

Holmes, J. (2000a) 'Politeness, power and provocation: how humour functions in the workplace', *Discourse Studies* 2, 2: 159–85.

Holmes, J. (2000b) 'Doing collegiality and keeping control at work: small talk in government departments', in Coupland, J. (ed.) *Small Talk*, London: Longman: 32–61.

Holmes, J. and Marra, M. (2002) 'Over the edge? Subversive humour between colleagues and friends', *Humor* 15, 1: 65–87.

Hopper, R. (1992) *Telephone Conversation*, Bloomington: Indiana University Press.

Hopper, R., Knapp, M. L. and Scott, L. (1981) 'Couples' personal idioms: exploring intimate talk', *Journal of Communication* 31, 1: 23–33.

Howarth, P. (1998) 'Phraseology and second language proficiency', *Applied Linguistics* 19, 1: 22–44.

Howden, M. (1984) 'Code and creativity in word formation', *Forum Linguisticum* 8, 3: 213–22.

Hudson, J. (1998) *Perspectives on Fixedness*, Lund: Lund University Press.

Huizinga, J. ([1944] 1949) *Homo Ludens*, London: Routledge and Kegan Paul.

Hutchby, I. (1999) 'Frame alignment and footing in the organization of talk radio openings', *Journal of Sociolinguistics* 3, 1: 41–63.

Hymes, D. (1996) *Ethnography, Linguistics, Narrative Inequality: Toward an Understanding of Voice*, New York: Taylor and Francis.

Jakobson, R. (1960) 'Linguistics and poetics', in Sebeok, T. (ed.) *Style in Language*, Cambridge, MA: MIT Press: 350–77.

Jaworski, A. (1993) *The Power of Silence: Social and Pragmatic Perspectives*, Newbury Park, CA: Sage.

Jaworski, A. (2000) 'Silence and small talk', in Coupland, J. (ed.) *Small Talk*, Harlow: Longman: 110–31.

Jeffries, L. (2001) 'Schema affirmation and white asparagus: cultural multilingualism among readers of texts', *Language and Literature* 10, 4: 325–43.

Johnson, M. (1987) *The Body in the Mind: The Bodily Basis of Reason and the Imagination*, Chicago: University of Chicago Press.

Jones, R. (2002) 'Computer mediated communication and youth culture in Hong Kong: linguistic educational and social dimensions: a participatory study', mimeo, Hong Kong: Hong Kong City University, Department of English and Communication.

Kaivola-Bregenhoj, A. (1996) 'Riddles and their uses', in Hasan-Rokem, G. and Shulman, D. (eds) *Untying the Knot: On Riddles and Other Enigmatic Modes*, New York and Oxford: Oxford University Press.

Kearney, R. (1998) *The Wake of Imagination: Ideas of Creativity in Western Culture*, London: HarperCollins.

Keenan, E. (1973) 'A sliding scale of obligatoriness: the poly-structure of Malagasy oratory', *Language in Society* 2: 225–43.

Kendon, A. (ed.) (1994) *Gesture and Understanding in Social Interaction* (special issue of *Research on Language and Social Interaction*), Hillsdale, NJ: Lawrence Erlbaum Associates.

Kennedy, G. (1991) *An Introduction to Corpus Linguistics*, Harlow: Longman.

King, A. (1981) 'Form and function in Hausa professional songs', in Abalogu, U. N., Ashiwaju, D. G. and Amadi-Tshiwala, M. R. (eds) *Oral Poetry in Nigeria*, Lagos: Nigeria Magazine: 118–35.

Kirschenblatt-Gimblett, B. (ed.) (1976) *Speech Play*, Philadelphia: University of Pennsylvania Press.

Kirton, M. (ed.) (1994) *Adaptors and Innovators: Styles of Creativity and Problem Solving* (2nd edn), London: Routledge.

Knowles, G., Taylor, L. and Williams, B. (eds) (1996) *The Corpus of Formal British English Speech*, Harlow: Longman.

Koester, A. (2001) 'Interpersonal markers in workplace genres: pursuing transactional and relational goals in office talk', unpublished PhD thesis, University of Nottingham.

Koestler, A. (1964) *The Act of Creation*, London: Hutchinson.

Kövecses, Z. and Szabó, P. (1996) 'Idioms: a view from cognitive semantics', *Applied Linguistics* 17, 3: 326–55.

Kramsch, C. (1993) *Context and Culture in Language Teaching*, Oxford: Oxford University Press.

Kramsch, C. and Sullivan, P. (1996) 'Appropriate pedagogy', *ELT Journal* 50, 3: 199–213.

Kris, E. (1952) *Psychoanalytic Exploration in Art*, New York: International Universities Press.

Kubie, L. S. (1958) *The Neurotic Distortion of the Creative Process*, Lawrence: University of Kansas Press.

Kuiper, K. (1996) *Smooth Talkers: The Linguistic Peformance of Auctioneers and Sportscasters*, Mahwah, NJ: Lawrence Erlbaum Associates.

Kuiper, K. and Flindall, M. (2000) 'Social rituals, formulaic speech and small talk at the supermarket checkout', in Coupland, J. (ed.) *Small Talk*, Harlow: Longman: 183–208.

Kuiper, K. and Haggo, D. (1984) 'Livestock auctions, oral poetry, and ordinary language', *Language in Society* 13: 205–34.

Labov, W. (1972) 'Rules for ritual insults', in *Language in The Inner City: Studies in Black English Vernacular*, Philadelphia: University of Pennsylvania Press.

Lakoff, G. (1987) *Women, Fire and Dangerous Things*, Chicago: University of Chicago Press.

Lakoff, G. and Johnson, M. (1980) *Metaphors We Live By*, Chicago: University of Chicago Press.

Lakoff, G. and Johnson, M. (1999) *Philosophy in the Flesh: The Embodied Mind and Its Challenge to Western Thought*, New York: Basic Books.

Lakoff, G. and Turner, M. (1989) *More than Cool Reason: A Field Guide to Poetic Metaphor*, Chicago: University of Chicago Press.

Lantolf, J. (1997) 'The function of language play in the acquisition of L2 Spanish', in Perez-Leroux, A. and Glass, W. R. (eds) *Contemporary Perspectives on the Acquisition of Spanish*, Somerville, MA: Cascadilla Press: 3–24.

Laurel, B. (1993) *Computers as Theatre*, Reading, MA: Addison-Wesley.

Lecercle, J. J. (1990) *The Violence of Language*, London: Routledge.

Le Page, R. and Tabouret-Keller, A. (1985) *Acts of Identity*, Cambridge: Cambridge University Press.

Levelt, W. J. M. (1989) *Speaking: From Intention to Articulation*, Cambridge, MA: MIT Press.

Lindenfeld, J. (1990) *Speech and Sociability at French Urban Market Places*, Amsterdam: John Benjamins.

Linell, P. (1982) *The Written Bias in Linguistics* (Studies in Communication 2), Linkoping: Linkoping University.

Low, G. (1988) 'On teaching metaphor', *Applied Linguistics* 9, 2: 125–47.

Lubart, T. I. (1999) 'Creativity across cultures', in Sternberg, R. J. (ed.) *Handbook of Creativity*, Cambridge: Cambridge University Press: 339–50.

McCarthy, M. (1998a) *Spoken Language and Applied Linguistics*, Cambridge: Cambridge University Press.

McCarthy, M. (1998b) 'Talking their heads off: the everyday conversation of everyday people', *SELL* 10: 107–28.

McCarthy, M. J. (2000) 'Mutually captive audiences: small talk and the genre of close-contact service encounters', in Coupland, J. (ed.) *Small Talk*, Harlow: Longman: 84–109.

McCarthy, M. (2001a) *Issues in Applied Linguistics*, Cambridge: Cambridge University Press.

McCarthy, M. (2001b) 'Discourse', in Carter, R. and Nunan, D. (eds) *The Cambridge Guide to Teaching English to Speakers of Other Languages*, Cambridge: Cambridge University Press: 48–55.

McCarthy, M. and Carter, R. (1994) *Language as Discourse: Perspectives for Language Teaching*, Harlow: Longman.

McCarthy, M. and Carter, R. (1995) 'Spoken grammar: what is it and how do we teach it?' *ELT Journal* 49, 3: 207–18.

McCarthy, M. and Carter, R. (forthcoming) '"There's millions of them": hyperbole in everyday conversation', *Journal of Pragmatics*.

McGlone, M. S., Glucksberg, S. and Cacciari, C. (1994) 'Semantic productivity and idiom comprehension', *Discourse Processes* 17: 169–90.

McRae, J. (1991) *Literature with a Small 'l'*, London: Macmillan/Prentice Hall.

Makkai, A. (1972) *Idiom Structure in English*, The Hague: Mouton.

Makkai, A. (1978) 'Idiomaticity as a language universal', in Greenberg, J. H. (ed.) *Universals of Human Language*, vol. 3, *Word Structure*, Stanford, CA: Stanford University Press: 401–48.

Maley, Y., Candlin, C. N., Crichton, J. and Koster, P. (1995) 'Orientations in lawyer–client interviews', *Forensic Linguistics* 2, 1: 42–55.

Mannheim, B. (1986) 'Popular song and popular grammar, poetry and metalanguage', *Word* 37: 45–74.

Mar'i, S. K. and Karayanni, M. (1983) 'Creativity in Arab culture: two decades of research', *Journal of Creative Behaviour* 16, 4: 227–38.

Martindale, C. (1999) 'Biological bases of creativity', in Sternberg, R. J. (ed.) *Handbook of Creativity*, Cambridge: Cambridge University Press: 137–52.

Maybin, J. (2003) 'Voices, intertextuality and induction into schooling', in Goodman, S., Lillis, T., Maybin, J. and Mercer, N. (eds) *Language, Literacy and Education: A Reader*, Stoke-on-Trent: Trentham Books: 159–70.

Meares, R. (1992) *The Metaphor of Play: On Self, the Secret and the Borderline Experience*, Melbourne: Hill of Content.

Mechling, J. (1984) 'High Kyobo floater: food and faeces in the speech play at a boy scout camp', *The Journal of Psychoanalytic Anthropology* 7, 3: 236–68.

Mertz, E. (1989) 'Sociolinguistic creativity: Cape Breton's Gaelic linguistic tip', in Dorian, N. (ed.) *Investigating Adolescence*, Cambridge: Cambridge University Press: 103–16.

Meyer, R. E. (1999) 'Fifty years of creativity research', in Sternberg, R. J. (ed.) *Handbook of Creativity*, Cambridge: Cambridge University Press: 449–60.

Moeran, B. (1984) 'Advertising sounds as cultural discourse', *Language and Communication* 4, 2: 147–58.

Monson, I. (1996) *Saying Something: Jazz Improvisation and Interaction*, Chicago: University of Chicago Press.

Moon, R. (1998) *Fixed Expressions and Idioms in English: A Corpus-Based Approach*, Oxford: Oxford University Press.

Moore, A., Candlin, C. N. and Plum, G. (2001) '"Making sense of viral load": one expert or two?', *Journal of Culture, Health and Society* 3, 4: 429–50.

Mukarovsky, J. (1932) 'Standard language and poetic language', in Garvin, P. (ed.) *Prague School Reader in Esthetics, Literary Structure and Style*, Georgetown: Georgetown University Press.

Mullany, L. (2003) 'Identity and role construction: a sociolinguistic study of gender and discourse in management', unpublished PhD thesis, Nottingham Trent University, Nottingham.

Myers, G. (1994) *Words in Ads*, London: Arnold.

Nash, W. (1998) *Language and Creative Illusion*, Harlow: Longman.

Nash, W. and Stacey, D. (1997) *Creating Texts*, Harlow: Longman.

Nelson, K. (1996) *Language in Cognitive Development: Emergence of the Mediated Mind*, New York: Cambridge University Press.

Norrick, N. (1993) *Conversational Joking: Humor in Everyday Talk*, Bloomington: Indiana University Press.

Norrick, N. (2000) *Conversational Narrative*, Amsterdam: John Benjamins.

Norrick, N. (2001) 'Poetics and conversation', *Connotations* 10, 2–3: 241–67.

Norton, B. (2001) *Identity in Language Learning*, Harlow: Pearson.

Ochse, R. (1990) *Before the Gates of Excellence: The Determinants of Creative Genius*, Cambridge: Cambridge University Press.

O'Dowd, E. M. (1998) *Prepositions and Particles in English: A Discourse-functional Account*, New York: Oxford University Press.

Ohmann, R. (1971) 'Speech acts and the definition of literature', *Philosophy and Rhetoric* 4: 1–19.

Ong, Walter J. (1992) *Orality and Literacy: The Technologising of the Word*, London: Methuen.

Osborn, A. F. (1953) *Applied Imagination* (revised edn), New York: Scribner's.

Otto, I. (1998) 'The relationship between individual differences in learner creativity and language learning success', *TESOL Quarterly* 32, 4: 763–73.

Palmer, G. B. and Jankiowiak, W. R. (1996) 'Performance and imagination: toward an anthropology of the spectacular and the mundane', *Cultural Anthropology* 11, 2: 225–58.

Pawley, A. and Syder, F. F. (1983) 'Two puzzles for linguistic theory: nativelike selection and nativelike fluency', in Richards, J. C. and Schmidt, R. W. (eds) *Language and Communication*, Harlow: Longman: 191–226.

Petterson, A. (1990) *A Theory of Literary Discourse in Aesthetics* 2, Lund: Lund University Press.

Phillips, S. U. (1975) 'Teasing, punning and putting people on', *Working Papers in Sociolinguistics* 28: 1–21.

Pile, J. (2000) *A History of Interior Design*, London: Laurence King.

Poincaré, H. (1913) *The Foundations of Science*, Lancaster, PA: Science Press.

Policastro, E. and Gardner, H. (1999) 'From case studies to robust generalizations: an approach to the study of creativity', in Sternberg, R. J. (ed.) *Handbook of Creativity*, Cambridge: Cambridge University Press: 213–25.

Pope, R. (1994) *Textual Intervention: Critical and Creative Strategies for Literary Studies*, London: Routledge.

Pope, R. (2002) *The English Studies Book* (2nd edn), London: Routledge.

Pope, R. (forthcoming) *Creativity* (Critical Idiom series), London: Routledge.

Porter, D. (ed.) (1996) *Internet Culture*, London and New York: Routledge.

Pratt, M. L. (1977) *Towards a Speech Act Theory of Literary Discourse*, Bloomington: Indiana University Press.

Preminger, A. and Brogan, T. V. F. (1993) *The Princeton Encyclopaedia of Poetry and Poetics*, Princeton, NJ: Princeton University Press.

Pulman, S. (1982) 'Are metaphors creative?', *Journal of Literary Semantics* 11: 78–89.

Ragan, S. L. (2000) 'Sociable talk in women's health care contexts: two forms of non-medical talk', in Coupland, J. (ed.) *Small Talk*, Harlow: Longman: 269–87.

Rampton, B. (1995) *Crossing: Language and Ethnicity among Adolescents*, Harlow: Longman.

Rampton, B. (1996) 'Crossing: language across ethnic boundaries', in Coleman, H. and Cameron, L. (eds) *Change and Language* (British Studies in Applied Linguistics 10), Clevedon: Multingual Matters: 89–102.

Rampton, B. (1999) 'Styling the other: introduction', *Journal of Sociolinguistics* 3, 4: 421–7.

Reddy, M. J. (1993) 'The conduit metaphor', in Ortony, A. (ed.) *Metaphor and Thought*, 2nd edn, New York: Cambridge University Press: 164–201.

Redfern, W. (1984) *Puns*, Oxford: Blackwell.

Rintel, E. S. and Pittam, J. (1997) 'Strangers in a strange land: interaction management on internet relay chat', *Human Communication Research* 23, 4: 507–34.

Roberts, R. and Kreuz, R. (1994) 'Why do people use figurative language?' *Psychological Science* 5: 159–63.

Rogers, C. (1990) *A Way of Being*, Boston, MA: Houghton Mifflin.

Rosch, E. H. *et al.* (1976) 'Basic objects in natural categories', *Cognitive Psychology* 8: 382–439.

Rossen-Knill, D. F and Henry, R. (1997) 'The pragmatics of verbal parody', *Journal of Pragmatics*, 27: 719–52.

Rothenberg, A. (1979) *The Emerging Goddess: The Creative Process in Art, Science, and Other Fields*, Chicago: University of Chicago Press.

Rubin, D. C. (1995) *Memory in Oral Traditions: The Cognitive Psychology of Epics, Ballads and Counting-Out Rhymes*, Oxford and New York: Oxford University Press.

Rumelhart, D. E. (1993) 'Problems with literal meanings', in Ortony, A. (ed.) *Metaphor and Thought* (2nd edn), New York: Cambridge University Press: 71–82.

Sacks, H. (1984) 'On doing "being ordinary"', in Jefferson, G. (ed.) *Structures of Social Action: Studies in Conversational Analysis*, Cambridge: Cambridge University Press: 413–29.

Sadock, J. M. (1993) 'Figurative speech and linguistics', in Ortony, A. (ed.) *Metaphor and Thought* (2nd edn), New York: Cambridge University Press: 42–57.

Sarangi, S. and Roberts, C. (1999) *Talk, Work and Institutional Order*, Berlin: Mouton.

Sawyer, W. K. (1996) 'Role, gender, voicing and age in preschool play discourse', *Discourse Processes* 22, 3: 289–307.

Sawyer, W. K. (1997) *Pretend Play as Improvisation: Conversation in the Pre-school Classroom*, Hillsdale, NJ: Lawrence Erlbaum Associates.

Sawyer, W. K. (1999) 'The emergence of creativity', *Philosophical Psychology* 12, 4: 447–69.

Sawyer, W. K. (2001) *Creating Conversations: Improvisation in Everyday Discourse*, Cresskill, NJ: Hampton Press.

Schave, D. and Schave, B. (eds) (1989) *Early Adolescence and the Search for Self: A Developmental Perspective*, New York: Praeger.

Schegloff, E. (1986) 'The routine as achievement', *Human Studies* 9: 111–51.

Scherzer, J. (1987) 'A discourse-centred approach to language and culture', *American Anthropologist* 89: 295–309.

Schiffrin, D. (1996) 'Narrative as self-portrait: sociolinguistic constructions of identity', *Language in Society* 25: 167–203.

Schneider, K. (1988) *Small Talk: Analysing Phatic Discourse*, Marburg: Hitzeroth.

Schneider, K. (1989) 'The art of talking about nothing', in Weigand, E. and Hundsnurscher, E. (eds) *Dialoganalyse II: Referate der 2. Arbeitstagung Bochum, 1988, I and II*, Tübingen: Niemeyer: I, 437–49.

Scott, M. (1999) *Wordsmith Tools*, software, Oxford: Oxford University Press.

Searle, J. (1975) 'The logical status of fictional discourse', *New Literary History* 6, 2: 319–32.

Semino. E. (2001) 'On readings, literariness and schema theory: a reply to Jeffries', *Language and Literature* 10, 4: 345–55.

Shepherd, V. (1990) *Language Variety and the Art of the Everyday*, London: Pinter Publishers.

Shippey, T. A. (1993), 'Principles of conversation in Beowulfian speech', in Sinclair, J. M., Hoey, M. and Fox, G. (eds) *Techniques of Description: Spoken and Written Discourse*, London: Routledge: 109–26.

Short, M. and Candlin, C. (1986) 'Teaching study skills for English literature', in Brumfit, C. and Carter, R. (eds) *Literature in Language Teaching*, Oxford: Oxford University Press: 89–109.

Shotter, J. (1993) *Conversational Realities: Constructing Life through Language*, Thousand Oaks, CA: Sage.

Simonton, D. K. (1984) *Genius, Creativity and Leadership*, Cambridge, MA: Harvard University Press.

Simonton, D. K. (1994) *Greatness*, New York: Guilford.

Sinclair, J. (1987) 'Collocation: a progress report', in Steele, R. and Threadgold, T. (eds) *Language Topics: Essays in Honour of Michael Halliday*, Amsterdam: John Benjamins.

Sinclair, J. (1991) *Corpus, Concordance, Collocation*, Oxford: Oxford University Press.

Spacks, P. M. (1985) *Gossip*, New York: Knopf.

Sperber, D. and Wilson, D. (1986) *Relevance*, Oxford: Blackwell.

Steen, G. (1994) *Understanding Metaphor in Literature: An Empirical Approach*, London: Longman.

Steiner, G. (2002) *Grammars of Creation*, London: Faber.

Stenstrom, A.-B. (1994) *An Introduction to Spoken Interaction*, London: Longman.

Sternberg, R. J. (ed.) (1988) *The Nature of Creativity*, Cambridge: Cambridge University Press.

Sternberg, R. J. (ed.) (1999) *Handbook of Creativity*, Cambridge: Cambridge University Press.

Sternberg, R. J. and Lubart, T. I. (1991) 'An investment theory of creativity and its development', *Human Development* 34, 1: 1–32.

Sternberg, R. J. and Lubart, T. I. (1999) 'The concept of creativity: prospects and paradigms', in Sternberg, R. J. (ed.) *Handbook of Creativity*, Cambridge: Cambridge University Press: 3–15.

Stockwell, P. (1999) 'The inflexibility of invariance', *Language and Literature* 8, 2: 125–42.

Stockwell, P. (2001) 'Towards a critical cognitive linguistics', unpublished manuscript, School of English Studies, University of Nottingham.

Stockwell, P. (2002) *Cognitive Poetics: An Introduction*, London: Routledge.

Stone, A. R. (1995) *The War of Desire and Technology at the Close of the Machine Age*, Cambridge, MA: MIT Press.

Storr, A. (1972) *The Dynamics of Creation*, London: Secker and Warburg.

Strässler, J. (1982) *Idioms in English: A Pragmatic Analysis*, Tubingen: Gunther Narr Verlag.

Street, B. (1993) 'Culture is a verb: anthropological aspects of language and cultural process', in Graddol, D., Thompson, L. and Byram, M. (eds) *Language and Culture*, Clevedon: BAAL/Multilingual Matters: 23–43.

Stubbs, M. (1986) *Educational Linguistics*, Oxford: Oxford University Press.

Stubbs, M. (1996) *Text and Corpus Analysis: Computer Assisted Studies of Language and Culture*, Oxford: Blackwell.

Stubbs, M. (1997) 'Language and the mediation of experience: linguistic representation and cognitive orientation', in Coulmas, F. (ed.) *The Handbook of Sociolinguistics*, Oxford: Blackwell: 344–57.

Stubbs, M. (1998) 'A note on phraseological tendencies in the core vocabulary of English', *Studia Anglica Posnaniensia* 23: 399–410.

Sullivan, P. (2000) 'Playfulness as mediation in communicative language teaching in a Vietnamese classroom', in Lantolf, J. (ed.) *Sociocultural Theory and Second Language Learning*, Oxford: Oxford University Press: 115–31.

Sweetser, E. (1990) *From Etymology to Pragmatics: The Mind–Body Metaphor in Semantic Structure and Semantic Change*, Cambridge: Cambridge University Press.

Tambling, J. (1988) *What Is Literary Language?*, Buckingham: Open University Press.

Tannen, D. (ed.) (1982) *Spoken and Written Language: Exploring Orality and Literacy*, Norwood, NJ: Ablex.

Tannen, D. (ed.) (1984a) *Coherence in Spoken and Written Language*, Norwood, NJ: Ablex.

Tannen, D. (1984b) *Conversational Style: Analyzing Talk among Friends*, Norwood, NJ: Ablex.

Tannen, D. (1989) *Talking Voices: Repetition, Dialogue and Imagery in Conversational Discourse*, Cambridge: Cambridge University Press.

Tannen, D. (1990) 'Silence as conflict management in fiction and drama: Pinter's *Betrayal* and a short story, "Great Wits"', in Grimshaw, A. (ed.) *Conflict Talk*, Cambridge: Cambridge University Press: 165–88.

Tannen, D. (1991) *You Just Don't Understand: Men and Women in Conversation*, London: Virago.

Tannen, D. (ed.) (1993) *Framing in Discourse*, Oxford: Oxford University Press.

Tannen, D. (1994) *Talking from 9 to 5: Women and Men in the Workplace: Language, Sex and Power*, New York: Avon.

Tedlock, D. (1975) 'Learning to listen: oral history as poetry', *Boundary* 2, 3: 707–26.

Tedlock, D. (1977) 'Toward an oral poetics', *New Literary History* 8, 3: 507–19.

Toolan, M. (1996) *Total Speech: An Integrational Approach to Language*, Durham, NC: Duke University Press.

Toolan, M. (2000a) 'Joke shop names', mimeo, School of English Language and Literature, University of Birmingham.

Toolan, M. (2000b) 'Quasi-transcriptional speech: a compensatory spokenness in contemporary Anglo-Irish fiction', in Bex, T., Burke, M. and Stockwell, P. (eds) *Contextualised Stylistics* (Studies in Literature 29), Amsterdam and Atlanta, GA: Rodopi: 153–72.

Torrance, E. P. (1974) *Torrance Tests of Creative Thinking*, Lexington, MA: Personnel Press.

Tracy, K. and Coupland, N. (1990) 'Multiple goals in discourse: an overview of issues', *Journal of Language and Social Psychology* 9: 1–13.

Tsui, A. (1994) *English Conversation*, Oxford: Oxford University Press.

Turner, M. (1991) *Reading Minds: The Study of English in the Age of Cognitive Science*, Princeton, NJ: Princeton University Press.

Turner, M. (1996) *The Literary Mind: The Origins of Thought and Language*, Oxford: Oxford University Press.

Turner, M. and Fauconnier, G. (1999) 'A mechanism of creativity', *Poetics Today* 20, 3: 397–418.

Turner, V. (1982) *From Ritual to Theatre: The Human Seriousness of Play*, New York: PAJ.

Tusa, J. (ed.) (2003) *On Creativity: Interviews Exploring the Process*, London: Methuen.

Uglow, J. (2002) *The Lunar Men*, London: Faber.

Van Peer, W. (1991) '"But what *is* literature?" Toward a descriptive definition of literature', in Sell, R. D. (ed.) *Literary Pragmatics*, London: Routledge: 127–41.

Verdonk, P. and Weber, J.-J. (eds) (1995) *Twentieth Century Fiction: From Text to Context*, London: Routledge.

Vernon, P. E. (ed.) (1970) *Creativity*, Harmondsworth: Penguin.

Vizmuller-Zocco, J. (1985) 'Linguistic creativity and word formation', *Italica* 62, 4: 305–10.

Voloshinov, V. N. (1986) *Marxism and the Philosophy of Language* (trans. L. Matejka and I. R. Titunik), Cambridge, MA: Harvard University Press.

Vygotsky, L. (1971) *The Psychology of Art*, Cambridge, MA: MIT Press.

Wallace, D. B. and Gruber, H. E. (eds) (1989) *Creative People at Work: Twelve Cognitive Case Studies*, New York: Harper and Row.

Ward, T. B., Smith, S. M. and Vaid, J. (eds) (1997) *Creative Thought: An Investigation of Conceptual Structures and Processes*, Washington, DC: American Psychological Association.

Ward Jouve, N. (1997) *The Female Genesis: Creativity, Self and Gender*, London: Polity Press.

Watt, I. (1948) *The Rise of the Novel*, Harmondsworth: Penguin.

Weisberg, R. (1986) *Creativity, Genius and other Myths*, New York: W. H. Freeman.

Weisberg, R. (1993) *Creativity: Beyond the Myth of Genius*, New York: W. H. Freeman.

Werry, C. C. (1996) 'Linguistic and interactional features of internet relay chat', in Herrig, S. (ed.) *Computer-Mediated Communication: Linguistic, Social and Cross-cultural Perspectives*, Amsterdam: John Benjamins.

Widdowson, H. G. (2000) 'On the limitations of linguistics applied', *Applied Linguistics* 21, 1: 3–25.

Widdowson, H. G. (2002) 'Verbal art and social practice: a reply to Weber', *Language and Literature* 11, 2: 161–7.

Williams, R. (1983) *Keywords* (2nd edn), London: Fontana.

Willis, P., Jones, S., Canan, J. and Hurd, G. (1990) *Common Culture: Symbolic Work at Play in the Everyday Cultures of the Young*, Buckingham: Open University Press.

Winner, E. (1988) *The Point of Words*, Cambridge, MA: Harvard University Press.

Winnicott, D. W. (1971) *Playing and Reality*, Harmondsworth: Penguin.

Wolfson, N. (1979) 'The conversational historical present alternation', *Language*, 55: 168–82.

Wray, A. (1999) 'Formulaic language in learners and native speakers', *Language Teaching* 32, 4: 213–31.

Wray, A. and Perkins, M. R. (2000) 'The functions of formulaic language: an integrated model', *Language and Communication* 20: 1–28.

Zelinsky-Wibbelt, C. (ed.) (1993) *The Semantics of Prepositions: From Mental Processing to Natural Language Processing*, Berlin: Mouton de Gruyter.

Index

Abrahams, R. D. 46
advertising: metaphors and 131; patterns 139 *See also* business
aesthetics: pleasure and 82
Aherne, Caroline 40–1
Airplane (film) 19
allegory 138
Amabile, T. 34, 37
Amis, Kingsley: *Lucky Jim* 65
Animal Farm (Orwell) 60
Antaki, C. 106
antonyms: core words 115–16
Armstrong, Isobel: *The Radical Aesthetic* 51
art, defined 18
artists: artisans and 18; as creative individuals 27–9; limits and 33, 35; thought processes of 32
Aston, G. 214
asynchrony 34
audience psychology 39–41
Austin, J. W.: speech acts 60

Babcock, B. A. 50
backchannelling 9
Bakhtin, Mikhail 85; framework for utterances 195, 196; heteroglossia 198; quoting others 204–5; voicing 67–9, 173, 211
Bali 43
Bateson, Gregory 86
Bauman, R. 62, 177
Beckett, Samuel 214
Beethoven, Ludwig van 33
Bennett, T. 84
Berlyne, D. 82
Bever, T. G. 82

biological paradigm 77–8
Black English Vernacular 96
Bloom, Harold: *Genius* 50
Bloomfield, L. 57
Boden, Margaret 24; on creativity 36; historical/personal creativity 66–7
Bohm, David 52
Bowen, J. R. 45
brainstorming 31
Breuer, Marcel 40
Briggs, C. L. 177
Britain: multicultural language 172–3
Brogan, T. V. F. 27
Brown, G. 85
Burke, P. 119
Bush, George W. 74
business: creative language 21–3; *see also* advertising

Cable News Network (CNN) 69
Caillois, R. 83
Cambridge University Press xiii, 150
Cameron, L. 126, 142
CANCODE corpus 4; context type data 149–50; data of 12, 89–90, 149–50, 150–1; development and use of 168; journalists' discourse 153–6; lifeguards' discourse 151–3; limitations of 160, 219, 221; morphological creativity 97–101; new words 222–6; patterns 100–1; punning and play 90–7; small businesses 163–4; snapshot of language 170–1; social context and 147–9, 167; transcription code 220
CANBEC corpus 168

Candlin, Chris 178, 179, 182–4; critical
    moments 208
Carter, R. 64, 67, 132, 214
Cattell, R. B. 49
chatlines, creativity of 191–4
Cherny, L. 201–4
Chiaro, D. 20
Chomsky, Noam 56, 77–8
Chukovsky, K. 76
Churchill, Winston 55
Clark, Timothy 50
clichés *see* formula phrases
clines: creativity in 139–40, 164–5, 166;
    of expression 127, 130–1; intimacy,
    intensity and evaluation 117–19;
    literary language 66–7
code-mixing: computer-mediated
    communication 175–7; multicultural,
    multilingual 172–3
cognition: aesthetic functions and 62
cognitive poetics 69–72
Cohen, D.: *Creativity* 51
Coleridge, Samuel Taylor: manifesto to
    Lyrical Ballads 28–9
Colligan, J. 43
communication: information and task-
    oriented 149–50
computer-mediated communication
    (CMC) 13; code-mixing 175–7;
    development of 189–90; features of
    chat 191–4; Goddard's case study of
    194–9; Internet Relay Chat 190–1;
    mimicry and voicing 204–5; more like
    speech 57–8; MUD interaction
    200–4, 207, 208; self-dramatisation
    197–9
connotations: core words 116
convergence 100–1
conversation: analysis of 78–80; creative
    subversion 23–4; for enjoyment 194;
    fluency 147; humour and 85; poetry
    within 8–9, 10
Cook, Guy 46, 62; on conversation 79,
    194; *Discourse and Literature* 59–60;
    Language Play, Language Learning 73–4,
    75–7; play 83; on puns 91
core vocabulary 115–17, 131–2
Cornbleet, Sandra 125
Couper-Kuhlen, E. 205
Coupland, J. 151; *Small Talk* 186–8

creation: four creator types 33–4;
    product/process 42
creativity: adversarial 173–4; Chomsky
    on 77–8; clinal nature of 139–40;
    cognitive skills 34–5; in common talk
    81–2; composition and 67; creation
    and 25–6; critical 47–8, 183–4;
    defined 47; degrees of 214–15;
    demotic 30; features and aspects of
    47–9; fiction and fact 76–7; function
    of 22–3; historical/personal 66–7;
    inspiration 25; interactive 107–11;
    invention and 29; journalists'
    discourse and 155–6; linguistic studies
    of 12; literary language and 81–2;
    morphological 97–101; novelty and
    appropriateness 29–30; ordinary
    language and 18–19, 209–10;
    originality and 26–7; paradigms of
    24–5; in performance 44–5; play and
    72–6; presence of 140–1;
    psychological approaches to 30–41;
    repetition 6–8; the self and multiparty
    discourse, 194 ff.; the self and
    dramatic effect, 197–9; social context
    of 164–7, 205–8; sociocultural
    approaches 42–7, 188; spoken 11;
    systems approach 37–9; in writing 54
Creole 172
crossing, *see* culture, identity
Crystal, David: on conversation 80;
    internet games 201; language play
    72–3
Csikszentmihalyi, Mihaly 37–8, 67, 83;
    systems theory 54
culture: East and West 42–4; identities
    47; knowledge in wordplay 21;
    limitations of approaches 46–7;
    multilingual 'crossing' 171–3;
    performance 44–5; sociocultural
    approaches and creativity 42–7;
    variability of creativity 48
Cupitt, Don 209

Dad's Army (television) 128, 132
Darwin, Charles 33; *On the Origin of
    Species* 28, 38
De Bono, Edward 31; *Serious Creativity*
    52
defamiliarisation 60

Derrida, Jacques 84
deviation theory 59
dictionaries and grammars 55
Discourse and Literature (Cook) 59–60
Zoltán Dörnyei 215
Dostoevsky, Fyodor 69
drama and theatre: cultural difference
and 45
duelling, verbal 45–6
Dunbar, R. 73
Duranti, A. 78–9, 147

Eagleton, Terry 62, 81
education: discourse of students 13;
foreign languages 213–14; writing
performances 54
Einstein, Albert 33
Eisenhower, Dwight: 'I like Ike' 59
Eliot, T. S. 33, 34
email *see* computer-mediated
communication
English language: multilingual 'crossing'
172–6; varieties of 90
ethnomethodology: conversational
analysis 78–9
ethnopoetics 78–80

Fairclough. N. 22
fiction: alternative realities 200–4;
defining literature 18; literal and non-
literal worlds 76–7; the novel 26;
Williams on 55
figures of speech 115; creativity and
139–40; expressive clines 130–1;
hyperbole 136–8; idioms 132–3;
metalinguistic awareness 126–7;
proverbial 134–5; social contexts 159;
uncreative 133–4; *see also* idioms;
metaphorF
Finke, R. 36, 51
Flindall, M. 187
foreign languages: creativity in the
classroom 213–14
formulaic phrases 109; fixed expressions
128–9; uncreative 133–4
Freeman, D. 84
Freud, Sigmund: case-study approach
33; creativity and 51; creator-type 33
Friedrich, P. 85

Galton, Francis: *Hereditary Genius* 33, 50
games: Multi-User Dungeon/Dimension
200–4
Gandhi, Mohandas K. (Mahatma) 33, 34
Garbutt, M. 178
Gardner, H. 33–4
gender 164; context and meaning 212;
interaction and identity 169
Geneplore model 36
genius 24, 48, 50; creativity and 28;
individuality and 27–9
Gibbs, R. W. 83, 84, 129, 138; on
metaphor 70–2; *The Poetics of Mind* 70;
proverbial phrases 134–5
Giora, R. 131, 141
Goddard, Angela: case study of chat-
rooms 194–9
Goffman, Erving: dramatisation 197–8;
everyday conversations 196; footing
shifts 153
Gordon, D. 135
Gossen, G. 46
graffitti 20
Graham, Martha 33, 34
Graves, Robert 25
Gruber, H. E. 33
Guilford, J. P. 51

Hall, G. 84
Halliday, Michael A. K. 56, 57, 58
Hallman, R. J. 42
Hanks, W. F. 86
Harré, R. 156
Harris, R. 83–4
Havranek, B. 57
Hayakawa, S. 135
Hereditary Genius (Galton) 33, 50
Herrnstein-Smith, B. 62–3, 84–5
Holliday, A. 84
Holmes, J. 163
Hong Kong: multilingual 'crossing' 174
Howden, M. 98
Huizinga, Johan 72, 74–5, 83
humour 18–21; rehearsed 111; *see also*
puns; wordplay
Hymes, D. 86
hyperbole 23; expressive clines and 119;
forms of 136; intensification with
136–8; simile and 125

identity: counselling convergence
179–82; culture and creativity 47, 48;
dynamic and mobile nature 199–200;
and language crossing 171–4
idioms 2, 3; displacement 109; evaluating creativity of 132–3; expressive
clines and 119; fixed expressions
128–9; principal patterns 141
improvisation: creativity, jazz and 112,
114, 147
individualism: biographical approaches
33–5; creativity and 24, 54–6
Indonesia 43, Gayo culture 45
inherency models: deviation and self-
reference 59
insults 46
intelligence quotient (IQ) tests 32
interdiscursivity 183, 188
internet communication *see* computer-
mediated communication
internet relay chat *see* speech
intonation 204–5
invention: creativity and 29
irony 23; journalists' discourse and 156

Jakobson, Roman 59
Jankiowak, W. R. 84
Johnson, M.: *Metaphors We Live By* (with
Lakoff) 69–70

Kaivola-Bregenjoj, A. 44
Karayanni, M. 50
Kearney, Richard 50
Keenan, E. 44
King, A. 44
Kirton, Michael: *Adaptors and Innovators*
52
Koestler, Arthur: *The Act of Creation* 50
Kövecses, Z. 128
Kramsch, C. 213
Kris, E. 32
Kubie, L. S. 32
Kuiper, K. 187

Lakoff, G.: *Metaphors We Live By* (with
Johnson) 69–70
language: corpus as snapshot of 170–1;
geography of 171; *see also* English
language; foreign languages;
ordinary/common language

Language Play, Language Learning (Cook)
73–4, 75–7
lateral thinking 31
Lecercle, J. J. 63
legal discourse 182–3
Levelt, W. J. M. 86
linguistics 10; cognitive 70–1;
generative/cognitive wager 70;
spoken language 56–7
literal and non-literal language 70–2,
76–7
literary language: Bakhtin's 'voicing'
67–9; borders of 62–3; clines and
values 66–7; examining 53–4;
inherency models 59; literature and
80–1; metaphor 70–2; models of 58;
properties of 'literariness' 63–6;
schema and refreshment 59–60;
speech acts 60–1; *see also* writing
Lubart, T. I. 49; on cognition 36; on
creativity 42; on imitation 30; on
inspiration 25; music in New Guinea
50; social dimension of creativity 37
Lucky Jim (Amis) 65

Macbeth (Shakespeare) 25, 26
McCarthy, Michael 57, 129, 132, 214;
CANCODE design 150; on discourse
creativity 216; on ordinary language
209
McGlone, M. S. 129
McRae, J. 84
Malevich, Kasimir 35
Maley, Y. 182
Manchester Metropolitan University 194
Mannheim, B. 85
Mar'i, S. K. 50
Marra, M. 163
Martindale, C. 36–7
Maybin, J. 85, 205
Mead, Margaret 43
metaphor 109, 139, 159; creativity and
120–2; 'dead' 122, 129; decoding and
processing 122–3; drawing analogies
119–20; expressive clines and 119;
literary language and 70–2;
metalinguistic awareness 126–7;
metonymy and 120; simile and 125
Metaphors We Live By (Lakoff and Johnson)
69–70

metonymy 139; metaphor and 120, 123–4
Mexico 46
Meyer, R. E. 31
Michael, George 20
mimicry: discourse intonation and 204–5; originality, creativity and 30
monosemy/polysemy 65–6, 70
morphology, creative 97–101
Mozart, Wolfgang A. 33
Mrs Merton (television) 40–1
Mullany, L. 163
Multi-User Dungeon/Dimension 200–4
multilingual communication 207; critiques of 177–8; Rampton on 'crossing' 171–3
multimodality 212

Nash, W. 64, 67
newspapers 170–1
Nigeria 44
Norrick, N. 85
novel 26
nursery rhymes 1–2, 3

offensive language 191–2
Ohmann, Richard 60–1
OK! (magazine) 163
On the Origin of Species (Darwin) 28, 38
Ong, Walter J. 55–6
online communication *see* computer-mediated communication
ordinary/common language 209; 'common' defined 18; creative wordplay 18–21; creativity and 209–10; 'ordinary' defined 17–18
originality 24, 48; creativity and 26–7; imitation and 30
Orwell, George: *Animal Farm* 60

Palmer, G. B. 84
pattern formation 101–2, 156, 164–5; collocational 116; communicative purpose 109, 110; fixed expressions 129; further research 210–11; repetition 100–1; social context 112, 141, 148; of sound 3; verbal play 95–7, 102–9, 162
Petterson, Anders: *A Theory of Literary Discourse* 61–2

Picasso, Pablo 33, 34, 35
The Poetics of Mind: Figurative Thought, Language, Understanding (Gibbs) 70
poetry: in conversation 8–9, 10, 107–8; metaphor 71
Poincaré, H. 36
Policastro, E. 33–4
Pollock, Jackson 35
Pope, R.: *Creativity* 51
Porter, D. 200
Potter, Beatrix 154, 156
Pratt, M. L. 61, 84
Preminger, A. 27
presentationality 61–2
professional communication *see* workplace communication
psycholinguistics 10
psychology 41; audience expectations 39–41; biological/neuroscientific 36–7; cognitive 35–6; creativity and 30–1; practical and pragmatic 31; psychodynamic 32–3; psychometric 31–2; social-personality 37; systems 37–9
puns 156; ordinary creativity 18–21; speech and creativity 90–7; *see also* wordplay

Rampton, B. 171–3
reading 111; *see also* writing
Redfern, W. 91
repetition 156; creativity and 6–8; echoing 109; *see also* pattern formation
research: context and 'objectivity' 177–8; meaning of contexts 212–13; multimodality 212; new words 224, 225; patterns 210–11; voicing 211
rhetoric 55
rhyme: patterned wordplay 107–8; *see also* poetry
Rogers, Carl 51
Romanticism: creativity and 26, 27–8; manifesto on 'language of men' 28–9
rule breaking 9

Sacks, H. 148
Samoa 43
sarcasm 23

satire 23
Saussure, Ferdinand de: *parole* and *langue* 56, 63
Sawyer, W. K. 82
schema and refreshment 85
Scherzer, J. 79
Searle, John 60
self-referentiality theory 59
sex: gender and banter 164; insults and abuse 46; puns with 5–6; *see also* gender
Shakespeare, William: as genius 27–8; *Macbeth* 25, 26
Shippey, T. A. 46
silence, creative 169, 212
simile 125; *see also* metaphor
Simonton, D. K. 37, 42
Sinclair, J. 141
Singapore Broadcasting Corporation 167
slang and intimacy 135
Small Talk (Coupland) 186–8
Smith, Steven: *Creative Thought* (with Ward and Vaid) 52
social contexts 10, 141; building relationships 8–9, 76, 188; CANCODE and 147–9; class and 212; creativity in 164–7, 205–8; expressive clines 117–19; flatmates' discourse 158–9; further research and 212–13; intimacy and slang 135; limitations of approaches 46–7; of new words 224, 225; patterned wordplay 107–12; puns and laughter 96–7; sociocultural approaches to creativity 42–7; student couple 160–2; *see also* workplace communication
social theory 13
speech: Bakhtin's 'voicing' 67–9; compared to writing 111; creativity and 11; Internet Relay Chat 190–1; limitations of CANCODE 219, 221; literary language and 55–7; mapping context and interaction 165; rehearsed humour 111; unplanned 139; values of 12; writing and 9, 57–8
speech acts 60–1
Sperber, D. 142

Steiner, George: *Grammars of Creation* 50
Sternberg, R. J. 49; on cognition 36; defining creativity 47; on inspiration 25; systems theory 39
Stockwell, P. 71, 142
Stone, A. R. 193–4
Storr, Anthony: *The Dynamics of Creation* 51
story-telling 45
Stravinsky, Igor 33
structuralism *see* Saussure, Ferdinand de
The Sun (newspaper) 163
Swedish students 194–9
synecdoche 124, 139
systems theory 54, 67; psychology and creativity 37–9
Szabó, P. 128
Talking Voices (Tannen) 7, 79–80
Tambling, J.: *What is Literary Language?* 63
Tannen, Deborah 83; repetition 101; *Talking Voices* 7, 79–80
A Theory of Literary Discourse (Petterson) 61–2
therapeutic discourse 13
Thomas, Dylan 59
thought: cognitive skills 34–5
Toolan, M. 22–3, 84
Torrance, E. P. 32
Turner, M. ix, 69–70, 84, 142
Turner, Victor 173, 183; liminality 86

Uglow, Jenny: *The Lunar Men* 51
understatement 3, 23
United States: African-American insults 46
universalism: Huizinga's study 74–5
University Challenge (television) 45

Vaid, Jyotsna: *Creative Thought* (with Ward and Smith) 52
Verdonk, P. 84
Vizmuller-Zocco, J. 98
vocabulary: core 115–17; new words 222–6
voicing 67–9; discourse intonation and 204; double- 173; further research 211

Voloshinov, V. N. 85
Vygotsky, Lev 86

Wallace, D. B. 33
Ward, Thomas: *Creative Thought* (with
    Smith and Vaid) 52
Weber, J. J. 84
Weisberg, R. 33, 50
What is Literary Language? (Tambling) 63
Widdicombe, S. 106
Widdowson, H. G. 84
Williams, Raymond: on 'common' 18;
    on creativity 25–6, 27; on 'genius' 28;
    on literature 55
Willis, P. ix, 170, 189
Wilson, D. 142
Wolfson, N. 45
Woolf, Virginia 33
word origins: core words 116
wordplay 12, 83; creativity and 72–6;
    'no queues' 1, 2; ordinary language
    18–21; puns 90–7; *see also* creativity

Wordsworth, William: creativity and 26;
    manifesto to *Lyrical Ballads* 28–9
workplace communication 12–13, 207;
    credit security controllers 157–8;
    doctor and AIDS patient 179–82,
    183; journalists 153–6; law and
    dispute resolution 182–3; lifeguards
    151–3; psychiatrist and patient
    178–9; slang and social context 135;
    small company meeting 163–4;
    supermarket small talk 186–8;
    supervisor and doctoral student
    184–6; teachers 162–3; therapeutic
    alliance 179–82, 183
writing: compared to speech 111;
    composition 67; creativity and
    54–6; Internet Relay Chat 190–1;
    speech and 9; *see also* literary
    language

Young, George 27
Yule, G. 85

Related titles from Routledge

The Routledge Guide to Modern English Writing

John McRae and Ronald Carter

This is that rare and admirable thing: a critical work that is both comprehensive and insightful, yet fresh, accessible and clear. It should be a
valuable resource for students, journalists, authors – anyone, in fact, with
an interest in literature and language in Britain today.
Sarah Waters, author of *Tipping the Velvet*, *Affinity* and *Fingersmith*
and one of *Granta* magazine's 'Best of Young British Novelists'

The Routledge Guide to Modern English Writing tells the story of British and
Irish writing from 1963 to the present. From the first performance of Tom
Stoppard's *Rosencrantz and Guildenstern Are Dead* in the 1960s to lad novels and
chick lit in the twenty-first century, the authors guide the reader through the
major writers, genres and developments in English writing over the past forty
years.

Written by the authors of prize-winning *The Routledge History of Literature in
English* (second edition 2001), *The Routledge Guide to Modern English Writing* is
essential reading for all readers of contemporary writing.

ISBN 0–415–28636–0 (hbk)
ISBN 0–415–28637–9 (pbk)

Available at all good bookshops
For ordering and further information please visit www.routledge.com

Related titles from Routledge

The Routledge History of Literature in English
Britain and Ireland

Second edition

John McRae and Ronald Carter

> An enormously ambitious and wide-ranging work . . . Students of writing are bound to be indebted to it – and it has a clarity of structure and analysis that everyone will welcome.
>> Andrew Motion, Poet Laureate and Professor of
>> Creative Writing, University of East Anglia

This is a completely updated and expanded second edition of the wide-ranging and accessible *Routledge History of Literature in English*. It covers the main developments in the history of British and Irish literature and has extensive accompanying language notes, which explore the inter-relationships between language and literature. With a span from AD 600 to the present day, it emphasises the growth of literary writing, its traditions, conventions and changing characteristics, and includes literature from the margins, both geographical and cultural. Extensive quotes from poetry, prose and drama underpin the narrative.

ISBN 0–415–24317–3 (hbk)
ISBN 0–415–24318–1 (pbk)

Available at all good bookshops
For ordering and further information please visit www.routledge.com